Nature Performed:
Environment, Culture and Performance

D1219427

A selection of previous *Sociological Review* Monographs

Sport, Leisure and Social Relations[†]
eds John Horne, David Jary and Alan Tomlinson
Gender and Bureaucracy*
eds Mike Savage and Anne Witz
The Sociology of Death: theory, culture, practice*
ed. David Clark
The Cultures of Computing
ed. Susan Leigh Star
Theorizing Museums*
ed. Sharon Macdonald and Gordon Fyfe
Consumption Matters*
eds Stephen Edgell, Kevin Hetherington and Alan Warde
Ideas of Difference*
eds Kevin Hetherington and Rolland Munro
The Laws of the Markets*
ed. Michael Callon
Actor Network Theory and After*
eds John Law and John Hassard
Whose Europe? The turn towards democracy*
eds Dennis Smith and Sue Wright
Renewing Class Analysis*
eds Rosemary Cromptom, Fiona Devine, Mike Savage and John Scott
Reading Bourdieu on Society and Culture*
ed. Bridget Fowler
The Consumption of Mass*
ed. Nick Lee and Rolland Munro
The Age of Anxiety: Conspiracy Theory and the Human Sciences*
eds Jane Parish and Martin Parker
Utopia and Organization*
ed. Martin Parker
Emotions and Sociology*
ed. Jack Barbalet
Masculinity and Men's Lifestyle Magazines
ed. Bethan Benwell

[†]Available from The Sociological Review Office, Keele University, Keele, Staffs ST5 5BG.
*Available from Marston Book Services, PO Box 270, Abingdon, Oxon OX14 4YW.

The Sociological Review Monographs

Since 1958 *The Sociological Review* has established a tradition of publishing Monographs on issues of general sociological interest. The Monograph is an edited book length collection of research papers which is published and distributed in association with Blackwell Publishing. We are keen to receive innovative collections of work in sociology and related disciplines with a particular emphasis on exploring empirical materials and theoretical frameworks which are currently under-developed. If you wish to discuss ideas for a Monograph then please contact the Monographs Editor, Rolland Munro, at *The Sociological Review*, Keele University, Newcastle-under-Lyme, North Staffordshire, ST5 5BG.

Nature Performed:
Environment, Culture and Performance

Edited by Bronislaw Szerszynski, Wallace Heim and Claire Waterton

Blackwell Publishing/The Sociological Review

© The Editorial Board of the Sociological Review 2003

Blackwell Publishing
9600 Garsington Road, Oxford OX4 2DQ, UK

and

350 Main Street, Malden, MA 02148-5018, USA

All rights reserved. No part of this publication may be reproduced, stored in a retrieval system, or transmitted, in any form or by any means, electronic, mechanical, photocopying, recording or otherwise, except as permitted by the UK Copyright, Designs, and Patents Act 1988, without the prior permission of the publisher.

Every effort has been made to trace copyright holders. The authors apologise for any errors or omissions and would be grateful to be notified of any corrections that should be incorporated in the next edition or reprint of this volume.

First published 2003 by Blackwell Publishing Ltd

Library of Congress Cataloging-in-Publication Data

ISBN 1-4051-1464-9

A catalogue record for this title is available from the British Library.

Printed and bound in the United Kingdom by Page Brothers, Norwich.

For further information on Blackwell Publishing, visit our website:
http://www.blackwellpublishing.com

Contents

Acknowledgements   vii

Introduction   1
Bronislaw Szerszynski, Wallace Heim and Claire Waterton

Part I—Making worlds   15

Performances and constitutions of natures: a consideration of
the performance of lay geographies   17
David Crouch

Ritual theory and the environment   31
Ronald Grimes

A passionate pursuit: foxhunting as performance   46
Garry Marvin

Part II—Living here   61

Green distinctions: the performance of identity among
environmental activists   63
Dave Horton

Performing safety in faulty environments   78
Peter Simmons

Public participation as the performance of nature   94
Stephen Healy

Part III—Embodying abstraction   109

Performing the classification of nature   111
Claire Waterton

Performing facts: finding a way over Scotland's mountains   130
Hayden Lorimer and Katrin Lund

Performing place in nature reserves   145
Matt Watson

Part IV—Unsettling life   161

Feral ecologies: performing life on the colonial periphery   163
Nigel Clark

Slow activism: homelands, love and the lightbulb   183
Wallace Heim

Technology, performance and life itself: Hannah Arendt and
the fate of nature   203
Bronislaw Szerszynski

Notes on contributors   219

Index   221

Acknowledgements

This book is one of the results of collaborations and conversations around Between Nature, an interdisciplinary conference held at Lancaster University in July 2000. Hosting academic papers, visual arts, performances and installations, the conference explored the interface between ecology and performance. The event came about through productive collaborations with our colleagues in the Department of Theatre Studies at Lancaster, Gabriella Giannachi, Nigel Stewart and Andrew Quick. Gabriella and Nigel are editing a companion to this volume for a performance studies audience, *Performing Nature: Explorations in Ecology and the Arts*, due to be published in 2005 by Peter Lang AG. We would like to thank them for all that they have contributed to our understanding of nature and performance.

We would also like to thank Robin Grove-White and Baz Kershaw for their encouragement for Between Nature, and to Sue Weldon for her invaluable support. Kate Lamb, Michelle Needham and Janet Hamid provided essential administrative assistance, and we would like to thank Kate for her continued assistance with this collection. We also are grateful for the financial support provided by the Global Environmental Change Programme of the Economic and Social Research Council, the North West Arts Board, The Granada Foundation, and Lancaster University.

We especially want to thank all the performers, contributors, helpers and technical staff who created that event. In developing this collection, we have had the pleasure of continuing some of the conversations that began at that event, and also of starting some productive new ones.

Introduction

Bronislaw Szerszynski, Wallace Heim and Claire Waterton

Across a range of disciplines, a number of researchers and theorists have moved towards seeing nature and nature–human relations in terms not of static structures and rules but *activity*. Our purpose in editing this book has been to gather together examples of this 'performative turn' in the study of environment and society. The contributors explore domains as diverse as allotments and bioinvasion, green politics and policymaking in terms of performance, using the rich layers of meaning embedded in this term to expand the way we look at nature and the human relationship to it. Other collections and books have helped inform the aspirations of the present volume, helping to mark out a space of inquiry to which it is a further contribution. Notable among those has been Gillian Rose and Nigel Thrift's special issue of *Environment and Planning D: Society and Space* on 'Spaces of Performance' (2000), which explored spatiality in terms of performance. Similarly, Phil Macnaghten and John Urry's collection *Bodies of Nature* (2001), and Adrian Franklin's monograph *Nature and Social Theory* (2001) both look at nature in more embodied, cultural terms which are broadly consistent with the approaches taken in this book. But this is the first collection that specifically focuses on performance and nature, and one that we hope will be useful to a wide readership.

Our aims in editing this book are not wholly academic and intellectual. Firstly, we would argue that the performative turn being described above is being driven not just by intellectual curiosity but also by an increasing sense that existing ways of thinking about nature are inadequate to contemporary needs. There is a growing understanding of the dynamic quality of both nature and society, a dynamism that is not well served by the noun-dominated languages used for describing both. This mismatch is if anything getting sharper, as technological and social change introduce an even greater volatility to our relations with the natural world. Secondly, the following chapters are not just abstract theoretical explorations, but are rooted in various real-world contexts and problems, often explored through detailed ethnographic work. As such, they present to the reader some radically different ways of thinking about nature, ways that might prompt more reflective practice in both academic and non-academic domains. Thus, while the main intended readership of the collection consists of students, researchers and academics in the social sciences, the book should also interest

© The Editorial Board of the Sociological Review 2003. Published by Blackwell Publishing Ltd, 9600 Garsington Road, Oxford OX4 2DQ, UK and 350 Main Street, Malden, MA 02148, USA

and provoke a wider readership in other disciplines and in the 'real-world' areas of environmental politics and policy. Towards the end of this introduction we consider some of the challenges posed by the work presented here for these and other domains.

What does it mean to bring 'nature' and 'performance' together in the ways to be found in this collection? Let us first consider the terms separately. Both of them, of course, are famously complex words. They are familiar yet ambiguous, classic 'keywords' in Raymond Williams' sense, their meanings 'inextricably bound up with the problems [they are] being used to discuss' (Williams 1976: 13). Any attempts by scholars to stabilize them in determinate, substantive definitions typically have the opposite effect, merely accentuating the proliferation of interpretations. They seem to yield their meanings more readily to approaches that are from the beginning oriented to their inherent multipleness. The contributions in this volume add to the density of interpretations of each term, giving the reader a number of entry points to the multiple readings of performance and nature.

Against such a background, it is not our intention in this introduction to provide a definitive survey of the various readings and approaches to the two terms taken separately. But we owe it to our readers at least briefly to set out a broad family of meanings for each of our terms in turn. As far as 'nature' is concerned, the complexity of this term is likely to be familiar to most of our readers (see Collingwood, 1945; Williams, 1976, 1980; Soper, 1995; Macnaghten and Urry, 1998). Briefly to pick out a few meanings, nature is firstly *materiality*—it is rock, ocean, biota, atmosphere. At many points in the collection nature in this sense is evoked—an organism, a hillside, a continent. But, secondly, nature can be *process*—causality, evolution or 'life itself'; it is this sense of nature that comes closest to the meanings of our other term, 'performance'. Thirdly, nature is also a world of meanings and significance, something 'good to think with' (Lévi-Strauss, 1962)—nature can be cosmos or lifeworld, an Eden or an object of dread, a signifier that calls forth a profusion of associations. Fourthly, nature can also be invoked as something *abstract*, a substrate underlying appearances; nature in this sense is not the signifier but the referent in processes of signification, the 'real', rendered through numbers and other abstractions.

The complexity of the term 'performance' is likely to be less familiar to our readers (for overviews see C. Bell, 1998; V. Bell, 1999; Carlson, 1996; Parker and Sedgwick, 1995; Schechner, 1988, 2002; Schieffelin, 1998; States, 1996; Thrift and Dewsbury, 2000; Dewsbury, 2000). As we discuss below, to call something a performance generally involves more than saying it is a process, but nevertheless this is an important component of its layers of meaning. Firstly, then, performance is something *done*, an activity. One particularly relevant cognate term of performance here is that of 'practice' (see Crouch, this volume; see also Bourdieu, 1977; de Certeau, 1984). But another related term is 'performativity',[1] generally used to express the idea both that language *does* something—that its power is not just to represent but to bring about effects—but also that certain phenomena only exist in the doing of them—that they have to be continually

© The Editorial Board of the Sociological Review 2003

performed to exist at all (Austin, 1962; Lyotard, 1986; Butler, 1997). As Clark (this volume) points out, some Australian feminists have extended this notion of performativity from language and culture to the body, arguing that bodies themselves can be seen as contingent and articulate, involved in the play of signification (see Grosz, 1995). And whereas in Judith Butler's classic application of the term (1990) it is gender that is shown to be performed, in the current volume it is nature itself that is revealed to be performative in this sense.

Secondly, some readings of performance emphasize the importance of repetition, the 'twice-done' in Schechner's (1988) theatrical terms, or the iterative as Butler (1990) theorizes it. Performances typically involve the repetition of gestures, tasks, actions, which might be seen as the following of scripts, or the acting out of codes (see Horton, this volume). But at the same time, in some sense a perfect reproduction of an earlier performance would not be a performance at all but a copy of one; similarly, the automatic acting out of a code would not have about it the 'spirit' of an appropriate performance according to that code. So, thirdly, as central as iteration to performance is the way that variation and difference emerge in the spontaneous, creative moments between iterations, and in the application of codes to contexts. Performance is the manifestation of agency and the action through which agency and creativity emerge. Performance is thus ephemeral, unpredictable, improvisatory, always contingent on its context. Indeed, pre-figured scripts and codes might be seen as not primary but secondary phenomena, mere abstractions from this flow of performance.

Fourthly, performance also of course carries with it an important range of theatrically derived meanings. As a created event, performance in this sense is marked out from the everyday, by ritualization, attendance to routine, theatrical convention, and generally—but not always—involves display to an audience (Schechner, 1988). But performance in this theatrical sense is also used as a metaphor to interrogate the activity of everyday life (Goffman, 1959, 1967; Sennett, 1986; Turner, 1974). Perhaps above all, in this cluster of meanings, performance is an 'event' (Deleuze and Guattari, 1994), an activity through which presence is created (Schieffelin, 1998).

It might said that the idea of *nature* as a performance was most dramatically asserted and sustained through biological perspectives that have built on Charles Darwin's evolutionary theory. Darwin put forward a view that the nature that we see (nature as *materiality*) is the ongoing product of a performance (by nature the *process*). In doing away with the concept of natural kinds belonging to fixed entities and orders, life itself could be seen, from his perspective, as an infinite evolutionary process obeying the simple principles of natural selection and the survival of those that fit. Biological, ecological and many other sciences continually build on these insights, now taken for granted. Thus 'nature'— biotic and a-biotic life intertwined—is 'naturally' seen as a co-performance of a number of different, interacting and evolving individuals, species and processes—including human beings. Nature performed, in this sense, might offer a sense of the essential vitality of all (including human) life, engulfing all the actions and processes that such life might entail.

© The Editorial Board of the Sociological Review 2003   3

It is important to stress that conjoining our two terms does not necessarily leave 'performance' unchanged—as if we were simply using one thing (performance) to shed a new, uncanny light on another (nature). In different ways, as the contributors to this collection extend performance beyond the human, they start to change its meaning. While using the term performance we often retain the traditional sense of it as belonging to the realm of culture, to human creativity and play. But once we view performance as obtaining not just to culture but to a life which encompasses the human and the non-human, then many things we think of as human activities—such as hunting a fox, settling a new land, gardening an allotment—begin to look more like mutual improvisations that highlight the agency of the non-human—the fox, the colonizing species, the germinating seeds. Out of this mutual improvisation one loses a sense of nature as pre-figured and merely being 'played out'; instead, the performance of nature appears as a process open to improvisation, creativity and emergence, embracing the human and the non-human.

Throughout the chapters of this collection we see examples of co-produced 'nature–cultures' (Franklin, Lury and Stacey, 2000) emerging from activity. Indeed, the cumulative sense one gets is that it is the concept of a nature *un*performed, one which simply endures as an object, which is problematic and needs explaining in terms of its historical emergence and plausibility. Instead, we glimpse an ontology where performance is the primal term, and stable objects and subjects are simply abstractions from this. Such an ontology would be consistent with a broader move in parts of the social sciences to more active metaphors for the natural and the cultural, including ideas of complexity (Urry, 2003) and liquidity (Bauman, 2000). Such metaphors also imply a sense of limit on our human capacity to 'know' enough, to 'get a grip' on the ever-evolving, complex world, epistemic implications which run through many of the chapters of this book. Performance is treated by many authors at once as a means by which we may come to know, and as something which necessitates a different way of thinking about knowledge—not as static, or passive, but as active, distinctly relational, forming distinctive events and experiences by which it is possible to know more. And as many of the chapters show this is as true of abstract and expert knowledge as it is of the lay, everyday knowing of vernacular nature.

The chapters

We have grouped the chapters into sections in order to bring out some of the patterns between the chapters. The first section, *Making worlds*, explores the ways in which performed action—everyday, staged or ritual activity—brings into being a felt and sensed world of experience in connection with the natural. In *Living here*, the chapters investigate the practices of identity formation and social action in specific locales and environmental contexts. The third section, *Embodying abstraction*, looks at the practices of quantification and abstraction of nature which at the same time infuse the embodied experience of a landscape

© The Editorial Board of the Sociological Review 2003

and render knowledges of nature and place mobile. And finally, in the chapters of *Unsettling life*, performance is understood as a process and as an event conjoining the human and the non-human in which intended and improvised actions set loose further, unpredictable actions into the world. Although these groupings imply a common theme within each section, other themes also weave in and out of many of the chapters—the emergent and creative qualities of performance and of nature, the iterative as coextensive with biological life, the conjoining of the aesthetic and the everyday, the ambiguity of the 'real' and the 'not real' in performance. Finally, the grouping of chapters in each section is also designed to bring out contrasts as well as commonalities between the contributions.

Making worlds

Each chapter in this section gives a sense of performance's power to create worlds of experience. Whether as everyday practice (Crouch), elaborated activity (Marvin), staged performance or ritual (Grimes), performance has the capacity to create meaningful worlds around those who perform, worlds which can often involve a deeply felt relationship with the natural world. In such world-making the dynamics between the human and non-human can engender strong emotional and sensual responses. Performances can be composed of ideas and values, the reasoned and the emotive, the embodied and the abstract. Pre-figured views of nature may be conserved and reinforced, but in the immediacy of performance, there may also be surprises, inventiveness and the experience of new relations, new meanings. Each of these chapters explores how that creative act can emerge between the human and 'the natural'.

David Crouch explores performance in the context of allotments, the provision in the UK of areas of public land for gardening. Crouch strongly contests the view that nature is wholly pre-figured, and that such already-given views can only be acted out or resisted. Rather, he suggests, nature is constituted and understood through practice. The multiple facets of ideas, values, and feelings which accompany nature are re-figured and created through embodied, material activity, in both everyday practice and staged performances. Crouch focuses on an allotment in Birmingham, with a diverse and multi-cultural group of allotment holders. An art event staged there, 'Bloom 98', gave a context for expressing and celebrating the symbolic and material practices of growing plants and the social-nature interactions in allotments, intertwining the real and the make-believe. But it is the narratives of everyday practices that reveal the enjoyment, love and care which inform an identification with nature and the allotment space. Through the feeling and embodiment of doing—tending plants, providing and sharing food, working in proximity to others—nature is a re-imagined and re-worked dimension of life. Performance, in both senses, is characterized by flow, adjustment and the potential for agency through which feelings and ideas of nature are changed, newly practised, and made meaningful.

In his chapter Ronald Grimes questions whether through newly made ecological rituals humans can re-learn a connection with their environments. He

© The Editorial Board of the Sociological Review 2003

argues that ethics alone are not enough, since they cannot motivate or shape behaviour in the way ritual—as 'sustained, value-laden practice'—can. He critiques two approaches: that of Eugene d'Aquili and the biogenetic structuralists, who see ritual as an adaptive, biological function of *homo sapiens*; and that of Roy Rappaport, who sees ritual as the basic social act that binds society together. Against the first, he argues that not all ritual is conducive to well-being or ecologically benign. Grimes then finds contradictions in Rappaport's theories, which he sees as too conservative, but more favourably agrees that the idea of ecology is a religious as well as scientific conception. Ritual, then, may or ought to perform ways of inhabiting a place, to orient the self in an enacted cosmos. For Grimes, then, *some* ecologically attuned rites may indeed 'enhance adaptability and thus the longevity of the human species on the planet earth'.

The world described in Garry Marvin's chapter is one that, for the participants, enfolds them in passionate and meaningful action. Marvin's insider, ethnographic description of English fox hunting evokes the presence and the excess of performance. The hunt is an elaboration of an ordinary activity, tacitly scripted by social codes and historical precedence, and one which performs more than a specific action. The sensual engagement of everyone participating, their movements and roles, create shared perceptions of the surrounding landscape. The hunt transforms the relations between the humans and the animals— the dogs, horses and fox—into those between performers, dependent and intimate as together they bring about a life-ending event. By taking a performative view of hunting, a subject long studied by anthropologists in other cultures, Marvin's chapter challenges some normative assumptions about what constitutes a deep connectivity to nature.

Living here

'Here', in these chapters, is a locale, a town, a human-settled place in which the actions and contingencies of living together are caught up with nature and nature–human relations. These actions are not merely symbolic or expressive, but have an efficacy in creating individual and group identities, in offering subtle and overt means of resistance to environmental conditions, and in instigating material changes. The range of 'performance' in the section is broadly drawn, from everyday practices (Horton), to social roles (Simmons), to role-play and the ontological performativity described in actor network theory (Healy). Likewise, 'nature' is variously manifested as values enacted and personified, as the materialities of human-affected environments, as the object of policy-making and public participation. Common across the chapters is an attention to the performance of agency in the strategies for choosing or rejecting identities within both cultural and environmental contexts.

Dave Horton describes the everyday performance of 'green values' in the private and public lives of environmental activists in a British city. Basing his study on Pierre Bourdieu's concepts of distinction and taste, Horton analyzes the performing of 'green identity' through the materialities which organize the

© The Editorial Board of the Sociological Review 2003

practice of a green lifestyle. Conforming to the cultural 'codes' and 'scripts' attached to food, the car and the locations of green sociability enables the expression of identity and the display of values which the activists would want others to adopt. Horton further examines this normative dimension by exploring how mis-performances or over-performances of appropriate behaviour can transgress the boundaries of acceptable green practice. Horton concludes by suggesting that environmentally sustainable behaviour might better be promoted by the provision not of information and education, but of a 'new, green architecture' of materialities, times and spaces conducive to green practices.

Using Erving Goffman's dramaturgical analysis of the presentation of self and his ideas of situational 'framing', where situations are defined in ways which which offer up certain roles and identities to those involved, Peter Simmons explores the way that 'safety' is performed in a residential area close to a chemical plant in the United Kingdom. He argues that a semblance of normal, everyday life in a situation of ongoing technological risk requires the production and maintenance of a tacit negotiated symbolic order between the chemical company, local leaders and members of the public. But this 'normalization of danger' depends on the power of the company's self-presentational activities to command certain interpretations, and thereby to call forth appropriate performances from other members of the community. He explores the way that the company's performances are in fact semantically unstable, producing a range of counter-readings amongst the public, thereby rendering them unable to induce the desired responses.

Stephen Healy uses concepts of performance to understand a case-study of local participation in decision-making about stormwater run-off in a densely populated area of Sydney, Australia. Going beyond a Habermasian idea of deliberation, Healy considers two contrasting yet mutually intertwining models of performance. Firstly, he suggests that performative approaches to community discussions allow the space and time for role-play, for experimentation and improvisation—a ' bricolage'—of differing approaches. The playfulness and improvisation of community performative participation, Healy suggests, can expand the choices available for institutional decision-making practices by suspending the constraints of rational discourse. Secondly, he uses actor network theory to explore stormwater management as an 'assemblage' of material, social and institutional practices that might be thought of as open-ended performances in the world. Such performances, Healy argues, require an appropriate institutional network to be in place.

Embodying abstraction

The third group of chapters presents ethnographic research that has explored ways in which nature has been rendered 'mobile' through practices of abstraction, quantification and standardisation. All focus closely on particular sites— a Lancashire hillside (Waterton), the mountains of Scotland (Lorimer and Lund), Dorset heathland (Watson)—places which are partly known through such abstractions. Each chapter illustrates, however, how these abstractions can simultaneously be seen as the products of locally situated practice. Attention is directed by these authors to the embodied, sensed, felt aspects of the practices that occur in these places as an integral part of the classifications and quantifications which in turn help to constitute the places themselves.

Claire Waterton's chapter describes an experiment designed to expose some of the performative aspects of classifying practices, exploring the way that classifications of nature incorporate two mutually sustaining ideas of performance: performance as *replication* and performance as *improvisation*. In the handing down of formalized knowledges about nature such as classificatory knowledge, a delicate balance is often struck between the two, whereby improvisation is 'done' but not always made visible or explicit. Waterton suggests that as we learn how to perform ways of classifying the natural world, we also learn to disguise the contingencies, the embodiments and the sensory disciplining involved in classification as an act as opposed to an abstract system. It is in the questions presented by the novice learning to 'do' classifications that the implicit knowledges involved can be unmasked. Waterton's experiment entailed the dual performing of classificatory practices of a patch of grassland, first by herself using the National Vegetation Classification system, and by a colleague, using a choreographic categorization related to movements of the human body.

Lorimer and Lund explore the phenomenon of Munroism. In the 'Tables', assembled by Hugh Munro in 1891, are recorded all Scottish mountains over 3000 feet. The 'Munro-bagger' traditionally climbs all 283 peaks, typically guided by maps, a compass, and various walking technologies and knowledges. On the surface, this is a highly disciplined performance, according to scripts of nationalism, cartographic abstraction, and quantification. Yet the authors catalogue some of the ways in which walkers adapt Munroism. Some devise their own rules—by refusing to keep records, by deliberately not completing the list, by refusing certain navigational technologies. More fundamentally, Lorimer and Lund argue that the very act of wayfinding involves not just following maps and 'rules of thumb' but an improvised, continuous adjustment between walker, map, compass and landscape. Through Lorimer and Lund's ethnography, counting is revealed in its materiality and performativity, with foot, body and hillside somehow on the *inside* of the action.

In his study of Godlingston Heath, part of the Studland National Nature Reserve in Dorset, England, Matt Watson describes the way that the concrete particularity of 'place' involves mobilizing abstract concepts and classifications. Watson highlights how such abstractions and classifications themselves can be traced as performative in origin. In demonstrating this he also illustrates how an excessively local and immediate understanding of place can elide the wider flows of ideas, people, materiality and agency that constitute a place. Building on but also departing from the work of Tim Ingold, Watson develops a conceptualization of place in which particular concrete practices—also described by Waterton—spiral out from place, then arc back into the local and help constitute its apparent solidity.

© The Editorial Board of the Sociological Review 2003

Unsettling life

In this last group, performance is an event and process that sets loose further actions, those actions eluding confinement. Performance and the performative are extended beyond deliberate human-centred action to the improvisation and exuberance exhibited by 'life', using the term both in its biological sense and in that of the hermeneutics of human experience and meaning. The social, aesthetic and biological are all already performative and conjoined in the performance of the world. Performance here is mutual creation, an adaptation with variation where organisms, ideas, activities and memories move into new contexts, transforming both themselves and these contexts in the process. It is a conversing—between human and human (Heim), human and nature (Szerszynski), or organism and environment (Clark)—and in all cases is an exchange with unpredictable outcomes as its effects continue into the future. Those unanticipated consequences, are, like the event itself, dependent on their contexts; and through these chapters, the shifting from the familiar context to the unfamiliar, the crossing of environmental and conceptual boundaries, can be an intentional act of transformation or inherent in life's ongoing performativity.

Nigel Clark extends a particular concept of performativity—as variation emerging out of repetition—from the cultural and discursive realms to those of the biological and geological. The 'performativity of life' is exemplified by the creativity and spontaneity of those species introduced to the antipodean islands as they adapt themselves to and modify those environments. Mutating, transplanted organisms, like the cultural, economic and political processes of colonization, present not a rupture with an essential 'nature', but an indication of inventiveness and the potential for making and re-making territories. These self-organizing processes through which new forms and structures emerge are inherent in all domains of existence, and Clark crosses between environmental history, biological and social theory, continental and feminist philosophy, and aesthetic performance in tracing the unpredictable generation—and deterritorialization—of home and territory. Like the feral, transplanted cultural and life forms can set loose unpredictable events and consequences which are potentially devastating and uncontainable. The exuberance of life may prevail, but among the lessons Clark proposes from the colonial experience is for caution and judgement in initiating mobilizing and unsettling experiments.

Wallace Heim's chapter continues with ideas of the disruption of territoriality and belonging in her interpretation of HOMELAND, a performance event by the social practice collective PLATFORM. Like other works in this aesthetic field, the event was a hybrid of conversation, art and activism. The event's persuasive intent was to bring participants to a recognition of how the production of London's electricity affects distant European landscapes. Heim focuses on the potency of the performative methods of the work, rather than on its overt content. As an installation, the work provided a surrounding of metaphoric, material elements, allowing for a reflective imagination to operate, creating an opening for new representations and configurations of nature–human relations

© The Editorial Board of the Sociological Review 2003   9

to emerge. But it was conversation between the artists and participants which animated the event. Carefully invited, the participants' stories and emotions of 'home' were narrated, and through the artists' questioning and listening, those feelings for home were to be extended and dispersed to those other homes and lands on which the city depends. The conversations were both uncharted and persuasive, a form of rhetorical culture and social reasoning, an occasion of ethical character. As 'slow activism', the event made a space for speaking about nature, from which the experience and stories of those conversations could be set loose, unpredictably moving into future spaces and experience.

The last chapter of the volume, by Bronislaw Szerszynski, develops an ecologically critical account of contemporary society on the basis of Hannah Arendt's analysis of the *vita activa* in *The Human Condition* (1958). Starting from Arendt's division of human activity into labour, work or fabrication, and action, he describes how their original ordering has become disturbed by the social, economic and technological changes of the last few centuries. Firstly, he describes how an invasion of the life-process's ceaseless performativity into the heart of the human world, dissolving meaningful work into repetitive labour and the products of work into objects of consumption, has threatened the capacity of that world to support meaning and purpose. Secondly, he describes how recent changes in the character of science and technology constitute a shift in their core activity from fabrication to action, from making things to initiating processes, thus introducing a radical uncertainty and irreversibility to human dealings with nature.

Nature performed: the challenges

Thinking about nature in performative terms can be challenging and disorienting, frequently giving a sense that conceptual closure is always just out of reach. But this thinking also opens up new vocabularies and experiences, enlarging the possibilities for forms of knowledge, broadening the spectrum of intersecting terms between nature, culture and society, and presenting necessary and incisive challenges to different domains of action and thought. In this closing section of the introduction we want to suggest what the scope and location of such challenges might be, to begin to show where and how the conceptual intertwining of nature and performance might have consequences both within and beyond an academic milieu.

Firstly, the areas of planning, environmental policy and regulation are dominated by static ideas about nature and nature–human relationships, ideas that might usefully be disrupted by the application of notions of performance, with their emphasis on activity, on ongoing 'doing' or 'making'. In such domains, however, there is often a tacit understanding of the performativity of nature–culture—an awareness, for example, of the messy, improvised character of knowledges about nature. Yet such awareness is generally kept 'backstage' as it were, often for sound pragmatic reasons, so that a 'front-stage', stable and

10

predictable nature can be acted upon, forecasted, known and controlled. The existing social, bureaucratic and political arrangements have evolved their own modes of human performance in response to and affirmative of that front-stage, predictable view of nature. Bringing to the fore not only the process qualities of nature, but the performative and often improvisatory actions and effects of nature–human relations can imply a demand for new institutional performances and arrangements, and these can be threatening. Working within the unpredictability of an on-going performative view of nature-culture would stretch the most flexible planners, policy and regulation-makers, since their responsibilities bind them into temporary stabilizations that allow them to define appropriate action.

Yet policymaking arrangements which can incorporate both the stable and the performative *are* being developed in some locations and at various scales, as shown in Healy's chapter. As Heim also shows from the domain of artistic practice, experiments in dialogue about nature can harness the very unpredictability and disruptive potential of conversation, a potential that might offer institutions greater self-knowledge and reflexivity. Furthermore, as Horton and Simmons demonstrate, acknowledging and understanding the way that local communities perform their identities and values in relation to nature and risk indicate particular ways in which policy initiatives to encourage responsible environmental citizenship might better go with the grain of the performativity of everyday life. But the performative offers more than procedural examples, novel means for negotiating lay and expert knowledges, or the framing of agendas in regulatory planning. It requires acknowledgement of a radical ambiguity as to what constitutes the 'real', a welcoming of adaptation and mutual change in relation with the natural world, and an openness to the emotive, sensual, and perceptual dimensions of natural–social relations.

Such aspects also influence another domain, that of applied environmental ethics, which shadows many of the chapters. Rather than nature—as living beings, entities or processes—being treated as a given, bounded system to which can be applied an ethical system from which judgement can be derived, nature as performed requires a re-consideration of the ethical as and in experience—as active, embodied, contingent. From the existing literature in feminist, ecofeminist, relational, dialogic and environmental ethics, there is support for views of the ethical as 'practiced' or 'done', or as based on qualities of character and relations of care (see for example Benhabib, 1992; Cuomo, 1998; Smith, 2001; Statman; 1997). The 'performative' perspective contributes further dimensions, of which we can only point towards a few. As Clark has shown, the performativity of life describes the world as fluctuating, complex, improvised and turbulent, and the relations between nature and the human as continuous within it. Responsibility and accountability for human intervention and actions become not only addressed to effects but also inhere as a component of the performative event itself, or of the conditions which allow an event to be initiated.

From such a perspective, ethical agency may not be wholly confined to human subjectivity, but found in other 'actants', in the network of relations. The ethical is found also within the small practices of the everyday in which 'know-how', or tacitly repeated habits, can be sites for ethical expression. And indeed the 'performing'—the action of an ethical approach to nature, the physical meeting between the human and the natural entity figured by human comportment, presence, relationality, emotion, abstraction, and principle—in itself creates the conditions in which knowledge of that other being or entity is created and made possible. In these senses, the ethical is not simply a judgement on the world; like the performative, it is itself creative of the possibilities of knowledge about the world (Cheney and Weston, 1999).

From a theatrical-performance domain, nature in performance troubles the delicate boundary between the staged event and the world outside that event, at times, bringing a too material and presenced 'reality' into a crafted simulacra. Conventional assumptions as to the licence of the performed event to transgress bounds of ethical norms, because it is within an arena marked-out from its 'real' or material effects, are questionable when other life-forms are brought within the event, and altered, created, or harmed. As those representational conventions and boundaries are loosened and crossed, both performance and nature are unsettled, re-created, re-defined (for a more systematic exploration of the natural in performance, see Giannachi and Stewart, 2005 forthcoming).

And finally back to the social sciences. Sociological and anthropological debates have lately explored numerous constructivisms with respect to nature (see Macnaghten and Urry, 1998; Burningham and Cooper, 1999; Irwin, 2001). The performative turn, as we have called it, can contribute to this exploration through the gifts of new vocabularies, metaphors and conceptualizations which can sometimes highlight, sometimes overcome, natural–cultural–social divides. Nature performed, in this context, implies a move to extract the social sciences from positivist, empiricist versions of the world and to embrace a multi-sited and multi-agential view of nature–human relations. However, the idea of nature as something that is performed has also been unsettling. Narratives of performance have recently been problematizing assumptions about the nature and reach of human agency—and even, as Szerszynski indicates, problematizing the assumptions embedded in talk of the social *construction* of nature, as if nature was a fabricated object. As Clark's chapter suggests, a new space and agency for the biological is being carved out within such narratives, with human action and intent beginning to be interpreted within larger spaces, timescales and non-human agencies. 'Nature performed—by what?' is a question that is creeping towards the borderlands of the natural and social sciences. Once again performance is pushing accepted conventions and idioms towards liminal spaces where new meanings might be created.

Notes

1 Sometimes in this volume 'performativity' is used in this more technical sense; at others it is used in a looser way, to denote the performance-like characteristics of something.

 © The Editorial Board of the Sociological Review 2003

Bibliography

Arendt, Hannah (1958), *The Human Condition*, Chicago: University of Chicago Press.
Austin, J. L. (1962), *How to Do Things with Words*, Oxford: Clarendon Press.
Bauman, Z. (2000), *Liquid Modernity*, Cambridge: Polity Press.
Bell, C. (1998), 'Performance' in M. C. Taylor (ed.), *Critical Terms for Religious Studies*, Chicago and London: University of Chicago Press, pp. 205–224.
Bell, V. (ed.) (1999), *Performativity and Belonging*, London: Sage/TCS.
Benhabib, S. (1992), *Situating the Self: Gender, Community and Postmodernism in Contemporary Ethics*, Cambridge: Polity Press.
Bourdieu, P. (1977), *Outline of a Theory of Practice*, tr. Richard Nice, Cambridge: Cambridge University Press.
Burningham, K. and G. Cooper (1999), 'Being Constructive: Social Constructionism and the Environment,' *Sociology*, 33(2): 297–316.
Butler, J. (1990), *Gender Trouble*, London: Routledge.
Butler, J. (1997), *Excitable Speech: A Politics of the Performative*, New York: Routledge.
Carlson, M. (1996), *Performance: A Critical Introduction*, London and New York: Routledge.
Chaudhuri, U. (1997), *Staging Place: The Geography of Modern Drama*, Michigan: University of Michigan Press.
Cheney, J. and A. Weston (1999), 'Environmental Ethics as Environmental Etiquette: Toward an Ethics-Based Epistemology', *Environmental Ethics* 21(2): 115–134.
Collingwood, R. G. (1945), *The Idea of Nature*, Oxford: Clarendon Press.
de Certeau, M. (1984), *The Practice of Everyday Life*, Berkeley: University of California Press.
Cuomo, C. J. (1998), *Feminism and Ecological Communities: An Ethic of Flourishing*, London and New York: Routledge.
Deleuze, G. and F. Guattari (1994), *What is Philosophy?* London: Verso.
Dewsbury, J.-D. (2000), 'Performativity and the Event: Enacting a Philosophy of Difference' *Environment and Planning D: Society and Space*, 18: 473–496.
Franklin, A. (2001), *Nature and Social Theory*, London: Sage.
Franklin, S., C. Lury and J. Stacey (2000), *Global Nature, Global Culture: Gender, Race, and Life Itself*, London: Sage.
Giannachi, G. and N. Stewart (eds) (2005 forthcoming), *Performing Nature: Explorations in Ecology and the Arts*, Bern: Peter Lang AG.
Goffman, E. (1959), *The Presentation of Self in Everyday Life*, revised and expanded edition, London: Doubleday.
Goffman, E. (1967), *Interaction Ritual: Essays on Face-to-Face Behaviour*, Harmondsworth: Penguin.
Grosz, E. (1995), *Space, Time and Perversion*, London: Routledge.
Irwin, A. (2001), *Sociology and the Environment: A Critical Introduction to Society, Nature and Knowledge*, Cambridge: Polity Press.
Lévi-Strauss, C. (1962), *The Savage Mind*, London: Weidenfeld.
Lyotard, J.-F. (1986), *The Postmodern Condition: A Report on Knowledge*, tr. Geoff Bennington and Brian Massumi, Manchester: Manchester University Press.
Macnaghten, P. and J. Urry (1998), *Contested Natures*, London: Sage.
Macnaghten, P. and J. Urry (ed.) (2001), *Bodies of Nature*, London: Sage.
Parker, A. and E. K. Sedgwick (eds) (1995), *Performance and Performativity*, New York and London: Routledge.
Rose, G. and N. Thrift (eds) (2000), *Environment and Planning D: Society and Space. Special Issue: 'Spaces of Performance'*, 18(4–5).
Schechner, R. (1988), *Performance Theory*, New York: Routledge.
Schechner, R. (2002), *Performance Studies: An Introduction*, London: Routledge.
Schieffelin, E. L. (1998), 'Problematizing Performance' in F. Hughes-Freeland (ed.) *Ritual, Performance, Media*. London and New York: Routledge, pp. 194–207.

Sennett, R. (1986), *The Fall of Public Man*, London: Faber and Faber.

Smith, M. (2001), *An Ethics of Place: Radical Ecology, Postmodernity, and Social Theory*, Albany: State University of New York Press.

Soper, K. (1995), *What is Nature? Culture, Politics and the Non-Human*, Oxford: Blackwell, 1995.

States, B. O. (1996), 'Performance as Metaphor', *Theatre Journal*, 48(1): 1–26.

Statman, D. (ed.) (1997), *Virtue Ethics*, Edinburgh: Edinburgh University Press.

Thrift, N. and J.-D. Dewsbury (2000), 'Dead Geographies—And How to Make Them Live, *Environment and Planning D: Society and Space* 18: 411–432.

Turner, V. (1974), *Dramas, Fields and Metaphors*, Ithaca, New York: Cornell University Press.

Urry, J. (2003), *Global Complexity*, Cambridge: Polity.

Williams, R. (1976), *Keywords: A Vocabulary of Culture and Society*, London: Croom Helm.

Williams, R. (1980), 'Ideas of Nature,' in *Problems in Materialism and Culture*, London: New Left Bookclub, pp. 67–85.

© The Editorial Board of the Sociological Review 2003

Part I
Making worlds

Performances and constitutions of natures: a consideration of the performance of lay geographies

David Crouch

Introduction

This chapter considers performance in relation to the negotiation of feelings and ideas about nature. Moreover, it concerns ways in which pre-figured notions of what nature may be may be negotiated through a process of doing. Doing is explored through ideas of embodied practice, grounded in the work of Maurice Merleau-Ponty (1962), that have informed recent debates on performance. Performance has become a plural notion that includes Butler's perspective of repetition and containment of identities whilst offering the possibility of resistance, and what Elizabeth Grosz refers to as its potential to open up and encounter the unexpected (Butler, 1997; 1993; Grosz, 1999). In the chapter, embodied practice is thus considered not only in terms of the reiteration of the mundane, habitual and the everyday, but also in terms of the potential of practice to be *practising*, to involve trying out life, exploration and experiment. Performance can also be regular, repetitive and work to a given choreography. As Grosz in particular asserts, however, it also has the potential of experimentation and of resistance.

In that sense, the terms 'practice' and 'performance' offer the potential of a two-way re-negotiation. Discourses on practice have recently acknowledged the power of subjective negotiation, and have contributed to the debate on performance in terms of a spectral consideration of the body-components of discursive encounters with space (see Crouch, 2003b forthcoming). In turn, performance has added to the debate on practice by elucidating the way that individuals have to work within the tension between *holding on* and of *going further* in things they do. In each case, however, there is an insistence on the active relation of each back to culture. In this chapter the 'performance' explored includes both staged performance and everyday performance. This is not intended to provide a detailed comparative critique in the light of different performance theories but to use the two in order to inform an understanding of everyday performance.

Recent debates on the construction and constitution of an ontology of nature have explored how the perception of nature is shaped by pre-figured notions of

© The Editorial Board of the Sociological Review 2003. Published by Blackwell Publishing Ltd, 9600 Garsington Road, Oxford OX4 2DQ, UK and 350 Main Street, Malden, MA 02148, USA

nature in the British landscape tradition, and how nature can be understood as constructed through practical events and available tools (Macnaghten and Urry, 1998; Franklin, 2001). Phil Macnaghten and John Urry acknowledge the possibilities of vision being modified by the engagement of the other senses (1998). This chapter seeks to take this further empirically by contesting the significance of pre-figured understandings of nature in literature and the arts, advertising and formal discourses such as management. Tim Ingold's notion of dwelling becomes pertinent here in relation to debates about performance, as a means of situating ideas and practical ontology in the world (Ingold, 2000).

Adrian Franklin's account includes a social history of the garden, preferences and practices of gardening; the influence of diverse influences of technology and the significance of embodied practice in the complexities of contemporary constructions of 'nature' (2001). His discourse on nature reflects the consumptionist perspective of objects and ideas worked on and made sense. This displaces Macnaghten and Urry's emphasis on constructions of nature that may deviate from the mainstream as being essentially 'resistant', exemplified by their reference to new age travellers and, using this author's work, allotment gardening (1998). In contrast, the argument developed in this chapter is that 'nature' is constituted in practice in any case, and that practice therefore provides a significant rather than merely deviant mode or process through which nature is understood, made sense. To argue thus is not to contradict the informing elements of wider context, but to complement them through an attention to practice. In this chaper, practice is considered through the particular debates on performance. Performance is framed as both staged event and the processes of self-actualization that are made in everyday life.

Nature is engaged in this debate through a consideration of practical objects and the encounter with them in allotment gardening. When considering the working of objects and ideas through allotment gardening into a practical ontology it is argued that not only a will to cultivation but also numerous other facets of life are performed (Crouch, 1999; Crouch, 2003a). It is through these numerous facets that ideas and values surrounding nature may be worked, constituted and, using diverse contexts, refigured. Ideas about allotment holding were performed in a staged artistic/theatrical event on an allotment site in England in 1998, called *Bloom 98*, at Uplands allotments, Birmingham England (Palmer, 1998). This was organized as an intervention into the world of allotment gardening by Harry Palmer, interventionist artist, who combined his own particular ideas about allotments with those elicited through the performers' encounter with people working allotments. It is significant that in neither of these performances—everyday allotment gardening and the intervention into it—was nature the single object or idea. This narrative account, however, demonstrates ways in which nature was drawn into performance.

At the centre of this discussion is the argument that this process of constituting nature can be inter-subjective; that ideas of nature emerge and are worked in complex processes that may be self-consciously grounded in ideas about nature and may be not. Ideas of nature emerge in the lives of the allotment

© The Editorial Board of the Sociological Review 2003

holders through what they do and how they feel. In both versions of performance it is argued that nature is incompletely understood in terms of prior 'givens', particular traditions, and cannot be understood outside the sphere of performance.

In exploring aspects of performance of these two kinds I intend to illuminate the role of practice in making sense of nature, the self, identities and subjectivities. I suggest that what we 'do' in practice may include facets of everyday life such as 'enjoyment', love and care, as well as frustration and tasking (Gorz, 1984) and that these may inform and be informed by processes of self-regulation and self-identification.

On two 'performances'

An allotment event

Uplands allotments in Birmingham were chosen for the staging of a multiple event of diverse art, called *Bloom 98*. Harry Palmer, an intervention artist from Hull, was the Director (Palmer, 1998). The use of the site was negotiated with allotment holders over several months through which a number of different artists sought to interpret what allotment holding meant for the people who used the place. The actual performance was staged one evening in July 1998 and attracted over one thousand 'spectators'.

This performance included a very explicit discourse on nature, a discourse which was politically subversive or at least alternative. An allotment was chosen for this event because it 'remains a quintessential British activity[1] which crosses boundaries, transcending monetary and class values despite the pressures for its alternative use seen as "more suitable", "more worthwhile" and "better for the economy" echoes of which are voiced from above'.[2] So this performance was situated very explicitly in a discourse of human, social and cultural/political relations. Uplands was chosen not only because it is a large space (400 plots) and spread over a hill, providing a dramatic setting for spectacle, but **also** because the plot-holders come from many different nationalities, displaying diverse ways of cultivation, ethnicities and a significant level of associative activity that includes activities involving the local community during the year. This provided a context for performing a number of ideas. All of this performance involved the use of 'natural' objects—earth, branches, seeds, and ideas of nature.

The performance evening included *Umbrella Gardening*, where one allotment plot was transformed into 'a field of umbrellas planted in the earth'. As Martin Burton, the artist behind the piece, put it: 'our expectations are confounded by a paradox of light and sound of rain'. Some one hundred umbrellas were 'planted' in the ground and lit from beneath as the evening progressed. This lighting was accompanied by the projected sound of falling rain that had an effect of sounding also like roots moving, growing in the earth, disrupting the idea of the silent growth of plants. In another part of the event one hundred plastic gloves were

© The Editorial Board of the Sociological Review 2003

'planted' in the ground of one plot, raised up like their plot-holders struggling—with their land, and with their rights to 'hold' land—but also unsettling the idea of growing nature. Of course, the history of allotment holding is one of struggle for the right to use land (Crouch and Ward, 2003). A third part of the performance was presented by *Blissbody* who 'tended their allotment/installation throughout the early evening, with a ritualistic performance at dusk' at which the artists lit fireworks and set light to planted twigs. Situated on the brow of a hill in this site this performance made a significant spectacle in the dark. In each case the staged event leant away from a direct use of natural objects yet was performed in relation to, and alluded to, ideas of nature. Each took place surrounded by many other plots where crops were growing.

Other features of this event included *Seedsaluv's* 'collaborative seed packet with alotmenteers to reflect and celebrate culturally diverse and organic gardening practices'. Seed packets they produced were designed by the artist and filled with seeds given by plot-holders, the seeds representing particular crops grown by different cultures: Afro-Caribbean, Indian, and so on. These packets were given away and engaged with ideas about the shared and inter-subjective character of plant use in allotment holding (Crouch, 1999). *Life Frame* by Jo Roberts included photographs: 'photo installations in cold frames pick up on the isolation of the allotment holder within his/her solitary activity of gardening'. Photographs of garden tools, the plot, and individual plants and vegetables were placed within a selection of cold frames (which are used to protect plants). Being a plot-holder can be solitary as well as communal, and can be a time for reflection, as discussed below.

With reference to his construction *The View from the Shed: Landscape of the Imagination* Greg Miller explored two dimensions of contemporary environmental concern. 'The wider universe is struck down to the scale of an allotment. Mechanical pieces interacting with its surroundings'. Through the construction he presented a discourse on global issues through a provocation of the local, and of the interaction between human, 'natural' and non-natural objects in human practice. In *Potted Histories* a potting shed was made interactive to 'reveal the secrets of both the plants and those who nurture them'; crude but ingenious mechanisms could be activated by the visitors. This author narrated allotment stories whilst meandering around the lanes that bisect the allotment site. Poems were recited in a series of marquees and multi-ethnic music performed in the lanes up and down and between the plots in expression of the cultural diversity of allotment holding.

These aspects of performance included both significant ideas of nature—in terms of global/local natures, cultivation care, nature in human exchange—and engaged the small scale of everyday engagement and encounter with nature. Nature in allotment holding is drawn out and celebrated in these performances. Felt, tangible nature is implicated with its metaphorical power: as a microcosm of global nature, as ethnic/multi-cultural diversity. The Uplands allotment organization describes itself as 'a melting pot of race, creed and culture united by their love of gardening' (Palmer, 1998). In all these performances nature is pre-

© The Editorial Board of the Sociological Review 2003

sented as engaged in the performed experience of the space in which allotment cultivation is practised.

In each of these performances the meanings of nature were explored through metaphor—in the upstanding gloves; in cultivated and 'natural' growth; in the encounter between symbolic artefacts and the idea and practice of growing; in the curious mutuality between plants and 'those who nurture them'. Ideas about the meaning of cultivating allotments were related to issues of local and global values about environment as nature, as well as to the material objects of nature that plotholders encounter. This produced a narrative of marginalization and inclusivity; of the local and the global; of the power of cultivation (over lives, over ways people think) and the practice of nature; and a celebration of space, nature and people's lives.

The character of this performance was not incidental. Palmer engineered the event as a whole to be a direct political intervention. He claimed that the event resonated with what allotment holders do. *Bloom 98* sought to explore the grounds for a direct but fluid relationship between the possibilities of staged performance and performance in everyday practice:

'The imagination of artists and allotment holders has captured the potential of cross cultural exchange forming a new possibility and working relationship. Allotments are still a special place where individual creative effort is on display within the urban environment. Individuality, value, meaningfulness and associations concerning marginalization—the hidden words of allotment activity and artistic practice induce pride and passion in what they do. Despite the ongoing pressure of the everyday and the struggle to maintain landscape and culture, it is hoped that this project shall indeed celebrate the adversities, break down the solitary conventions and demonstrate new ways of collaboration. In this instance, between the allotment owner and the artist' (Palmer, 1998).

The ideas of nature performed in *Bloom 98* were not incidental. They included the material and metaphorical realm in which solitariness can be realised; the connectivity of local and global; the cultivation of plants; the chance to work land and nature. These features were extended to human interactions, in ritual, celebration and encounter. Nature provided the crucial metaphors and materiality through which this performance worked—plants, earth, seeds, and so on. Allotment sites are cultivated, ordered and dominated thrugh human control (Crouch, 2003a). Allotments, however, can also be sites of partnership with nature through which particular ideas can be worked. At *Bloom 98* ideas and objects of nature were drawn through and related to human actions and feelings expressed in sound, growth, light and words. These different themes are explored in the next section through a consideration of the performance of everyday allotment life.

Everyday allotment performance

In this section of the chapter I present a series of brief narratives of the experience individuals have of doing allotments. Allotment holding involves plant cultivation. In this sense it is much the same as gardening anywhere. However, there are particular characteristics of being an allotment holder that are distinctive. These include the close contact with others that comes from the use of small pieces of land adjacent to each other without interruption. Moreover, in order to have an allotment one must make a conscious act of securing a plot, as the plot does not simply 'come with the house' as in the case of the home garden. For whatever reason an individual may take on, or rent, an allotment, this may involve a particular kind of commitment. The reasons for having an allotment are many and can include: to grow food, to grow food of a particular kind (notably organic food) or simply to provide food cheaply; a search for escape from the home, possibly to be with other people, or simply to be alone. These diverse reasons are not all explored in this section but rather, selectively, as examples of individuals explicitly and implicitly engaging with the act of cultivation. These are therefore not presented as typical of allotment holders but indicative of ways in which individuals work ideas and actions in performance.

Linton Carby is a plot holder at Uplands allotments. He was one of the plot-holders who provided seeds for *Seedsaluv*. He talked about the social activity of giving crops away as part of the enjoyment of growing, cultivating and friendship:

'If you give somebody anything they say—where did you get it from?—I say I grew it myself. You feel proud in yourself that you grows it, you know, if you get it from the shop, some of it don't have any taste. On the allotment you plant something and it takes nine months to come to' (Crouch and Ward, 2003: vii).

He implicates nature in the exercise of human relations and identities. What he has grown through the season becomes an object of social encounter. Love and care and developing non-commodity values in self-identification are marked by Deirdre, from Northampton: 'My allotment means relief from stress, creativity, the love of creation . . . it means everything to me. I don't know where I would be without my garden'.

Another plot-holder, Carol Youngson, demonstrates the close physical significance and making of values that she associates with allotment cultivation, simply in feeling her way around what she grows, how and where she grows it:

'. . . working outdoors feels much better for your body somehow . . . more vigorous than day-to-day housework, much more variety and stimulus. The air is always different and alerts the skin, unexpected scents are brought by breezes. Only when on your hands and knees do you notice insects and other small wonders. My allotment is of central importance in my life. I feel strongly that everyone should have access to land, to establish a close relationship with the earth . . . essential as our surroundings become more artificial' (Crouch and Ward, 2003: 157).

Carol describes what she does—and what she makes of this activity through what she does—in terms of how her body engages in the intimacy of space, in terms of movements amongst multi-sensual encounters. Carol touches, bends and kneels. She moves her body amongst the spaces between vegetation, earth,

 © The Editorial Board of the Sociological Review 2003

insects and the air and herself. She finds her feeling of life through what her body does there. In this extract there is greater ambivalence between the content and the process of performance, and reference to pre-figured intentions and how those ideas are worked through doing. In the extract she talks first of her performance, and then refers that back to contexts, which could be regarded as double-checking or confirming performance with reference to prior context. It would appear that performance and prior context are engaged simultaneously in the way she makes sense of what she is doing.

Two plotters expressed the value of ethnicity and cultural exchange in cultivation:

'We learn from each other. You are very social and you are very kind. You make me feel good, you don't come and call at me. Things in your garden you always hand me, little fruits . . . which I have valued so much'.

'And I've learnt from him. I've learnt some ways of planting, I've learnt real skills about planting, Jamaican ways of growing and cooking . . . And I've also learnt about patience and goodness and religion, too. It all links in' (Crouch and Ward, 2003: ix).

Ideas of nature that are performed in plotting include the desire to cultivate plants and work the ground, and thereby involve escape, self-discovery and self-assertion in relation to nature. Ideas of nature are also figured in giving, in the sensuous feeling and awareness of body-contact, in constituting values. Nature is both an object of expression and constitutes a feeling through which the body can express itself. In the following section I consider how these components work. Nature does not appear to be conceptualized, or imagined, as something outside everyday experience. Instead it is engaged in and through what individuals do, not in isolation of other informing contexts, but in relation to them. Moreover nature is not a separate entity of existence but engaged through and alongside other trajectories of human action.

The nature of performance

Nature is dynamically empowered and its power signified in the performances discussed. Rather than being simply 'there' for observation, nature is mobilized in a different way, as partner in action; its character progressed into multiple possibilities of significance through what the individual does. Such an interpretation can be followed through a consideration of debates about performance in relation to embodiment and space (Thrift, 1997; Thrift and Dewesbury, 2000; Nash, 2000; Crouch, 1999, 2001). The significance of embodiment in performance may be focused through the feeling of doing (Harré, 1993). The feeling of doing highlights our grasp of the world around us as felt, as not only imagined and concentrated in mental reflexivity. Harré's discussion of the feeling of doing draws upon Merleau-Ponty's extensive exploration of the multi-sensuality and multi-dimensionality of life-practices and the practice of the body in (its) body-space (1962).

© The Editorial Board of the Sociological Review 2003   23

Merleau-Ponty's particular contribution is in his consideration of the physicality of everyday doing and of movement in space, of individuals being engulfed by it rather than acting in detachment. This contribution is increasingly being engaged with in terms of the metaphorical and imaginative/poetic content and character of practice (Crouch, 2003b forthcoming). Nick Crossley has explicated the ways in which embodied practices are progressed intersubjectively, rather than in terms of isolated individual action (Crossley, 1995). Consistently, the constitution of embodied practice is thought of in terms of a subjective negotiation with the cultural contexts in which individuals live. Furthermore Alan Radley (1995) has explored the expressive content of practice. Just as space can be encountered in a process of spacing so we may consider nature too as encountered in a process of 'naturing'. The idea of space as constituted through performance incorporates the significance of contexts and representations, but challenges their frequent privilege (Crouch, 2001). Rather, individuals negotiate contexts and representations through their performance of space or nature. To go further, individuals may constitute their ideas of nature through their experience of performance, ideas that need not be pre-figured by context but discovered, uncovered, in the performance itself.

As exemplified in the case of Carol, talking of her relationship with the earth, the doing body informs what she makes of the performance, discursively and pre-discursively. Space is grasped through the doing, not as an object 'out there' or merely 'felt' through the body, rather as constituted of the numerous feelings, sensualities and, in particular, the expressive character of these together. Radley points to the significance of expressivity in the way individuals do things, and thereby the way in which performance is felt in a relationship with others, including objects and space, and things are changed (1995). Expressivity is in the encounter, in the performance, the body-performativities in touch with other sensibilities, body-thinking and feeling. In the act of performing they are there, at the moment, doing. As Deleuze argues, 'all begins with sensibility' (1994: 144 quoted in Harrison, 2000: 497). Moreover they do not merely perform in response of the pre-figured to the performative, or to a space or to others. Neither do they perform a given self through particular moments, or intentionally do things in an exploration of the self.

Carol's case has similarities with Harry Palmer's self-conscious pursuit of allotments, in being prefigured by a particular position of concern about environment. However, whereas Palmer's intervention seeks to represent ideas, albeit through a practised encounter amongst the performers and the allotment holders, Carol approaches it differently. Her performance is significantly unexpected and diverse; she seeks to cultivate and discovers other things. Her notions of nature are unsettled, enlarged and focused in the performance she makes. She builds, refigures and reworks nature through her lay knowledge. And she expresses herself through the process of performance.

Ways of doing things and the elements of doing can express and invoke our constant monitoring of the self and of others (Goffman, 1959, 1967; Malbon, 1999; Crang, 1994). Nature, then, may be figured, discovered, made sense of,

© The Editorial Board of the Sociological Review 2003

challenged, constituted, refigured in the multi-sensuous and expressive content of both everyday and crafted performance. Such an approach contrasts with many treatments of nature that tend to prioritize nature as essentially prefigured (see discussion in Macnaghten and Urry, 1998). Discussion on nature(s) has tended also to be made in terms of an English association of nature with landscape, visual content and a more formal enculturation supported through a popular culture of advertising and product branding (Franklin, 2001). Notions of nature contextualized through landscape and thereby as essentially visual can be contested through its consideration as enveloping, relating to Merleau-Ponty's conceptualization of the body in the world and working sensuously in relation to it (Crouch and Toogood, 1999).

The materiality of nature may be practised in relation to artefacts through which memory, identity and a sense of being in the world may be forged, artefacts encountered and valued through doing things and that become significant in the way we make sense of the world. Radley (1990, 1995) and Crossley (1995, 1996) have emphasised the importance of body-engagement or encounter with artefacts such as these—that Maffesoli calls body tactics (1996), worked by our expressive body-interaction with them, and inter-subjectively in our bodily relation with others. Crucially too Julia Kristeva's work (1996) on the imaginative/poetic self interacting body in the world brings the tactical content of body-encounter to bear on these other dimensions.

Nature emerges as a means and as an expression of making sense of the world and of ourselves; in turn, nature is made sense of through practical action. John Shotter discusses ontological and practical knowledge as worked and won in doing (Shotter, 1993). This refiguring of nature, as bricolage of objects, renderings and ideas, resembles consumer goods. Contextualized, they are each worked on through what the individual does with them and makes of them (Miller, 1998).

Micropolitics is a further dimension of what may critically constitute performance in both staged and everyday terms. In the two examples considered micropolitics emerges in different ways. In *Bloom 98* politics is foregrounded, and nature is manipulated in the process of argument. Amongst allotment holders (whose individual politics may be as varied as that of the population as a whole) ideas, attitudes and values concerning nature can be reformulated through performance. Recent discussion on the constitution of 'nature/s' has pointed to the possibility of practising nature in determinate ways which oppose the commercialization of nature and the seeking after alternative human values and 'green awareness', explored by Macnaghten and Urry in terms of the examples of new age travellers and, using this author's work, of allotment holding (1998). Allotment performance certainly has the potential to adjust individuals' ontology and even encourage resistance and alternative values on nature, but does not necessarily do so. The grasp of nature is less easily polarized and instead the classical presumptions of what may be understood as nature are not only unsettled through a consideration, valuable though it is, of directly oppositional practices. Rather, the argument that develops from this consideration of performance in everyday life is that ideas of 'nature' can be progressed across a wide range of apparently mundane and habitual everyday practices. As Thrift has argued, the diversity of empowering practices of individuals is as interesting and as informative as the overtly and self-declared 'resistant' in an understanding of the multiple character of what nature means and how and in what processes it is engaged in life (Thrift, 1997).

Ideas of nature may be worked and refigured in relation to a kaleidoscope of activities, materials, imaginings, relationships. Particular dimensions of human values and feelings may be encountered, discovered and progressed (Domosh, 1998). In addition to ideologically-prefigured and explicitly exercised activities, micropolitics in the everyday offers potential grounds through which we may understand nature in everyday ontology, indeed to construct the grounds for a more practical ontology in everyday life and apparently mundane practices (Nast and Pile, 1998). The possibility that these processes may have wider consequences for individuals' attitudes and actions towards other issues of 'nature' is not the focus of this discussion, which is rather the possibility of individuals progressing their ideas concerning nature through performance.

Butler has argued that performance can be conservative, repetitive and ritualistic (Butler, 1997). In recent debate, however, it has been argued that performance may be characterized by a potential to reconfigure, break, adjust or negotiate contexts such as gender, ethnicity and values (Lloyd, 1996; Thrift and Dewesbury, 2000). Thus performance may be considered the effect of context or the affecting of context. It is suggested, then, that context is refigured in performance and does not remain the same. Performance has been figured as modulating life and discovering the new, the unexpected, in ways that may reconfigure the self, in a process of '. . . what life (duration, memory, consciousness) brings to the world: the new, the movement of actualization of the virtual, expansiveness, opening up' (Grosz, 1999: 25). It may be that individuals perform in ways that feature across the spectrum of what these different interpretations offer and work their own way through them in the doing.

In terms of theatre, 'performance' has become increasingly contested territory. Judith Butler argues that ingredients of the performative succeed 'only because it is ritualised practice, echoing prior speech actions and therefore "citing" prior authoritative practices' (Tulloch, 1999). In contrast Cindy Patton claims that the performative can embody tactics of coping and strategy for alternative discourse (Patton, 1999). John Tulloch (1999) connects the possibilities of both theatre (considered in this chapter through the example of the staged performance of *Bloom 98*) and everyday life as holding a critical potential.

Dimensions of performance as risky, critical, and potentially subversive of dominant discourses, as 'becoming', may be considered through Ingold's distinction between thinking and doing, articulated in his reworking of Heidegger's notion of 'dwelling' (1995, 2000). On the one hand he acknowledges prefigured, determined and closed ideas for things, spaces, and so on. On the other he identifies the motor of 'dwelling' that sustains the present, that can dislodge prefigured meanings, and that can enable a refiguring of what things mean,

© The Editorial Board of the Sociological Review 2003

from which contemplation, in flows, can occur. Ingold's discussion progresses from a consideration of cultivation (Ingold, 2000). In the examples considered, nature is crucially not only a mental construct or subject of mental reflexivity but encountered, physically and materially too. Performance can be significant in making sense, temporally, unevenly, non-linearly, multiply and perhaps chaotically, as performative structures of feeling constructed of numerous movements, encounters and reflections (Harrison, 2000). Through performance individuals are also able to feel; through performance they are able to think and rethink.

Naturing

In this chapter it is less the intention to interpret performance and its performativities in terms of whether they are critical/subversive or conservative than to explore ways in which nature may be worked and (re)figured through the working of performance. It is evident that in both examples the potential is there for both of these modes. It is argued, however, that performance enables the movement away from (rather than necessarily in opposition to) prevailing/ dominant versions of what nature is and in what ways it may matter, or indeed be apprehended and 'made sense'. In any case, it emerges from this consideration of two cases that nature may be less 'made sense' than unevenly incorporated in the flows and adjustments that are characteristic of performance. Amongst the spectators of *Bloom 98* and its explicit performers there is the potential for agency; allotment holders share this potential (Tulloch, 1999: 8). In situating the performance through and amidst plot-holders, *Bloom 98* provided a spectacle that may have made illusion and reality more difficult to disentangle, or more easy because of its elements of the surreal.

Considering these two cases together offers interesting insight into the performance of nature. Everyday allotment holding is a means of 'getting on' with life where nature is persistently its material and is felt; in publicly staged *Bloom 98* nature provided the material and ideas for a negotiated intervention. Plotting is a private practice that is also public, because it happens in proximity to others and by its expressive potential in relation to others. Staged performance is public and on this occasion engaged the intimate feelings of those allotment holders who participated in the event. In each case, nature is celebrated and is the content of celebration; in getting on with life and making intervention there is a micro-politics of discovery and negotiation. Everyday allotment holding is felt to be an intervention in other everyday practices, body-sensuousness, expressivity, discovering identities and human relations and these are mobilized also in the staged event. Each encounters the everyday and is extraordinary in the sense of transcending the mundane. Cultivation engages a working of space, nature, sociality and the self. The materiality of 'nature' is clearly implicated in the way in which *Bloom 98* was constructed and in the everyday practice of allotments; nature as metaphor significant in each.

© The Editorial Board of the Sociological Review 2003

In making sense of nature in performance numerous objects that may be used to refer to nature are incorporated. Twigs, earth, bugs, plants and water are directly handled, felt, wielded. Artefacts can become important signifiers in memory (Radley, 1990). Moreover, these artefacts are given power through not only mechanical use but through expressive encounter. Things are given value through the feelings transmitted in the event (Radley, 1995). A plant is not merely something to grow but is transformed through the care, tedium, challenge, tenderness or commitment the individual may associate with it. Furthermore the significance of things can be rendered through the cultural and social relations through which they are used (Crossley, 1996).

It is possible to develop from this discussion a notion that nature is constituted performatively. The nuances and facets of performance may be reflexively constituted as embodied semiotics (Crouch, 2001). Anne Game presents the idea of material semiotics constituted through body-encounters (Game, 1991). Through bodily performance pre-figured notions of nature and our relationships with(in) it, practical knowledge may be produced. Rather than nature being a construction outside the self, whether as a scientific entity, as peace and the sublime, or as landscape and its contents as shaped in high or popular culture, the material and metaphor of nature is encountered. Such 'outward' notions are engaged, inter-twined and reworked through performance. Nature is not merely grasped as 'something to visit' or something to observe, but as encountered in life-practices and through encounter also with the self and others. The meanings and symbols of nature that may emerge from this process can be significantly embodied. It is suggested that 'doing' can be given the power to figure, and to refigure nature. In this process, however, ideas of nature can be disrupted and challenged or sustained; lives and values adjusted through the performance experience, as nature is worked through such as feelings, care and ideology with the possibility of their being strengthened, challenged, reworked.

Bloom 98 explicitly performed a significant politics in its formative statement and in its appropriation of the several issues of nature discussed. It engaged and challenged ideas of nature. It engaged a more subtle everyday micropolitics amongst allotment holders. The latter is a more gentle, negotiated finding and working of alternative, often non-commercial and sometimes anti-commercial positions and values that plotters hold in an actualization of the self. These are exemplified in love and care, varieties of human relations and relations also with nature in both metaphor and materiality, often conveyed through objects of nature.

'Ideas' emerge as recursive, and what is context in terms of nature become problematized (Barnett, 1999). Natures is practised, in a process of naturing the world, our bodies and our identities.[3] Nature is acknowledged through the practice less as a stand alone (and even simply ideologically good) artefact or 'goal' than a constituent of ontology, a culturally related but distinctively practised constituent that is a sensuous, expressively felt and imagined practice. Nature may be practised in a naturing of the world, and our identities may be natured. In this—certainly awkward—language it is possible to translate nature from

© The Editorial Board of the Sociological Review 2003

objectified 'thing' to ongoing, fluid parts—or dimensions—of our lives that is practised, reworked, reimagined, made in working human relationships, felt, made sense, ontologically.

Nature can be rendered as sensuous through the ways in which the individual may encounter it; made as part of expressive practice; characterised as multi-sensual/dimensional through the ways in which the individual does things. Through imagining and feeling nature, ideas of the self and human relations can be refigured and values discovered, constituted, with cultural contexts of film, art and design drawn in as resources in the process. In discursive and pre-discursive encounters of performance nature is not merely pre-figured or pre-given but produced, and any pre-figured representations of 'nature' are constantly refigured. It is in the performance, in the wider practice of nature that nature is constituted, and through which everyday unstable versions of nature are made sense.

Notes

1 In fact, allotments, under various nomenclature, are a global phenomenon (Crouch and Ward, 2003).
2 These themes were explored by the author in *The Plot*, BBC2, 1994.
3 Nature in the performance of artwork is considered through the painting and constructions of Peter Lanyon (Crouch and Toogood, 1999). Making painting is explored in terms of the artist's performance in nature, landscape or space in sensuous/expressive and poetic ways, in his awareness of nature/space/landscape all around him, sensing diverse realities in space walked inside rather than observed in a detached way. Performance of this kind is translated in the enactment of knowledge of nature in the painting, in physical movement that expresses these complex practices of moving in nature. The performance of painting translates into the presence of the completed work and in its relation with people who use similarly complex body movements and imagination in encountering paintings.

References

Barnett, C. (1999), 'Deconstructing Context: Exposing Derrida', *Transactions of the Institute of British Geographers*, 24(3): 277–293.
Butler, J. (1993), *Bodies That Matter: On The Discursive Limits Of Sex*, London: Routledge.
Butler, J. (1997), *Excitable Speech: A Politics of the Performative*, London: Routledge.
Crang, M. (1994), 'On the Heritage Trail: Maps of and Journeys to Olde England', *Environment and Planning D: Society and Space*, (12): 341–355.
Crossley, N. (1995), Merleau-Ponty, the Elusive Body and Carnal Sociology, *Body and Society*, 1(1): 43–63.
Crossley, N. (1996), *Intersubjectivity: The Fabric of Social Becoming*, London: Sage.
Crouch, D. (1999), 'The Intimacy and Expansion of Space', in D. Crouch (ed.), *leisure/tourism geographies*, Routledge: London, pp. 257–276.
Crouch, D. (2001), 'Spatialities and the Feeling of Doing' *Social and Cultural Geography*, 2(1): 61–75.
Crouch D. (2003a), *The Art of Allotments*, Nottingham, Five Leaves Press.
Crouch, D. (2003b), 'Spacing, Performing and Becoming: Tangles in the Mundane', *Environment and Planning A*, 35(11): 1945–1960.

© The Editorial Board of the Sociological Review 2003

Crouch, D. and M. Toogood (1999), 'Everyday Abstraction in the Art of Peter Lanyon', *Ecumene*, 6(1): 72–89.

Crouch D and C. Ward (2003), *The Allotment: Its Landscape and Culture*, 4th edition, Nottingham: Five Leaves Books.

Deleuze, G. (1994), *Difference and Repetition*, London: Athlone Press.

Domosh, M. (1998), '"Those Gorgeous Incongruities": Polite Politics and Public Space on the Streets of Nineteenth-Century New York', *Annals of the Association of American Geographers*, 88: 209–226.

Franklin, A. (2001), *Nature*, London: Sage.

Game, A. (1991), *Undoing Sociology: Towards a Deconstructive Sociology*, Buckingham: Open University Press.

Goffman, E. (1959), *The Presentation of Self in Everyday Life*, revised and expanded edition, London: Doubleday.

Goffman, E. (1967), *Interaction Ritual: Essays on Face-to-Face Behaviour*, Harmondsworth: Penguin.

Gorz, A. (1984), *Paths to Paradise*, London: Pluto Press.

Grosz, E. (1999), Thinking the New: Of Futures Yet Unthought, in E. Grosz (ed.), *Becomings: Explorations in Time, Memory and Futures*, Ithaca, NY: Cornel University Press.

Harre, R. (1993), *The Discursive Mind*, Cambridge: Polity Books.

Harrison, P. (2000), Making Sense: Embodiment and the Sensibilities of the Everyday', *Environment and Planning D: Society and Space*, 18: 497–517.

Harvey, D. (1996), *Justice, Nature and the Geography of Difference*, Oxford: Blackwell.

Ingold, T. (1995), 'Building, Dwelling, Living: How Animals and People Make Themselves at Home in the World', in M. Strathern (ed.), *Shifting Contexts: Transformations in Anthropological Knowledge*, London: Routledge, pp. 57–80.

Ingold, T. (2000), *The Perception of the Environment: Essays in Livelihood, Dwelling and Skill*, London: Routledge.

Kristeva J. (1996), *The Portable Kristeva*, New York: Columbia University Press.

Lloyd, M. (1996), 'Performativity, Parody and Politics', in V. Bell (ed.), *Performativity and Belonging*, London: Sage, pp. 95–214.

Macnaghten, P. and J. Urry (1998), *Contested Natures*, London: Sage.

Maffesoli, M. (1996), *The Time of the Tribes: The Decline of Individualism in Mass Society*, London: Sage.

Malbon, B. (1999), *Clubbing: Dancing, Ecstasy, Vitality*, London: Routledge.

Merleau-Ponty, M. (1962), *The Phenomenology of Perception*, London: Routledge.

Miller, D. (ed.) (1998), *Why Some Things Matter*, London: Routledge.

Nash C. (2000) 'Performativity in Practice: Some Recent Work in Cultural Geography', *Progress in Human Geography*, 24(4): 653–664.

Nast, H. and S. Pile (1998), 'EverydayPlacesBodies', in H. Nast and S. Pile (eds), *Places Through the Body*, London: Routledge, pp. 405–416.

Palmer, H. (1998), *Bloom 98*, Hull: Harry Palmer.

Patton C. (1995), 'Performativity and spatial distinction: the end of AIDS epidemology', in A. Parker and E. Kosofsky Sedgwick (eds), *Performativity and Performance*, London: Routledge, pp. 173–196.

Radley, A. (1990), 'Artefacts, Memory and a Sense of the Past', in D. Middleton and D. Edwards (ed.), *Collective Remembering*, London: Sage, pp. 46–59.

Radley, A. (1995), 'The Elusory Body and Social Constructionist Theory', *Body and Society*, 1(2): 3–23.

Shotter, J. (1993), *Cultural Politics of Everyday Life: Social Constructionism, Rhetoric and Knowing of the Third Kind*, Buckingham: Open University Press.

Thrift, N. (1997), The Still Point: Resistance, Expressive Embodiment and Dance', in S. Pile and M. Keith (eds), *Geographies of Resistance*, London: Routledge, pp. 124–154.

Thrift, N. and J.-D. Dewesbury (2000), 'Dead Geographies – and How to Make Them Live', *Environment and Planning D: Society and Space*, 18: 411–432.

Tulloch, J. (1999), *Performing Culture*, London: Sage.

© The Editorial Board of the Sociological Review 2003

Ritual theory and the environment[1]

Ronald L. Grimes

We are in a mess. The ecological fabric has been ripped, and the fleet-of-foot rescue teams have arrived already. The not so fleet are still on their way. Some passers-by are fleeing the scene. A few are stopping, offering advice and band-aids or even bulldozers. Other, less metallic, resuscitation devices are showing up too—among them, ritual.

Few people consider rites an effective means for saving the planet from environmental destruction. Ask the ordinary person, 'Should we expect anything of environmental significance from ritual or performance?' and the reply will probably be, 'No. Why would anyone even raise such a question?' Yet we are witnessing the emergence of groups and individuals who consider it obvious that ritual is one, if not *the*, answer to the environmental conundrum. They consider it urgent that humans learn, or re-learn, ritual ways of becoming attuned to their environments.

Let me give you some examples. The story of evolution is being told as myth and used as a script to inspire ritual activities. Miriam Therese McGillis leads the Cosmic Walk, a symbolic reenactment of the epic of evolution as told by Thomas Berry and Brian Swimme in *The Universe Story* (Swimme and Berry, 1992). Participants meditatively walk a path marked by a coil of rope representing the chronology of earth's emergence and evolution.

Ecological restorationists such as William Jordan III are attempting to spark the ritualizing of pragmatic actions, such as prairie burnings, that restore degraded environments (Jordan, 1993; Jordan, 1992). *Restoration Management & Notes*, a publication that Jordan edits, issued a playful but serious call for scientist-shaman-performer-storytellers who might help construct eco-rituals:

> Immediate opening for people who know the story of the earth and can tell it in a compelling manner. Candidates must be initiated into one or more of the contemporary scientific mysteries (physics, chemistry, geology, biology, ecology, climatology, cosmology, astronomy) and be willing to share the meaning of what they know. Ability to celebrate the rituals of the scientific tradition essential. Chanting and drumming skills useful, but not required for entry level position (Briggs, 1994: 124).

Australian John Seed has developed an event called the Council of All Beings (Seed *et al.*, 1988; Bragg, 1998). He and Ruth Rosenhek lead a series of

© The Editorial Board of the Sociological Review 2003. Published by Blackwell Publishing Ltd, 9600 Garsington Road, Oxford OX4 2DQ, UK and 350 Main Street, Malden, MA 02148, USA

're-earthing' rituals and workshops, some of which include a welcoming of species and an honouring of local indigenous people, as well as mourning and bonding exercises. Seed and Rosenhek believe that people will act morally and politically on the planet's behalf if they experience the depth of their own planetary despair and cultivate a felt connection with the earth and its creatures. In a culminating phase of one event, participants arrive masked as animal 'allies'. When the event concludes, folks take off their animal selves and assume their usual, human masks, thereby learning that 'human' is just one among many masks that animals wear.[2]

A few mainline religions too have begun constructing environmentally oriented rites. Buddhist monks in Thailand, for instance, are ordaining trees, thereby making them into Buddhas and forcing bulldozer drivers into a crisis of conscience over clearcutting the land (Darlington, 1998). And artists too are working in concert with some of these movements or else creating events of their own. Canadian composer Murray Schafer has been engaged in what he calls 'theatre of confluence' (Schafer, 1991a; Schafer, 1991b). In wooded rural areas, a series of ritualized musical performance rites called *Patria* (homeland) began in 1966 and continues today. It aims at nothing less than a recovery of a sense of the sacred, one not bound to either the anthropomorphism of Christianity or Renaissance humanism. Schafer writes:

> We need to breathe clean air again; we need to touch the mysteries of the world in the little places and the great wide places; in sunrises, forests, mountains and caves and if need be snowfields or tropical jungles. For too long the clement temperatures of our theatres have neutralized our thermic sensibilities. Why not a concert under a waterfall or a dramatic presentation in a blizzard? And why should we not feel the rain on our faces when we sing or a distant mountain throw back to us the voice we have just sent out to it? Why do we fail to notice the grass at our feet, the darkening of the sky or the sharp green eyes in the night air? Here are the divinities of our holy theatre, now so exceptional for having been ignored so long as to be overpoweringly real. These are the miraculous arenas of living drama inviting us to interaction; and the experience is absolutely free (Schafer, 1991b: 97).

Accordingly, Schafer conducts events in the woods that might be loosely called musical, but really they are ritualized enactments in which world mythology provides much of the content and in which landscape is a primary actor.

The surge of popular interest in the ecological possibilities of ritual is fed by a rich, publicly consumed ethnographic literature, some of which depicts rites as a primary means of being attuned to the environment. An environmentally attuned ritual sensibility is not characteristic of every indigenous ritual system, but it is of some small-scale ones. The import of this ethnographic testimony is that ritual participants believe ritual activity enables them to cultivate a bond with animals and plants, even rocks, mountains, bodies of water, and specific places. In such societies people are expected to behave with humility and receptivity. They realize that they are not more powerful than other creatures, so the human task is not only to use creatures but also to be receptive to their teach-

© The Editorial Board of the Sociological Review 2003

ings. In the traditional world presented by ethnographies, what we in the West think of as nature is animate. In rites, animals and plants and places are addressed with respect as equals, even superiors. Animals and plants and places are people too. So the nature/culture divide either does not exist or it is not so pronounced as it is in technocratic societies. In Native and alternative circles, one encounters the assertion that ritual performance is a primary way of becoming attuned to the planet and that, attuned, people behave more responsively, thus more responsibly.

Responding ritually to environmental crises is not typical of the religious mainstream of the Euroamerican West. When religious liberals, for example, make their peculiar offerings, hoping to appease the ravaged planet, they typically bring ethics, statements about what ought to be, hoping to stem the tide of what is. The currency tendered usually does not consist of plans for renewed cities, scientific procedures aimed at stemming the tide, or musical scales calculated to earn the affection of plants and animals. Rather codes of moral behaviour are the obvious means. If rites are on the table at all, they are there only to buttress moral persuasion. Rites are construed as variables dependent upon, and illustrative of, moral values and religious beliefs.

It would be difficult to deny that ethical reformulations and new laws are essential to the protection of the planet. Who would not subscribe to the sonorous principles of The Earth Charter?[3]

- Do not do to the environment of others what you do not want done to your environment.
- Respect Earth and all life. Earth, each life form, and all living beings possess intrinsic value. . . .
- Share equitably the benefits of natural resources. . . .
- Treat all creatures with compassion. . . .

It is worth being in concert with the aims of the Earth Charter, but the striking feature of religiously attuned environmental activism is the recurrent, liberal-Protestant-sounding assumption that the obvious way to proceed is by formulating ethical principles and then putting them into action by drafting laws and challenging political institutions.

This strategy is necessary but insufficient, because moral principles and new legislation do not by themselves ground world views or form attitudes. Attitudes are not merely emotional, nor world views merely intellectual. Each collaborates with the other in determining how people act, what they perform, and therefore how they behave. A sailboat's attitude is its tilt, the result of a complex negotiate between wind, water, and rudder. Human attitudes, too, are complex expressions of one's characteristic tilt in and toward the world.

So asked whether ritual is good for the environment, I am inclined to say yes. For attitudes to become definitive they must be cultivated by practice. And the name for sustained, value-laden attitude practice is ritual. In ritualizing, human beings discover, then embody and cultivate their world views, attitudes, and ethics. Rites are not only about confirming views that people already hold but also about divining ways to behave.

The notion, however, that rites might have an ecological function can sound outrageous even to religious studies scholars and theologians. Typically, both groups treat ritual as having expressive value but not causal force or formative power. For instance, Sallie McFague in *The Body of God: Toward an Ecological Theology* does not include a single index entry on ritual, ceremony, liturgy, or worship (McFague, 1993). If one asks, 'What are all those bodies in her book *doing*?', the answer is that they are thinking, imagining, or acting ethically. What they are *not* doing is ritualizing. The connection between ethics and ritual is not at all obvious in the popular mind, in religiously motivated environmental activism, or in ritual theory.

Ritual theory, performance, and efficacy

If one turns from liberal religious ethics and theology to functionalist ritual theory and poses the ritual-and-environment question, the answer is not an obvious yes. Rather it is, 'No, ritual has no significant connection with the environment. Rather, ritual is a way of maintaining the social-political status quo and of keeping in power those who are already in power'.

Theorists of ritual are no better equipped than religious liberals to make sense of environmental ritualizing. Few theories accommodate the facts of ritual change, ritual innovation, and ritual performance. Theoretically speaking, it is not at all obvious that one should speak of ritual, arts, and performance in the same breath, much less bring ritualistic, artistic, and performative sensibilities to bear on environmental problems.

Even theories that seem to embrace performance are not necessarily congenial to it. For instance, Stanley Tambiah has proposed a performative definition of ritual as:

> a culturally constructed system of symbolic communication . . . constituted of patterned and ordered sequences of words and acts, often expressed in multiple media, whose content and arrangement are characterized in varying degree by formality (conventionality), stereotypy (rigidity), condensation (fusion), and redundancy (repetition) (Tambiah, 1979: 119).

Tambiah recognizes that rites are adapted locally and that they have variable components, but he defines ritual as rigid, redundant, and formal, making it difficult to think of it as related to performance, since performance is often associated with the creative, experimental, and playful. The danger, as I see it, is not that of studying rites which are in fact rigid but in granting this characterization of ritual definitional status and thereby implicitly setting ritual against performance, play, and creativity.

In addition to disagreeing about ritual's creative and adaptive possibilities, theorists are divided over its efficaciousness. Some are willing to consider a rite

© The Editorial Board of the Sociological Review 2003

an effective tool for achieving a specified end, usually a social or psychological one; others argue that rites cannot be properly said to 'work' at all. Samuel George Frederick Brandon, illustrating the first predilection, defines ritual as 'action of an imitative or symbolical kind designed to achieve some end, often of a supernatural character, that could not be achieved through normal means by the person who performs it or on behalf of whom it is performed' (Brandon, 1973: 99). Some would say that when a rite aims at observable results (even if by mysterious or supernatural means), it is more properly labelled 'magic'.

Other theorists regard the question, How do rites work? as nonsensical. The assumption of ritual efficacy, they say, misses the point in the same way it would it would be a mistake to ask whether a piece of art 'works'. Liturgical theologians, for example, regularly define liturgy so as to remove it from means-end reasoning. Worship rites, like works of art, are not supposed to work or cause; they just are. So the theoretical dilemma is this: Neither what ritual *is* nor what ritual *does* seems appropriate to the task of environmental restoration.

But there are alternative theories. Theatre director Richard Schechner circumvents the dilemma by treating performance as the 'showing of a doing' (Schechner, 1977). By this definition, both ritual and theatre qualify as kinds of performance. The difference, according to Schechner, is that ritual performance emphasizes efficacy, whereas theatrical performance highlights entertainment, even though ritual also entertains and theatre also effects. His view of ritual performance would allow for the possibility of creative and adaptive ways of responding to planetary and environmental dilemmas. If one can assume that ritual efficacy and ritual creativity are possibilities, it becomes easier to understand why people might carry ritual impulses to scenes of environmental degradation.

Definitional wrangling is largely beside the point unless one inquires into its theoretical foundations. If ritual is to have anything more than a buttressing role, dependent for its worth on the moral prescriptions that it acts out or the groups that it consolidates, there is need for an alternative conception which articulates ritual's roots in human biology and the natural environment. Simply redefining ritual so that its performative aspects are more obvious is necessary but insufficient.

By the conventional account, ritual is cultural rather than natural. It is not at all the sort behavior one *cannot help* doing. Ritual is not like eating, sleeping, digesting, and breathing, or even copulating and speaking. Ritual is optional— one can choose *not* to engage in it. Whereas being alive requires eating and sleeping, it does not require ritualizing. Even if one claims that humans and other animals exhibit an inherent urge to ritualize, responding to that urge is optional, and because it is optional, ritualizing is cultural rather than natural. The dichotomy, cultural versus natural, is familiar. It is a staple of Western thought with its dualistic tendencies.

In my view, it is wrong to overstate the separation between culture and nature, since a less polarized view is possible. One can argue, for instance, that it is perfectly *natural* for humans, given their upright postures and large brains, to

© The Editorial Board of the Sociological Review 2003

be *cultural*. Or one might point out that cultural activities, when sustained for a sufficient time in the right environmental niche, can have genetic, which is to say, evolutionary, consequences. In other words, even though a noticeable cultural/natural *distinction* characterizes much human behaviour, it is unnecessary to think of it as *an impassible divide*. We might imagine it as a membrane rather than a chasm or wall. The distinction between things cultural and things natural is relative rather than absolute, so it is conceptually possible that ritual, (like language but unlike digestion) is both natural and cultural—a cultural edifice constructed on a natural foundation.

According to a few, alternative theories, ritual behaviour is not an archaic or merely expressive device that groups add to their usual activities in order to provide group cohesion or to shield the powerful from the deprived. Rather, ritualization is hard-wired into the structure of the brain and nervous system, a function of primate biological hardware rather than of merely human, cultural software. Even if one tries to escape explicit rites, tacit ritualization nevertheless emerges unbidden. If, for instance, people do not initiate their youth into adulthood, young peers will (perversely in all likelihood) initiate themselves. By this account, all social behaviour is not only ritualized but *necessarily* ritualized. In ordinary interaction, ritualizing, like dramatizing, is a universal, a given among humans and other animals. Our very biosocial being is dependent upon these twin foundational activities. Even if people avoid formal rites and stage plays, they cannot escape ritualizing and dramatizing. These impulses are essential to being human; they permeate human actions the same as they do the mating and aggressive behaviour of birds and fish.

Ritual and biogenetic structuralism

The foundation for an ecologically relevant theory of ritual has already been partly laid. In 1965 Julian Huxley organized a discussion on ritualization among animals and humans, the proceedings for which were published in 1966 by the Royal Society of London (Huxley, 1966). The transactions of that conference are important documents for considering ritual's relation to the environment. In attendance were an unusually large number of thinkers whose ideas would shape ritual theory for the next several decades. Among them were Konrad Lorenz, Victor Turner, Desmond Morris, R. D. Laing, Erik Erikson, Edmund Leach, Myers Fortes, and N. Tinbergen. Huxley proposed this formal definition:

> Ritualization may be defined ethologically as the adaptive formalization or canalization of emotionally motivated behaviour, under the teleonomic pressure of natural selection so as: (a) to promote better and more unambiguous signal function, both intra- and inter-specifically; (b) to serve as more efficient stimulators or releasers of more efficient patterns of action in other individuals; (c) to reduce intra-specific damage; and (d) to serve as sexual or social bonding mechanisms (Huxley, 1966: 250).

He also offered a shorter definition: '. . . the adaptive formalization and canalization of motivated human activities so as to secure more effective communi-

© The Editorial Board of the Sociological Review 2003

catory ('signalling') function, reduction of intra-group damage, or better intra-group bonding' (Huxley, 1966: 258). Huxley thought that ritualization (as distinct from ritual) was a biosocial asset rather than a liability. It had survival value. Ritualization was not, as Freud had seemed to imply, dysfunctional. Huxley knew there were differences between human rites and animal ritualization; he assumed they were the result of human ritual's basis in cultural rather than genetic transmission. But he was also insistent that there are important continuities.

Now, after the turn of the millennium, it is more common to assume continuities between animal ritualization and human liturgy, the 'bottom' and 'top' ends of the ritual spectrum.[4] Among those espousing such a view are anthropologist Charles Laughlin and psychologist Eugene d'Aquili, along with several of their colleagues. By the 1970s they were articulating some of the strongest theoretical arguments in favor of ritual's adaptive import and its fundamental rootedness in the human brain and nervous system. They refer to their theory under various labels, most commonly *neuropsychology*, *neurophenomenology*, or *biogenetic structuralism*. The theory emerges from a confluence of ideas from evolutionary, biological, genetic, ecological, neurophysiological, structuralist, psychological, ethological, and phenomenological thinking. Methodologically, the biogenetic structuralists espouse a wedding of what they call 'mature contemplation' (a species of ritual activity) with neuroscience. This combination, they argue, is the most holistic form of consciousness and the most effective means of conducting scientific research.

To invoke terms from structural linguistics, the biogenetic structuralists study *competence* rather than *performance*. The objects of their theorizing are the backstage (or, underlying) structures presupposed by frontstage (or, performative) activity. And these structures are, in their view, systemic, universal, and usually imperceptible to actors (hence, their metaphor 'deep' and my metaphor 'backstage'). Like rules of grammar, one has to infer them from actual, up-front usage, or performance. Accordingly, performance is regarded as a surface *transform* of these deep, or preconscious, structures.

The biogenetic structuralists have tendered several variations of their definition of ritual. A typical one holds that ritual is

> a sequence of behaviour that: (1) is structured or patterned; (2) is rhythmic and repetitive (to some degree at least), that is, tends to recur in the same or nearly the same form with some regularity; (3) acts to synchronize affective, perceptual-cognitive, and motor processes within the central nervous system of individual participants; and (4) most particularly, synchronizes these processes among the various individual participants (d'Aquili and Newberg, 1999: 89–89).

Two of the biogenetic structuralists' most far-reaching claims are (1) that ritualization is hard-wired—not only cultural but also a necessary function of the biological system—and (2) that ritual activity is evolutionarily functional rather than dysfunctional. Ritual, they say, emerged along with encephalization and is crucial for both the control and the transformation of consciousness.

© The Editorial Board of the Sociological Review 2003

Employing various driving mechanisms such as drumming, chanting, dancing, and ingesting, as well as ordeals and privations, rites are means of retuning, or returning balance, to the autonomic nervous system. Ritual activity facilitates the penetration and embodiment of symbols into human selves and societies, entraining these symbols into an effective system. In short, there are remarkable similarities between the propositions of biogenetic structuralism and ethnographic testimony concerning ritual's environmental significance.

The biogenetic structuralists posit a drive toward wholeness in all biological systems, and consider rites a primary means for achieving both social and neuropsychological wholeness. Ritual practices facilitate in the brain a simultaneous discharge of the ergotropic (excitation) and trophotropic (relaxation) systems, thereby coordinating them into a larger whole.

The biogenetic structuralists stop short of claiming that rites are the *only* means of practicing wholeness and interconnectedness. And since they say many of the same things about both play and contemplation as they do about ritual, it seems that ritual is not the exclusive agent of wholeness (unless, of course both play and contemplation are conceptualized as kinds of ritual).

Although I consider biogenetic structuralism a major, provocative theory of ritual, I have two reservations about it.

(1) The biogenetic structuralists' claims are more appropriate to some kinds of ritual than to others. What they say about ritual's ability to affect the nervous system and brain applies mainly to trance dance and meditation, at opposite ends of the scale of ritual exertion. These two activities require, respectively, either sustained exertion and driving or else the stilling of physical and mental activity. More than mainline worship and decorous liturgy, these kinds of ritual activity stimulate the extremes of the autonomic nervous system, thus facilitating the 'crossing over' that biogenetic structuralists treat as the primary biological virtue of ritual. So, unlike the biogenetic structuralists, I would distinguish quotidian ritualization from formal rites, and I would not claim that ritual *in general* attunes, only that *certain kinds* of rites, under certain circumstances, attune.

(2) However true it may be that certain kinds of ritual activity can precipitate measurable changes in brain functioning, this fact alone does not mean that ritual is either necessary ('hard-wired') or a good thing. As far as we know, there is no 'ritual gene,' and if sonic driving synchronizes the activities of brain hemispheres, such synchrony may serve evil as readily as it serves good. One can ritually destroy an ecosystem as surely as one can ritually redeem it.

There is also the obvious fact that some cultures minimize ritual while others maximize it. In my view, there is not yet a demonstrable connection between the amount of ritualization and the degree of either mental health or ecological sensitivity. So I am less certain than the biogenetic structuralists that ritualization is hard-wired, and I am more insistent on the necessity for an ethical critique of ritualistic means. Even though I take issue with the ethics-first or ethics-alone strategies of religious liberalism, I do not assume a ritual-ethics *dis*connection either.

© The Editorial Board of the Sociological Review 2003

Ritual and ecological anthropology

Another key source of theorizing about ritual and the environment is the writing of anthropologist Roy Rappaport. Sometimes he is referred to as an ecological anthropologist, and his theory as an ecological theory of ritual, but the label is not entirely accurate. Rappaport's writing is certainly informed by cybernetic and ecological perspectives, but when he writes more generally on ritual and liturgy, much of his ecologism is displaced by formalism. Unlike the biogenetic structuralists, he claims to study the 'obvious' (or performed) rather than the 'deep' structures of ritual.

The second edition of Rappaport's *Pigs for the Ancestors* (1984) was quite concerned to correct the excessively ecological misreading of the first edition. Rappaport says his demonstration of ritual's crucial role in regulating Maring ecology does not imply that ritual plays such a role elsewhere (Rappaport, 1984: 358). His early claims about ritual's ecological function were, he says, culture-specific, a matter of empirical observation of Maring warfare, ritual, and exchange, rather than a general assertion about the function of ritual everywhere. He does not claim, for instance, that the mass and the synagogue Sabbath service help balance the ecosystems in which they are enacted. So, labelled more accurately, Rappaport's is a formalistic theory of ritual articulated in the context of an ecological world view.

The concluding chapters of his final book, *Ritual and Religion* (1999), do not say that rites *in fact* exercise ecological functions, rather that they *should*. The ecological framing of his formalistic theory is prescriptive rather than descriptive. Rappaport's ethic assumes or requires a ritual grounding. He articulates what he takes to be the logical (rather than empirical) entailments of ritual form. And his formalism leads to an explicit universalism which resembles that of the biogenetic structuralists. However varied and culture-bound the *contents* and *purposes* of a rite, Rappaport says, ritual *form* is universal:

> . . . [Ritual,] the performance of *more or less* [my emphasis] invariant sequences of formal acts and utterances *not entirely* [my emphasis] encoded by the performers, logically entails the establishment of convention; the sealing of social contract; the construction of the integrated conventional orders we shall call *Logoi*; the investment of whatever it encodes with morality; the construction of time and eternity; the representation of a paradigm of creation; the generation of the concept of the sacred and the sanctification of conventional order; the generation of theories of the occult; the evocation of numinous experience; the awareness of the divine; the grasp of the holy; and the construction of orders of meaning transcending the semantic (Rappaport, 1999: 27).

This is Rappaport's most comprehensive summary statement. A staggeringly complex assertion, it takes him a book's worth of exposition to clarify. His theory is the most doggedly 'ritocentric' of all current theories of ritual. For him, not only the sacred and religion, but also social convention, morality, and cosmology are entailments of ritual. Ritual is *the* basic social act.

© The Editorial Board of the Sociological Review 2003

The 'more or less' and 'entirely' of his definition are concessions to the possibility of ritual change, revision, and creativity. In my view, they are fragile patches on the dike of his theory. They allow him to make concessions to more processual theories without having to take such alternatives with sufficient seriousness. For instance, he does not really engage the major alternative to his own view of ritual, that of Victor Turner. Whereas for Turner ritual is essentially creative, for Rappaport ritual is essentially conservative.

But both agreed that ritual, whatever else it is, is performative. Without performance, Rappaport says, ritual is merely a dead artifact. Ritual exists properly, fully, in the performing of it. He takes considerable issue with those who believe that myth and ritual express the same things, just in different media. Since many theorists talk as if ritual had many other functional equivalents (social structures capable of doing the same work), Rappaport's is an elevated conception of ritual. He makes ritual not merely interesting or even important but *necessary* for human social survival on the planet. Ritual, he insists, is the *only* way certain kinds of meaning can be expressed. The performative ritual form contains a meta-message—a declaration of certainty and sanctity—that no other form can or does.

Rappaport does not think performance is unique to ritual, so he compares it with dramatic and athletic performance. He makes the usual contrasts: participating ritualistic congregations versus spectating theatrical audiences; ritual's establishment of invariant orders versus theatre's problematizing of such orders; ritual's earnestness versus theatre's playfulness, and so on. The comparisons are conventional, but the conclusion is controversial, namely, that ritual, drama, and athletics are not equal partners. Drama and athletics are sanctified by their association with ritual, not the other way around. Logically and formally (not necessarily empirically), all other kinds of performance are subordinate to ritual performance.

For Rappaport ritual is 'a performative,' by which he means a conventional procedure for achieving a conventional effect. Ritual is a complex, not a simple, performative, since one of its primary tasks is that of *establishing* conventions of obligation. Since ritual not only uses convention but also actually establishes it, ritual is, properly speaking, meta-performative. So the sense of the term 'performance,' as Rappaport uses it, is not only, or even mainly, theatrical. Rather, like J. L. Austin, Rappaport considers a performative to be any embodied accomplishment or doing. 'Participants [in rites] enliven the order that they are performing with the energy of their own bodies, and their own voices make it articulate. They thereby establish the existence of that order in this world of matter and energy; they *substantiate* the order as it *informs* them' (Rappaport, 1999: 125).

Whereas Turner and Schechner use the notion of performance as a wedge against the solidity of the prevailing metaphors of structure and text, Rappaport understands 'performativeness' (his term) to be the means of establishing, rather than challenging or undermining, social convention. To perform a rite is to establish and accept a canonical order. Acceptance, by his definition, is not

© The Editorial Board of the Sociological Review 2003

a private state of mind but a fundamentally social, public act (Rappaport, 1979: 194). Acceptance, he argues, is intrinsic to ritual performance, and one is bound by it even when violating it, just as one can break a law while acknowledging its validity.

For Rappaport, ritual is *the* paradigmatic means of establishing obligation, thus of generating social and ecological order. Ritual is *the* basic social act without functional equivalents. 'In sum, ritual is unique in at once establishing conventions, that is to say, enunciating and accepting them, and in insulating them from usage' (Rappaport, 1979: 197).

Holiness and sacrality are the ultimate social-environmental insulators. For Rappaport, holiness is inexpressible, but sacrality is 'that [discursive] part of the holy [which itself is nondiscursive] that can be expressed in language and that, as it were, faces conscious reason and discourse' (Rappaport, 1979: 228; cf. Rappaport, 1979: 213). In this terminological division of labour, the holy is characterized largely by recourse to Rudolf Otto's phenomenology (except on occasions when holiness is given a reductionist twist by being spoken of as a 'product of emotion') (Rappaport, 1979: 215). Rappaport renders Otto's phenomenology of the holy in such as way as to make ritual performance the origin of religion: 'Divine beings . . . remain nothing more than inductions from mystified performativeness' (Rappaport, 1979: 216).

For Rappaport, religion and ritual, however adaptive and necessary for human survival, are mystified modes of human, utterly human, performance. Even though he makes other statements that seem to contradict this view, the logic of his argument echoes the claims of Ludwig Feuerbach and Karl Marx: 'The vitality that the worshipper feels in the divine object is his own projected upon what he takes to be other or 'concompassing'. Ritual, then, is possibly the furnace within which the image of God is forged out of the power of language and of emotion' (Rappaport, 1979: 216).

In sum, for Rappaport, ritual is essential to planetary survival not because God created it but because it created God. Rappaport credits ritual generally and liturgical order specifically with the origin of God, religion, rationality, morality, and language. Ritual is *the* self-contained, self-regulating system, hence its importance in modelling social and ecological systems.

There is a stunning paradox at the heart of Rappaport's sweeping vision. On the one hand, ritual utterances ('ultimate sacred postulates') are vacuous; on the other, they are the paradigms of cultural creativity and environmental regulation. On the one hand, liturgies are not 'encoded' by performers. On the other, social actors construct meanings (Rappaport, 1979: 158). If this is not to be a blatant contradiction, readers of Rappaport must posit two distinctly different points of view, that of liturgical performers who do *not* know that they are constructing meaning, and that of scholars who *do* know that ritualists construct both meanings and gods.

Rappaport crystallizes these two points of view into two models, 'cognized' and 'operative'. Liturgies, in his view, are cognized models; they are emic, issuing from ritual participants. Operative models, on the other hand, are etic; they are the explanatory schemes of theorists. Neither model *is* the environment; both attempt to comprehend it. Both are maps that can never coincide entirely with each other or with the territory to which they refer.

Rappaport's 'anthrocentric theology' (my term) is perhaps encapsulated in the single phrase 'fabricated sacred truths' (Rappaport, 1999: 453). It is common to assume that the sacred precludes fabrication and that anything fabricated cannot possibly be sacred. But Rappaport is utterly serious about both adjectives and about holding them together. The outcome is an ironically sacral anthropology that has many of the features of a theology.

Rappaport's conservatism regarding ritual arises in part from his holding Romer's rule as an ultimate sacred proposition in his own theoretical system. Romer's rule states that 'the initial effect of an evolutionary change is conservative in that it makes it possible for a previously existing way of life to persist in the face of changed conditions' (Rappaport, 1979: 229–30). Rappaport says nothing about subsequent (as opposed to initial) effects. Holding this rule to be the case in the evolutionary, biological world, Rappaport seems also to believe it true of the socio-cultural world. Thus, he not only views ritual as conservative, his view of ritual is conservative.[5]

On the surface, it seems that Rappaport's definition and theory might render ritual utterly anti-ecological, incapable of adaptive change. But Rappaport is quite aware that conventions must be flexible and adaptable for humans to survive. For him, however, the proper location of flexibility and versatility is in language. No longer reliant exclusively upon genetic change, humans adapt by using symbolic means, especially language. The problem with language, he observes, is the lie, the fact that symbols can be divorced from what they signify. With language comes the possibility of lying and disorder, of disordered versatility, innumerable possibilities.

The role of ritual action is opposite to that of language. Ritual is the means of grounding change, establishing order, and ensuring certainty in an uncertain world, whereas language is the means of adaptability and change but also of lying. Rappaport, it seems, does not take seriously the possibility of the gestural (as opposed to the linguistic) lie.

Rappaport seems intent, even desperate at times, to defend, restore, or invent ritual's authority, hoping it can close the maws of several great beasts: desertification, ozone depletion, species extinction, and environmental degradation (Rappaport, 1999, 452). Against the Goliath of quality-denying, 'monetized' epistemologies based on cost-benefit analysis (which he clearly considers maladaptive), he marshals the slingshot of ritual, hoping its emphasis on complementarity and reciprocity can displace the forces of disintegration. The difference between Rappaport and me is that he believes he is describing 'the obvious aspects of ritual' whereas I believe he is prescribing long shots.

Rappaport is more willing than most anthropologists to admit that the very idea of ecology is as much a religious conception as it is a scientific hypothesis.

42

© The Editorial Board of the Sociological Review 2003

Ecosystemic conceptions which, in some non-Western societies, approach ultimate sacred status, are thus worthy of high sanctification by the religions of the West as well. High and explicit sanctification of such conceptions and the actions they encourage not only might contribute to the preservation of the world's wholeness in the face of pervasive fragmenting and dissolving forces but could contribute to the revitalization of those religions in an age of increasing scepticism and cynicism toward them (Rappaport, 1999: 460).

Rappaport uses the idea of an ecosystem not just as a scientific hypothesis but as an active intervention, a guide for how to act in the world. And ecological thinking, it seems, requires ritual performance. 'Weakened or not, ritual and related forms of action should not be ruled out of attempts to establish a new Logos grounded in the concept of the ecosystem' (Rappaport, 1999: 460). Rappaport goes even further. For him, humanity 'is that part of the world through which the world as a whole can think about itself' (Rappaport, 1999: 461). So ritual performance is not merely a means for humans to illustrate ideas about the environment. Ritualizing is the way the world itself tries to ensure its own persistence. This is a deeply provocative suggestion, coming as it does from one of the United States' most respected anthropologists.[6]

Conclusion

Is ritualizing good for the planet? Ritual studies does not give an unambiguous answer to the question. Whereas conventional ritual theory and mainline post-protestant practice do not even raise the question much less support the claim, some indigenous peoples, a few alternative practitioners, and a small group of provocative theorists suggest otherwise. They have not *proven* that ritual is good for planetary health, but they have performed its possibility and argued its plausibility on the basis of well grounded but speculative theory.

Western scientistic and technocratic true believers look with scepticism on the claims of ethnographically presented ritualists. At best, their testimony is soft rather than hard evidence. Ethnographic reports present stories, beliefs, descriptions, even tacit hypotheses, but not demonstrated facts or replicable conclusions. So the best one can claim, and still honour the sacred tenets of scientism, is that certain kinds of ritual practices *may* have survival value. They *may* enhance adaptability and thus the longevity of the human species on the planet earth.

One must reiterate the 'may' as long as we have not eliminated the alternative, namely, that deeply ritualized human life can render participants one-dimensional, stereotyped, and inflexible—in short, maladaptive. If 'stereotypy' (to recall Tambiah's term) were ever a virtue in some other place and time, it is, in the Darwinian universe that many of us inhabit, a vice. Loss of postural and gestural diversity and flexibility would not stand us in good stead with Natural Selection, the reigning deity of the current Darwinian myth.[7] Loss of bodily or cultural flexibility, like loss of cultural and biological diversity, risks jeopardizing human health and longevity. If ritualizing implies rigidifying, we may be courting earthly extinction rather than planetary salvation by engaging in certain forms of it. So everything depends on which kinds of ritualizing we practice and which kinds we forego.

In my view, the convergence of ethnographically recovered indigenous views with ecological and neurobiological theory was one of the most promising of the last century, but it remains incomplete. There is need for synthesis, teasing out implications, critique, and the reformulation of basic definitions of ritual. For me, religious ritual is the predication of identities and differences (metaphors) so profoundly enacted that they suffuse bone and blood, thereby generating a cosmos (an oriented habitat). In such rites people enact a momentary cosmos of metaphor. Ritually, people do not dance merely to exercise limbs or to impress ticket-buyers with their skills or even to illustrate sacredly held beliefs. Ritualists dance, rather, to discover ways of inhabiting a place. This is the noetic, or the divinatory, function of ritual; ritual helps people figure out, divine, even construct a cosmos. A cosmos is not merely an empty everywhere. It is everywhere as perceived from somewhere, a universe as construed from a locale. A cosmos is a topocosm, a universe in this place, an oriented, 'cosmosized' place, a this-place which is also an every-where (Gaster, 1987).

Cosmologies are as important for what they tell ritualists *not* to perform as for what they tell them *to* perform. In the middle-of-the-road world many of us inhabit, we are not ritually supposed to sweat, stay up all night, sleep in the sanctum, enter trance, or let wild sounds escape the throat. All rites, even the holiest of liturgies, express time-bound values and space-bound peculiarities. They are suffused by the same spiritual and intellectual pollution that we all breathe in order to stay alive. So neither ritual theories nor ritual systems are free of the obligation to serve the ground we walk on, the water we drink, the air we breathe. Like Rappaport, I am speaking about what rites *ought* or *might* do. We will not know what ecologically attuned rites *actually do* apart from ritual experiment and critique. To wait, hoping for certainty *before* acting, is a greater risk than hoping to learn *by* acting.

Notes

1 Parts of this chapter are modifications of Grimes (2002) and Grimes (forthcoming).
2 A workshop manual for The Council of All Beings can be found at http://forests.org/ric/deep-eco/cabcont.htm. It was prepared by Eshana (Elizabeth Bragg).
3 Earth Charter web site: http://www.earthcharter.org/. See also Callicott (1994).
4 See, for example, Driver (1998).
5 Frederick Turner (Turner, 1992) also attributes to ritual a conserving role, comparing it with the role of genes in conserving patterns (cultural, of course, rather than genetic), but he also attributes to it a transforming role.
6 Rappaport served as president of the American Anthropological Association.
7 See, for instance, Pinker (1997) and Jones (2000).

© The Editorial Board of the Sociological Review 2003

References

Bragg, E. (1998), *The Council of All Beings Workshop Manual: A Step by Step Guide* [http://forests.org/ric/deep-eco/cabcont.htm].

Brandon, S. G. F. (1973), 'Religious Ritual', in P. Wiener (ed.) *Dictionary of the History of Ideas*, New York: Scribners, p. 99.

Briggs, B. (1994), 'Help Wanted', *Restoration & Management Notes*, 12(2): 124.

Callicott, J. B. (ed.) (1994), *Earth's Insights: A Multicultural Survey of Ecological Ethics From the Mediterranean Basis to the Australian Outback*, Berkeley, CA: University of California Press.

d'Aquili, E. and A. B. Newberg (1999), *The Mystical Mind: Probing the Biology of Religious Experience*, Minneapolis: Fortress.

Darlington, S. M. (1998), 'The Ordination of a Tree: The Buddhist Ecology Movement in Thailand', *Ethnology*, 37(1): 1–15.

Driver, T. F. (1998), *Liberating Rites: Understanding the Transformative Power of Ritual*, Boulder, CO: Westview.

Gaster, T. H. (1987), 'Ancient Near Eastern Ritual Drama', in M. Eliade (ed.) *The Encyclopedia of Religion*, New York: Macmillan, pp. 446–450.

Grimes, R. L. (2002), 'Performance Is Currency in the Deep World's Gift Economy: An Incantatory Riff for a Global Medicine Show', *Interdisciplinary Studies in Literature and Environment*, 9(1): 149–164.

Grimes, R. L. (forthcoming), 'Ritual and Nature', in B. Taylor and J. Kaplan (eds) *Encyclopedia of Religion and Nature*, New York: Continuum International.

Huxley, J. (ed.) (1966), 'A Discussion on Ritualization of Behaviour in Animals and Man', *Philosophical Transactions of the Royal Society of London, Series B*, 251.

Jones, S. (1999), *Darwin's Ghost*, New York: Random House USA.

Jordan, W. R. III. (1992), 'Restoration and the Reentry of Nature', in P. Sauer (ed.) *Finding Home: Writing on Nature and Culture From Orion Magazine*, Boston: Beacon, pp. 98–115.

Jordan, W. R. III. (1993), 'Rituals of Restoration', *The Humanist*, November/December: 23–26.

McFague, Sallie (1993), *The Body of God: An Ecological Theology*, London: S.C.M. Press.

Pinker, S. (1997), *How the Mind Works*, New York: Norton.

Rappaport, R. A. (1979), *Ecology, Meaning, and Religion*, Berkeley, CA: North Atlantic.

Rappaport, R. A. (1984), *Pigs for the Ancestors: Ritual in the Ecology of a New Guinea People*, new, enlarged edition, New Haven, CT: Yale University Press.

Rappaport, R. A. (1999), *Ritual and Religion in the Making of Humanity*, Cambridge: Cambridge University Press.

Schafer, R. M. (1991a), 'The Theatre of Confluence I', *Descant*, 22(2): 27–45.

Schafer, R. M. (1991b), 'The Theatre of Confluence II', *Descant*, 22(2): 87–103.

Schechner, R. (1977), *Essays on Performance Theory, 1970–1976*, New York: Drama Book.

Seed, J., J. Macy, P. Fleming and A. Naess (1988), *Thinking Like a Mountain: Towards a Council of All Beings*, Philadelphia: New Society.

Swimme, B. and T. Berry (1992), *The Universe Story From the Primordial Flaring Forth to the Ecozoic Era: A Celebration of the Unfolding of the Cosmos*, San Francisco: HarperSanFrancisco.

Tambiah, S. J. (1979), 'A Performative Approach to Ritual', *Proceedings of the British Academy*, 65: 113–169.

Turner, F. (1992), *Natural Classicism: Essays on Literature and Science*, Charlottesville: University of Virginia Press.

© The Editorial Board of the Sociological Review 2003

A passionate pursuit: foxhunting as performance

Garry Marvin

Early in the morning a farmer, dressed in dull green and brown work clothes, a dog at his side, leaves his house and walks quietly along a hedgerow towards a wood. At the edge of the wood he takes two cartridges from his pocket and puts them into his shot gun. He removes the safety catch. With the gun ready he continues slowly and quietly along the edge of the wood—an unobtrusive presence in the landscape. All of his senses alert, his eyes scan the near distance. He is not interested in the occasional pheasant that flaps out of the trees and into the field, nor the rabbits feeding along the hedgerows. His aim, if his aim is true, is to shoot one of the local foxes that might turn their attention to his poultry or lambs.

There is intense activity by mid-morning in a grassed paddock in front of a farm-house. Dozens of people, dressed in highly polished boots, cream jodhpurs, red or black coats and velvet-covered hats, are mounted on immaculately groomed horses. It is a convivial social gathering. Each of them take a drink offered on trays by members of the farmer's family and move on to greet and chat with friends. At the edge of the assembling riders is a man dressed in formal riding attire with a red jacket;[1] around his horse are a score or so of increasingly restless hounds. Although he talks with those who greet him, his attention is on the hounds and he occasionally raises his voice to one which attempts to slip away from the pack. Mixing with this group of riders are men, women and children, dressed in everyday country clothing, who pat the hounds, stroke horses while talking with the riders, share a drink and joke with other people on foot. The man with the hounds raises his horn to his lips and blows. The hounds move off excitedly, the crowd parts to let him through. The riders will follow when he is at some distance from them, and those on foot follow on behind. A foxhunt has begun.

In a sense each of these practices are foxhunts—in each there is an attempt to find and kill foxes—but the similarity ends at this very basic level. Although both take place in the spaces of the English countryside, and both centre on interactions between humans and animals, the nature of these interactions are differently configured and differently performed. The first example is a private, individual, everyday working practice and unmarked; the second is a public, communal, and highly elaborated event. Nobody attends to watch the farmer in his attempt to kill foxes whereas on any hunting day large numbers of people, on foot and on horseback, will gather to follow the activities of the Huntsman[2] and his hounds as they attempt to bring about the death of a fox. The over-

© The Editorial Board of the Sociological Review 2003. Published by Blackwell Publishing Ltd, 9600 Garsington Road, Oxford OX4 2DQ, UK and 350 Main Street, Malden, MA 02148, USA

elaboration of means compared with ends, the order and structure of the event, the formal rules of procedure and engagement, the extensive, but unwritten, rules of etiquette, the importance attached to dress codes, the complex descriptive vocabulary, the forms of address between participants, the sounds provided by the Huntsman's horn and the baying of the hounds, and the cultural elaboration of all of the animals involved might suggest to an outsider seeking to understand foxhunting that this is a highly complex ritual, ceremonial, performative event. The farmer out with his gun is an unadorned practice; it has a simplicity, an immediacy, and a utilitarian quality compared with the mounted fox hunt which is marked by excess and intensification. It is this excess and the complex procedures to achieve what could be achieved in much simpler and perhaps more immediate ways—a dead fox—that suggest that foxhunting can be interpreted as a cultural performance and a performance of a different order from the farmer with his gun.

Practice and performance

My central concern in this chapter is to explore some of the performative and expressive elements of foxhunting.[3] Such a performative approach attends to the complexity of the event as it is enacted in the spaces of the countryside but it is an approach that must be adopted with care. Those who participate in foxhunting do not consciously set out to create a cultural performance and they certainly do not, in my experience, ever consciously think of the event, in its totality, as *a* performance. They certainly make judgements in terms of the qualities of performance, or capabilities, of certain participants within the event, but such judgements are connected with the immediacy of the event as it is being created around them and by them, rather than a distanced reflection on its meaning. Edward Schiefflen has commented that in recent years anthropologists interested in cultural performances, however they are defined:

> . . . have increasingly moved from studying them as systems of representations (symbolic transformations, cultural texts) to looking at them as processes of practice and performance. In part this reflects a growing dissatisfaction with purely symbolic approaches to understanding material like rituals, which seem to be curiously robbed of life and power when distanced in discussions concerned largely with meaning. 'Performance' deals more with actions than text: with habits of the body more than structures of symbols, with illocutionary rather than propositional force, with the social construction of reality rather than its representation (1998: 194).

Meanings can certainly be imposed on the event or drawn out of it but my concern here is to explore the 'life and power' of foxhunting through a consideration of the elements and activities out of which it is composed, how it achieves its aims, how the participants, both human and animal, are involved in its construction and enactment and what cultural sense it has for them: in total, how the performance works. I will attempt to follow, in part, a path indicated by Schieffelin:

Performance is also concerned with something that anthropologists have always found hard to characterize theoretically: the creation of presence. Performances, whether ritual or dramatic, create and make present realities vivid enough to beguile, amuse or terrify. And through these presences, they alter moods, social relations, bodily dispositions and states of mind (1998: 194).

Presence is fundamental for the foxhunt. Whereas the farmer with his gun attempts to be a non-presence, the Hunt openly and deliberately announces itself in the countryside. Through its processes it engages and connects human and animal bodies, generates excitement and emotion, both mental and visceral, and dramatically enacts a set of relationships with the natural world.

The pursuit of the fox

It is necessary at the outset to offer a short description of some of the key elements of what actually occurs in a hunt. A significant point to emphasize here is that, unlike the case of the farmer out with his gun, the human participants in foxhunting are not directly hunting their prey. They do not themselves attempt to find, pursue and kill foxes; this is done by the hounds, their agents.

When the Huntsman arrives at the place, perhaps a small wood or hedgerow, where he intends to begin the day's hunting, he will use his horn and his voice to encourage the hounds to begin searching for the scent of a fox. In this form of hunting the hounds do not *look* for a fox using their eyes. These are scent hounds rather than gaze hounds. At this point they might catch the strong scent of a fox which has been recently disturbed by their arrival or they might catch the faint and evaporating scent of a fox which passed that way some time before. If there is any scent at all, those hounds that pick up on it will begin to whimper excitedly; a sound that draws other members of the pack to them. They will move off in the direction of the scent and, if it becomes more definite, the whimpering and squeaking becomes a more convincing baying. The Huntsman will make sure that all the pack is engaged and he will gallop after them. Once the hounds and Huntsman have been given enough distance, so that there is no danger that they will be interfered with, the Field Master[4] will lead the mounted riders after them. If the hounds maintain contact with the scent of the fleeing fox, the countryside begins to resonate with the baying of the hounds, the encouraging horn calls of the Huntsman and the sounds of horses galloping across the landscape. The hunt is in full cry. Such intensity might be built up over many, fast-paced miles or it might last only a few minutes. The hounds can, at any moment, lose the scent. Scent can evaporate quickly so that the hounds are left with nothing to follow; their cries cease and their fast, directed run subsides and finally comes to a halt.

A fox which is aware of the danger behind it may become evasive, change the direction of its flight, cross and re-cross its path, apparently attempting to disguise its scent by running through livestock, along a stream or road. It may seek the safety of terrain where it is difficult for hounds to follow. If the hounds

© The Editorial Board of the Sociological Review 2003

cannot reconnect with the scent then the Huntsman will gather them around him, move to another potential site and begin the process over again in the hope of picking up the scent of another fox. If, however, the hounds are able to hold onto the scent they will begin to gain ground on the fox and begin to outpace it. At a certain moment they will lift their heads to see their prey and, surging forward, increase their speed to catch and kill the fox on the move. The Huntsman, and the following riders will arrive to see a swirling mass of hounds tearing at a dead fox. The Huntsman will blow 'The Kill' on his horn. The hunt has come to a successful conclusion. After a pause, to allow the horses, hounds and riders to regain their breath, the Huntsman will lead them off to begin again.[5]

This short description does not adequately capture the dramatic ebbs and flows of the event, the pulsing between activity and excitement and waiting and stillness, the successes, false starts and failures, the surprising turns in the relationships between the hounds and the fox, the personal dramas of, and dangers for, the riders as they succeed or fail in jumping hedges, gates, ditches and streams, or in staying on their horses at the gallop to keep up with the hunt. What it does point to are the highly complex relationships between humans, hounds, horses, foxes and the countryside that are integral to, and constitutive of, foxhunting. Foxhunting is present in the countryside in very different ways from everyday practices of fox killing. In foxhunting humans and hounds do not attempt to engage with foxes directly, quietly, efficiently and unobtrusively. They announce their presence in the countryside and draw attention to themselves both visibly and audibly, and they expect the encounter with the fox to be convoluted, difficult, challenging. The rules of hunting both allow the fox the possibility of escape and restrict the possibilities of its capture and thus they open a space for an encounter of a different order.

Based on an original perceived need to control a rural pest, participants in foxhunting have, over the last two hundred years, transposed fox killing from the mundane into another register and have created what is arguably the most complex performative event in the English countryside. Central to this chapter will be a concern to attend to the ways in which foxhunting is present in the spaces of this countryside and how the nature and structuring of its presence can be interpreted as constituting a set of performances in and with the natural world. To continue this exploration it is necessary to consider the spaces in which foxhunting is enacted.

Spaces, setting and scenery

At the national level the countryside is framed for foxhunting. England[6] is divided into named Hunt[7] 'countries' by the Masters of Foxhounds Association. These are constituted as territories over which the Hunt, registered to each 'country', has the right to operate and Hunts may not, except in exceptional circumstances, hunt foxes in the territory of adjacent Hunts.

Those who go foxhunting do not, in the main, travel to different parts of the country to hunt. They become members or supporters of the Hunt in area in which they live[8] and such membership might have been continuous in families for generations. Hunt members are immensely committed to their Hunt, express a deep sense of belonging to a particular Hunt 'country'. It is a countryside of which they have a close and intimate knowledge because of their hunting experiences. It is not a countryside they visit, it is a countryside that they are *of* and to which they belong. Going hunting does not involve an outward movement to elsewhere but rather an inwards movement towards the spaces and places that the participants see, experience and often inhabit on a familiar, daily basis. On a hunting day, however, the inward movement, the movement towards a more immediate connectedness, results in the heightening and intensification of being in the countryside. The very landscapes and that which they contain are transformed into a performance space for the day. But that transformation, although new, fresh and full of immediate potential on each hunting day also has a long history that gives it a powerful depth and resonance for those who have regularly hunted across it. As I have argued elsewhere, for the participants, hunting converts the countryside into another space:

> ... a sacred space of deep emotional significance and social and cultural resonance. This is not a mere landscape of more or less beauty; it consists, as Michael Mayerfield Bell has commented, of 'sites of story and memory' (Bell, 1994: 170). The performance of hunting—often continued for hundreds of years—in this space imbues it with a set of sensual and experiential qualities that become enriched with each hunting event. The memories are of what has or has not happened there before; the present excitement is one of potential, what might occur and what experience it will generate (Marvin, 2000: 109–10).

It is highly significant that foxhunting is staged and enacted within the spaces of the worked, agricultural, countryside. Although mounted Hunts will enter landscapes of 'wild' countryside—for example, moorland and forest (depending very much on the location of the particular Hunt)—in the main it takes place across grasslands and cultivated fields, along hedgerows and through small woods. These are spaces of human activity rather than of untouched wilderness. The significance of this is to be found in the attitudes to and perceptions of the central character—the fox. One of the central reasons given for hunting foxes is that they are considered or perceived to be rural pests by many farmers and by those who hunt: intrusive and destructive animals which prey on poultry, lambs and other livestock. The fox has been the focus of their attention and concern in the countryside for centuries because, instead of being a wild animal which directs its attention to other wild animals as a source of food, it is thought to intrude improperly into human affairs in its search for food. As such, it is seen as a trespasser and poacher which leaves the wild places and enters fields and farmyards to steal and kill. For those who hunt, the fox is a creature which disturbs the proper rural order in terms of the relationships between humans and the animals they raise for their purposes. In part,

© The Editorial Board of the Sociological Review 2003

foxhunting is an attempt to bring this order back into balance through pursuing and killing foxes and to do so it is necessarily conducted in the lived space of this central animal and of those people who are most concerned with it.

The landscapes of the countryside are not merely a stage or a setting for the event but rather they are essentially constitutive of foxhunting. They demand a knowledge and awareness of them and an immersion into them for hunting to take place and to be successful. The animals, configured as performers (as will be shown below), respond to and interact with all the elements that make up the richly textured physicality of the countryside. The nature of the terrain itself, the places for hiding or of exposure, the wind, rain and sunshine, the presence of other animals, buildings, paths and roadways are all responded to and used by the fox in its attempt to escape the attention of the hounds. For all the participants, both human and animal, there is an intense, immediate and visceral engagement with the natural world during hunting. All of them sense, feel and respond to the weather conditions; all watch the countryside for signs of significance; all hear the sounds of the countryside and react to them in different ways; all are aware of the presence of others. Hounds draw the scent of foxes into their bodies while ignoring other scents that assault them. Humans can sometimes pick up the faint trace of fox scent but they are certainly aware of the smells of the countryside and the rich animal odours of hounds and horses as they come close. Riders have their bodies closely and sometime precariously connected with their horses and must be alert to anything that might disturb that equilibrium.

During its enactment foxhunting demands and creates a sustained awareness, responsiveness, sensuousness and thoughtfulness about the countryside and the lives it contains. The event is shot through with the everyday concerns of the working countryside, but it also bursts through this everyday life. Radiating out from the participants is a space that becomes, through the desires, demands and practices of hunting itself, a space in which everything is imbued with, and takes on, a greater significance, in which the experience of the ordinary is magnified, heightened and intensified. None of the participants, neither human nor animal, can participate unless they are alert and responsive to the totality of the countryside. On a non-hunting day the movement of a flock of sheep, the barking of farm dogs, the wind direction, the rising or falling temperature, the density of undergrowth in a wood or the height of a particular crop may not be things that people pay attention to, but they become immensely significant on a hunting day because they are all elements that might indicate where a fox has gone or where one might be found.

The over-arching theme here is that foxhunting reconfigures the countryside as a challenging space and it is the variety and intensity of these different challenges that constitute part of the multi-faceted enjoyment of hunting. In an important sense the countryside is not a 'setting' for foxhunting, and certainly neither an illusionary space nor a space of illusion as in other performance events, but rather it is an active constituent of the event itself.

© The Editorial Board of the Sociological Review 2003

Human participants, performers and spectators

Within the event all of those involved—humans, horses, hounds and foxes—have their participation and contribution variously and differently configured and judged in terms of how capably they perform by the people who partici-pate. It is important to stress that such perspectives are internal to the event and come from those who are themselves participants. Foxhunting does not take place, nor is it enacted, for anyone other than those who are part of it. At the most general level I would like to suggest that there is no distanced, uncon-nected, audience for foxhunting, there are no spectators who are outside of the event itself and that there are no mere observers of it.[9] Yi-Fu Tuan's comments about participation in local festivals resonates well with the case of foxhunting. He suggests that people attend festivals for a variety of reasons but all of them:

> ... go to immerse themselves in *life*—that is a confusion of sounds, colours, and movements that nevertheless are undergirded by a sense of order and common purpose. No one would want to have a bird's-eye view of a festival as a whole. To do so would require the sort of distancing that is antithetical to the celebration of life (1990: 240).

Similarly, people go foxhunting for a wide variety of reasons and they respond to it in different ways but all of them are participants who feel themselves to be connected and engaged with it. No one going hunting attempts to find a posi-tion from which they have an overview of the event: each of them seeks to be part of it and in the thick of it. Foxhunting, in its totality, *requires* their pres-ence for it to exist as an event.

Richard Schechner's notion of the 'accidental audience' and the 'integral audience' is one that can here usefully be extended from theatre and ritual to the fox hunt (1988: 193–196). The 'accidental audience' of a theatrical event is comprised of those who have seen advertisements, or in other ways found out about the event, and choose to attend something that is open to all. Similarly, they are like tourists watching a ritual ceremony. The 'integral audience' is one that is comprised of people connected with the theatrical world, friends of the performers—an audience of people who know each other, who 'know what is going on'. These differently comprised audiences are significant for performance in many different ways but what is particularly relevant here is, as Schechner points out, that:

> ... an accidental audience comes 'to see the show' while the integral audience is 'nec-essary to accomplish the work of the show'. Or, to put it another way, the accidental audience attends voluntarily, the integral audience from ritual need. In fact the pres-ence of an integral audience is the surest evidence that the performance is a ritual (1988: 195).

I cannot fully explore the notion of foxhunting as ritual here but Schechner's sense of the almost moral obligation felt by certain people to attend an event

© The Editorial Board of the Sociological Review 2003

and the need for them to be there for there to be an event at all is particularly important for foxhunting. During my fieldwork I was struck by the commitment to hunting from those involved in it. There was a strong sense that, as members of a particular Hunt, they ought to be out with them on as many days as possible during the season. Certainly this was connected with the obvious point that they found immense pleasure in the event. Beyond this, however, there was a strong sense that as foxhunting people it was *proper* to be out with the Hunt on a hunting day; that, although it was not as strong as a compulsion, there was a sense of obligation that it was necessary to make time for hunting. A Huntsman out with his hounds on his own could certainly hunt foxes but this would be a much reduced and impoverished sense of foxhunting and much more akin to the solitary farmer with his gun. The 'integral audience' is necessary for the totality of foxhunting as an event.

There is one point on a hunting day in which the Hunt is, as it were, on display and at which point there will possibly be an audience or spectators who view the Hunt as a spectacle. If the Meet, described earlier, is held outside a pub, on a village green or any similar public space there will be people who arrive as spectators of the gathering: an 'accidental audience' with no particular connection with the event. Even though they might live locally such people are *sightseers* who attend to observe a moment of what is treated as a colourful tradition that stands out from everyday life.

To return to the sense of the obligation to hunt, having made this general claim, it is necessary to offer a more nuanced account of the gradations of participation. It might seem that an obvious distinction could be drawn between the horse-mounted participants in their formal equestrian dress and those who attend on foot, dressed in everyday country clothing. The former might seem more obviously connected with the main activities of foxhunting, and constitutive of those activities, whereas the latter might seem to form more of an audience whose participation is limited to watching. This distinction is, however, misleading and would only be made by an outsider, someone unconnected with the foxhunting world. All of the people who come together on a hunting day are part of that Hunt's local world and all of them would regard themselves as fully, although differently, participating in what constitutes a day's hunting.

It is only the Huntsman and his hounds who are directly hunting the fox. No other participants are permitted to attempt to find, chase or kill foxes in foxhunting. Both those on horseback and those on foot are *following* the central activity of Huntsman, hounds and fox and may not directly intervene in that activity which is the performative core of the event. The ebbs and flows of the relationships between the fox and the hounds dictates and governs the rhythms of the hunt in its totality. The mounted riders have, perhaps, a more immediate relationship to this than those on foot or following in cars in that they hope to follow closely where the fox and hounds lead, although they must remain in a group under the guidance of the Field Master who will lead them across the countryside. While the Huntsman is stationary and waiting for his hounds to explore a particular terrain; the riders will be at rest, hoping and waiting for the hounds to find a scent and begin a pursuit. If the Huntsman is ambling along with the hounds as he follows them through a wood or along a hedgerow they will be allowed to follow at a suitable distance behind him, as they will if he trots or canters to a new location. For some riders, those who are *aficionados* of the practice of hunting itself, the fact that they are in sight of the Huntsman working with his hounds is the central pleasure of the day. For the majority of riders however, this is hardly the excitement they hope for. Once the hounds have picked up a scent and begin to increase their pace in a very directed way then the potential exists for a much more challenging performance of equestrianism. To keep up with the hounds they must cross the countryside at speed and confront the obstacles that present themselves. Here riders judge their horses and those of others in terms of their performance—how they have jumped or faltered, who showed skill, style and daring, who got in the way of other riders, who was competitive, who fell and who was able to keep up with the action.

Those who follow on foot will also comment on the equestrian aspect of hunting but this is not their passion. They are not there to see an equestrian show. The spectacular nature of the foxhunt is of no particular interest to them and is rarely commented on. Their passion consists of being in a position from which they can observe the hounds at work. This brings me back to the point suggested above. Those who participate on foot do not do so in order to see the pageantry of the hunt as it flows across the countryside but rather to enter the flows of hunting itself. Few foot followers actually walk across the countryside all day. The vast majority make use of motor vehicles of various kinds on the roads and lanes that crisscross the landscape to get them to a point where will be able to walk to see the best of the action. Unlike the mounted followers who must follow the hounds, the foot followers will attempt to predict where a fox might be found and how it might run and attempt to get there as efficiently as possible. They too must know the countryside and how to get across it. They make judgements about the local conditions, about how the hounds might respond, where a fox might lead them and they then act on these judgements. Foot followers are enormously proud of their skill and ability to be in the right place at the right time and many have a high reputation for this. Years of experience of hunting in the same country makes them extremely knowledgeable. To successfully predict how the hunt will develop and to be present at its key moments is the aim of most foot followers and is, in itself, a perfect performance for them. One regularly hears foot followers proudly announcing, 'I was the first to see the fox', 'I was at the corner of the wood when the hunted fox came past me,' or 'I was there when the hounds were right with their fox'.

This is not simply the skill of getting to the right places, it is also a narrative performance: they tell stories about what happened at a particular location in the past and they recount their previous experiences. Conversations consist of commentaries on what is going on, predictions about the chances of finding foxes, views on how the hounds are hunting, opinions on what might be expected given the conditions of that particular day and judgements about where next to move in order to view the predicted developments. People will disagree with each

© The Editorial Board of the Sociological Review 2003

other: some will stay where they are, convinced that the main activity will quickly swing back towards them, others will move off in different directions, each convinced that they have best understood the relationship between the fox, hounds and terrain. This deep knowledge of hunting is not simply directed towards informing a critical, distanced judgement of the performance of others but it is rather an understanding directed towards an experience in and of the natural world for themselves. It allows them to be fully, immediately and actively present.

Animal participants and performers

In foxhunting what is sought is an engagement between a fox and hounds that has duration across time and space, an engagement which, in terms of the perceptions of the human participants, allows both sets of animals to reveal and display their particular qualities and to create a performance. The importance of the development of a relationship is highlighted by its opposite. It sometimes happens that hounds, entering a wood or undergrowth, will find and immediately kill a fox. This is referred to as 'chopping' a fox. When I first witnessed such a killing I was surprised by the evident disappointment of the people present. I suggested to them that this was a good 'result': the hounds had quickly found a fox and killed it with no effort. The hounds had been both efficient and effective. Their response was that this was not what hunting was about; it was not hunting at all. It was not that the hounds had done anything wrong but it was, as it were, a waste. There had been no contest and challenge, and no interest and excitement. Although the people with whom I spoke about this did not express it in these terms, the expression 'chopping' conveys a sense of sudden and immediate violence, perhaps even destruction. The fox offered potential but it was 'cut down' before it could reveal it. It was killed as an unknown animal, one with which no relationship had been developed.

The fox should have the time and space to present a series of challenges to the hounds as it attempts to avoid being found, pursued and caught. The fox is unwittingly and unwillingly drawn into the performance of the hunt and its behaviour in this context is interpreted, commented on and judged as a performance. A fox, when it is aware that it is exposed and the subject of the attention of the hounds, will take evasive action. It might run through difficult terrain or across spaces containing livestock whose scent might disguise its own; it might run straight and fast or in potentially confusing loops; it might attempt to conceal itself or seek refuge somewhere that hounds cannot enter. All of this behaviour is of intense interest to the human participants who comment on it in terms of a set of opinions, views and cultural beliefs about the nature and character of foxes. For them, foxes are regarded as clever animals, wily rogues and tricksters, which are not easily caught and hunting allows them to display their essential 'foxness'. During a hunt they are admired for the skills of deception that they are judged to be employing to outwit the hounds, and for their bravery, strength, drive and stamina when under pressure. In the commentaries on the behaviour of a hunted fox there was a clear sense that what the fox was doing was something beyond responding to or relying on its natural instincts; it was no mere automaton driven by its biology but rather a thinking, aware, creature who was an active agent and who in some sense understood the processes of hunting and who created a performance out of the demands of the situation.

As a final point here it is also important to emphasize that the failure to catch and kill the hunted fox does not indicate a complete failure for the human participants. A fox which has created a series of interesting challenges for the hounds but who has finally outwitted or out run them is admired by those who have been present. Such a fox has been a worthy opponent and a worthy victor of the contest, one which has out-performed the hounds which have pursued it.

Although the issue of animal performance for the foxhounds is more complex than that for the fox there is a shared element in that the actions of the fox-hounds are perceived to be governed by something other than a response to their biological nature. Foxhounds have a long history and pedigree through which they have been selectively bred and trained to fulfil one role only—that of hunting foxes. However these animals are not simply bred for their physical conformation and robust stamina but also in terms of aesthetic qualities such as the colour of their coat and the melodious quality of their 'voice' and for other qualities directly related to their role in foxhunting—their scenting ability and the more difficult to define quality of 'fox sense' which refers to how humans think that foxhounds understand and respond to foxes.

There are two levels of performance associated with what is expected of a foxhound. At a minimal level a hound is expected to be effective in fulfilling its role as a hunting hound. It should be able to find the scent of a fox, be skilled and active in following it and have the necessary stamina to pursue the fleeing fox. There is, however, a more complex notion of performance in terms of what the human participants expect of an individual hound and of the pack as a whole. There is a strong sense that these animals have an awareness of, and respond to, a sense of responsibility to the breed of which they are a member. Although hounds are referred to as working animals it is not expected that the work of hunting should be a chore for them. Hounds are spoken of as not only expressing a willingness when hunting but also a joy. A significant part of the aesthetics of foxhunting (an aesthetics constructed by the people who hunt) is carried by the hounds. Not only are they admired as pedigree animals and physical specimens, the embodiment of 'foxhoundness', but in terms of how their behaviour can be interpreted as performance. Individual hounds will be singled out for attention and comment, but the performance of any individual is expected to contribute to the total performance of the pack. Many Huntsmen commented to me that within their pack they had particularly good individual hounds—one might have an uncanny ability to sense where a fox might be found or where it might have gone; another that could find the slightest trace of a scent and hold that scent in the most difficult conditions; one would always persevere

© The Editorial Board of the Sociological Review 2003

when the rest of the pack was becoming dispirited. Such individuals were valuable but, the Huntsmen would add, they should not become 'star performers' or indulged '*prima donnas*'. The individuality of the pack should be expressed in the quality of the pack not in terms of the qualities of its individual members.

On the hunting field people comment on how hounds work at a scent, how they communicate finding the first traces of a scent to others in the pack, the quality of their 'voices' (their baying, also known as 'the music of hounds'), how they form into a close pack (often described as being so close that one could 'throw a handkerchief over them') flowing rhythmically across the countryside. Although the hounds are expected to be effective hunters—they should regularly find and kill their prey—this is not expected to be a mechanical process and the hounds are not regarded as efficient killing machines. The pleasure for those who participate in order to watch hounds hunting is the style in which they do so. This is a performance of another order and more akin to interpreting and expressing a role.

To conclude this section it is necessary to consider the role of the person who is the catalyst of the relationship between the central animal performers. The Huntsman must exercise control over his hounds despite having no physical contact with them. At all times he is expected to strike a fine balance between leaving them alone and helping them along. He should feel, sense and understand the natural world around him and be responsive to everything that makes up that world. The nature of the landscape, the relationship between open fields, hedgerows, woods and roads, the changes in local climate, the direction of the wind and the rising or falling of temperature, the condition of the very ground over which he is riding are all elements that have an influence on the progress of the hunt.

Throughout the day people will comment on the Huntsman's performance. There will be different views about whether he is leaving his hounds alone too much or whether he is interfering when they are best left alone; about whether he is using his voice and horn too much or not enough to encourage the hounds; about whether he has really understood and responded to the conditions properly. He might be criticized for being too out of touch with his hounds when they have found a scent and then not being able to keep up with them, or he might be admired for the way he brought the pack back to him when he was convinced they were not on the true line of the hunted fox. Different groups on the hunting field will also evaluate his performance differently. Those who participate in order to ride will be enormously pleased with a Huntsman who moves along at a cracking pace, whether or not the hounds have convincingly settled onto the line of a fox, and creates plenty of opportunities for an exciting ride. Others, who often consider themselves purists in such matters, will be disappointed with a Huntsman who is too hurried and does not allow the hounds to display their full hunting capacities.

One of the key images often used of the relationship between the Huntsman and his hounds is that of 'the invisible thread' that connects them. The Huntsman and his hounds should form an *ensemble* linked by mutual purpose,

© The Editorial Board of the Sociological Review 2003

understanding and feeling. Although a pack of foxhounds is often spoken about as being a natural hunting unit they are not hunting for their own purposes; they are hunting with and for the Huntsman. He should not continually impose his will on them, he must not continually command, but neither should he blindly follow where they lead. The thread by which they are connected is composed of the inflections of voices, both human and canine, commands and obedience, encouragement and reprimands, understanding and mutual respect. It is a thread that sometimes has to be given out and sometimes drawn back in, sometimes it is taut, often it snaps.

This performance is at the heart of foxhunting. Human imagination and agency have created a domesticated animal to engage with a wild animal within the variously configured natural and cultural spaces of the countryside. The people who hunt come, in part, to witness this performance—not as distanced spectators who merely observe, criticize, or praise, but as participants who immerse themselves in the excitement, the disappointments and sometimes the boredom it creates.

Conclusion

My anthropological claim is that foxhunting can be interpreted as an enactment and celebration of a deep connectivity felt by the human participants with the natural world, with the lives within it and with the landscapes that both contain and constitute it. This is the world that surrounds them as part of their daily life and one that creates a foundation for much of their sense of community. Foxhunting both depends on that everyday connectivity but, out of key elements of it, creates something of particular significance: a cultural performance. James Peacock has asked how such performances relate to everyday day life and suggests that they should be considered as condensed, distilled, concentrated life, but marked as set apart and distinct from the ordinary routines of life. He comments:

> A performance is not necessarily more meaningful than other events in one's life but it is more deliberately so; a performance is, among other things, a deliberate effort to represent, to say something about something (Peacock, 1990: 208).

This event *is* deeply meaningful for those who participate in foxhunting. It does, in a Geertzian sense, 'say something about something' but the notion of 'saying' must be extended to expressing in a non-verbal idiom. Those who hunt are able to reflect on and speak about what hunting means to them, but that only occurs when it is over. During the time and space of its enactment and through the performances that constitute it, foxhunting is directly and immediately expressive of a set of relationships between humans, animals and the countryside.

Foxhunting should be both effective and affective. Just as there is work to be done in the routine event when the farmer takes his gun to shoot a fox, so there is work to be done in this excessive event. Foxes must be found, pursued and

© The Editorial Board of the Sociological Review 2003

killed—foxhunting should be an effective practice. This is performance defined as practical achievement but it is also one that allows a more evocative accomplishment to emerge. Foxhunting requires more from its participants for it to be affective, for fox killing to be transformed into foxhunting. For it to fulfil itself as foxhunting in its totality, to become fully performance and to fully accomplish this performance, it must create an emotional engagement between all its participants and the natural world in which they are immersed. They must give themselves up to *being* in the countryside in a more intense, aware, responsive way than they normally would. If all of its elements can be brought together, if this connectivity is achieved, then foxhunting becomes a passionate pursuit.

Acknowledgements

I would like to thank Bill Andrewes and Rebecca Cassidy for their insightful comments and suggestions about this piece and Stephanie Schwandner-Sievers who read too many versions and who always found ways to kick start it when it had ground to a halt. My particular thanks are to Wallace Heim for her careful pruning, editing and comments and for her patience with my battle against deadlines.

Notes

1 There is no space here to elaborate on the complexity of dress codes. There are other people, Masters of Foxhounds, Hunt Servants and those who have been invited to do so who are significantly marked out by red coats.
2 The Huntsman, who can either be a professional or an amateur, is responsible for the actual processes of hunting with the hounds. There will only be one in each Hunt.
3 It is important to state that my research into foxhunting has consisted, in large part, in a long-term engagement with the lived social worlds of several Hunts. I have been trusted and welcomed into those worlds and been given access to all the information I asked for because, I believe, it was understood that I wished to explore foxhunting as a social and cultural event from the perspectives of the participants. Foxhunting is a hugely contested event morally and politically but I have adopted the position of not engaging directly with those issues, although this is, in itself, a moral and political stance. In keeping with this particular personal and anthropological position I do not here deal with the legitimacy or illegitimacy of foxhunting or with foxhunting as a contested performance.
4 The Field Master, who can be male or female, is the person responsible, on a hunting day, for maintaining the discipline of the mounted riders. The Field Master must ensure that the riders do not interfere with the Huntsman, hounds and the processes of hunting and that the riders move across the countryside in a considerate manner. Of particular concern here is to make sure that there is minimal damage to hedges, fences and agricultural land, minimal disturbance to livestock and minimal inconvenience to other people if they are on roads.
5 Any hunt is likely to develop in much more complex ways and there are rules and regulations about what may or may not be done should a fox seek refuge in particular places.
6 Foxhunting also takes place in Wales, Scotland and Northern Ireland but for the sake of simplicity here I have referred only to England.
7 Hunt with a capital 'H' refers to the fox hunt as a social entity rather than to the practice of hunting itself.

8 There will be exceptions to this. Many Hunts will have members and supporters who live in urban areas.

9 In some ways this is a simplified exposition. There could be a fleeting audience for any hunt—for example the people who see it while driving across the countryside. On some occasions—for example on Boxing Day—Hunts deliberately engage in display and pageantry. There is another potential audience for the foxhunt—the anti-hunting protesters. It is impossible to engage here with the complexity of this issue but they, too, constitute a body of engaged (although, from the perspective of the Hunt, unwelcomed) participants in the event. They are not present merely to observe but actively to disrupt it. One could certainly explore, in terms of their dress codes, language and practices, the performative quality of their interjections into the performance of hunting.

References

Bell, M. M. (1994), *Childerley. Nature and Morality in a Country Village*, Chicago and London: University of Chicago Press.

Marvin, G. (2000), 'Natural Instincts and Cultural Passions: Transformations and Performances in Foxhunting', *Performance Research*, 5(2): 108–115.

Peacock, J. (1990), 'Ethnographic Notes on Sacred and Profane Performance', in R. Schechner and W. Appel (eds), *By Means of Performance*, Cambridge: Cambridge University Press, pp. 208–220.

Schechner, R. (1988), *Performance Theory*, London: Routledge.

Schieffelin, E. (1998), 'Problematizing Performance' in F. Hughes-Freeland (ed.), *Ritual, Performance and Media*, London: Routledge, pp. 194–207.

Tuan, Y. (1990), 'Space and Context' in R. Schechner and W. Appel (eds), *By Means of Performance*, Cambridge: Cambridge University Press, pp. 236–244.

© The Editorial Board of the Sociological Review 2003

Part II
Living here

Green distinctions: the performance of identity among environmental activists[1]

Dave Horton

Introduction

With increasing media attention to 'the environment', a dominant representation of environmental activism is of spectacular and often confrontational events in the public sphere. Many studies of social movements, tending primarily to focus on political protest, follow this preoccupation with the most visible and dramatic manifestations of contemporary environmentalism. Although some scholars are interested in analysing the 'non-political' dimensions of social movements like environmentalism, this interest is often circumscribed by the extent to which 'the cultural' can be used to explain 'the political', which remains for most theorists the proper concern of social movement research.

Environmentalism is a political force and high-profile environmental controversies are important objects of study. But environmentalism is also about the everyday. Some activists might occasionally participate in media-friendly stunts, but as part of their green campaigns most activists also issue press releases, write letters, organize town centre stalls, and attend public inquiries. And beyond these public performances exists a less visible world of continuous action. All social movements are sustained by 'submerged networks' (Melucci, 1985, 1989), and within the submerged networks of 'the green movement' activists organize and attend meetings, study a whole range of environmentally relevant texts, and grapple with the development of green cultural practice. This sphere of everyday life is an important, and frequently overlooked, part of contemporary environmentalism. Material culture is a hugely significant constitutive component of this sphere of 'the everyday'. Particular objects, and particular ways of living with the material world, are vital to the production and reproduction of both the everyday lives of environmental activists and environmentalism as a whole.

This chapter explores the importance of materialities to the performance of identity. It argues that distinctive and distinguished green lifestyles depend on the material objects environmental activists tend to live with and without. Further, it argues that activists' material relations are themselves performative of distinctive green lifestyles. The case of environmental activists provides a clear demonstration of the wider significance of materialities to the performance

© The Editorial Board of the Sociological Review 2003. Published by Blackwell Publishing Ltd, 9600 Garsington Road, Oxford OX4 2DQ, UK and 350 Main Street, Malden, MA 02148, USA

of identity, a significance which remains relatively unexplored within contemporary social science.

How does one earn 'green distinction', the markings of a green identity? This chapter argues that among environmental activists green distinction is not earned through the rational articulation of green perspectives or the correct espousal of green political ideology, so much as through the embodied performance of appropriate green identity. Through following the logic of their habitus, playing according to green cultural codes, activists perform an identity which earns them distinctively green distinction.[2] It should be clear that by performance I do not mean the occasional and ephemeral staging of an ordinarily hidden identity, but rather the ongoing, repeated and routinized enactment of the green cultural codes promoted by the discourses of contemporary environmentalism, which brings forth a distinctive way of life. The green identities of environmental activists are, in other words, performed throughout everyday life.

The setting

My ethnographic research, comprising participant-observation alongside a set of focus groups and a series of individual interviews, was centred on the green networks of Lancaster, England. Situated in a relatively remote and rural part of the north-west, between the sands of Morecambe Bay and the moors of the Forest of Bowland, the city is close to the upland National Parks of the Lake District and Yorkshire Dales. With good road and rail links, and near to some of Britain's most prized landscapes, Lancaster's location makes it something of a 'gateway' to important areas of outdoor recreation.

Lancaster's population of around 50,000 includes very significant numbers of students, who come to study at its two institutes of higher education. The city's green networks are comprised almost entirely of people who originally came to the city to study, and who decided to remain once their formal education was complete. These green networks are unusually vibrant. Since Lancaster University's foundation in 1964, the city has developed a reputation as a centre for new social movement politics (Bagguley *et al.*, 1990), and in recent years this reputation has become distinctively greened. There has been longstanding and very effective opposition to proposed road and housing developments, occasional 'radical' environmental protest events such as Reclaim the Streets and Critical Mass, and prominent campaigns by local members of national environmental organizations such as Friends of the Earth and Transport 2000. Currently, the area also has the highest number of elected Green Party councillors in the country.

There are visible signs of the city's green distinction. Most obviously, close to the city centre is a 'green complex', comprising three important spaces: a vegetarian wholefood workers' co-operative; a vegetarian café, the favourite informal meeting place of environmental activists; and a basement office, currently housing a 'radical' environmental project and the site for various activist initia-

© The Editorial Board of the Sociological Review 2003

tives over the years. Beyond this 'green complex', a short distance across town lies a thriving community centre which is the site of many 'green meetings', both the formal, planned meetings of specific groups and campaigns, and the informal and often unplanned meetings of the city's environmental activists. These signs of an 'alternative culture' can be found in other British city centres; in Lancaster, however, such places act as important supports to a green community larger than would be expected from the city's relatively small size.[3]

The activists

My fieldwork concentrated on post-1960s expressions of environmentalism. The label 'environmental activist' therefore includes people aligning themselves with well-known if relatively 'new' environmental organizations such as Friends of the Earth and the Green Party, as well as people more resistant to organizational labels and, whilst identifying with groups such as Reclaim the Streets and Earth First!, tending to form loose and ephemeral networks around specific direct actions. The category 'environmental activist' thus conflates important differences in the forms of politics practised by individuals. Broadly, the 'reformists' tend to recognize and work within existing political structures, while the 'radicals' tend ordinarily and deliberately to bypass the established political system, and instead favour 'direct action'.

These different styles of environmental activism are performed by, and performative of, different material assemblages, and result in distinctive green lifestyles. At the 'radical' extreme, for example, activists often favour highly mobile and 'close-to-nature' modes of dwelling, such as yurts and benders. 'Radical' activists also sometimes embody a 'counter-cultural' ethos through transgressive styles of dress and hair. At the other extreme, the lifestyles of some 'reformists' differ in remarkably few ostensive ways from the lifestyles of people beyond the boundaries of green culture.

At one point in the research process a group of locally-based activists engaged in fierce (and predominantly 'online') debate around the reformulation of the traditional 'reformist'/'radical' split according to the dress codes of 'fleece' and 'khaki'. Beyond acting as visible boundary markers, and contributing to the constitution of collective identities, these two broad styles of dress are powerfully symbolic of different predispositions to the 'natural world': among 'reformists' the wearing of 'fleece' fabrics (as well as walking boots and hi-tech waterproofs) signals an ever-present orientation to the outdoors, a willingness to be out in, engage with, but ultimately move through 'nature'; among 'radicals' the wearing of khaki (and many layers of more 'natural' fabrics) symbolizes a desire to dwell more permanently, and perhaps even to make a home, in 'the natural world'; to merge in an embodied way, and become one, with 'nature'.

Whether primarily 'radical' or 'reformist' in orientation, activists tend to be educated to at least degree level. Activists with the strongest green identities tend to be in their late-20s or 30s, to be childless, and to be committed to activism as 'a way of life', either surviving without much paid work or finding ways of getting paid to be an activist. Many other activists, not such central actors in the local green networks, are employed in health, education and social welfare professions, and maintain their green political commitments alongside career and parenthood. If people tend to enter green networks in search of sociality among like-minded others, they tend eventually to reduce their involvements, and sometimes altogether leave these networks as a result of growing commitments to family and work (see Klatch, 2000). This does not mean the pursuit of a green lifestyle is a passing fad; but it does mean that for many people the phase of group-based political activism which forcefully contributes to the greening of lifestyle tends to be of limited duration.

What unites activists is a willingness to perform environmental commitment in public. Activists seek to demonstrate their understandings to and impress their concerns upon others (Barry, 1999). Whether they do so rumbustiously or quietly, these activists are in their different ways responding to, and acting on behalf of, a variety of 'natures under threat'. Typically, activists' concerns include: the planet and its people; confronting the relentless spread of capitalism, consumerism and related ills such as 'climate chaos'; a geographically proximate and intimately known 'local nature', jeopardized by roads, urban sprawl and polluting factories; and their own bodies, bombarded by an increasingly complex cocktail of chemicals with highly uncertain consequences.

The greening of distinction

People in affluent societies are experiencing weakening identification with, and corresponding loss of commitment to, a whole range of institutions around which strong identities were once built (Bauman, 1993, 1995). Ties to locality, class, work, religion, politics and family which once structured a person's orientation to the world, are all now in various states of flux and rupture. In contrast to the more prescribed collective identities of the past, today's search for social solidarity and sense of belonging tends increasingly to revolve around lifestyles, with their shared values, interests and commitments (Hetherington, 1998; Maffesoli, 1996). Environmentalism is an important recipient of this contemporary search for new forms of community.

In the high consumption societies at least, environmentalism tends to be a class-based politics. In line with previous studies (Berglund, 1998; Cotgrove and Duff, 1980; Eckersley, 1989; Jasper, 1997; Lichterman, 1996), Lancaster's environmental activists, almost without exception, belong to the educated fractions of what is often called 'the new middle class' (Butler and Savage, 1995). Yet, like other 'new social movements', environmentalism seems to be values-led, and to lack clear class interests. In other words, environmentalism is 'of a class' but not 'for a class' (Offe, 1985). Environmentalism is a critique of the untrammelled pursuit of economic growth, and challenges the hegemony of material affluence

© The Editorial Board of the Sociological Review 2003

and conspicuous consumption as routes to distinction. Environmental activists, in questioning the value of economic capital, seek to promote new versions of legitimate taste, prioritizing the earning of what might be called 'green capital'.

'Taste classifies, and it classifies the classifier. Social subjects, classified by their classifications, distinguish themselves by the distinctions they make' (Bourdieu, 1984: 6). Bourdieu's analysis of lifestyles in 1960s France can be applied to the green lifestyles developed among environmental activists in Britain today. In particular, Bourdieu's descriptions of the lifestyles of 'the intellectuals', those high in cultural capital and low in economic capital, seem apposite. Environmental activists distinguish themselves by the 'austerity of elective restriction', the 'self-imposed constraint' of 'asceticism', which is one strategy through which the dominated fractions of the dominant class demonstrate their freedom from 'brutish necessity' on the one hand and profligate 'luxury' on the other, and assert the distinctive power of their cultural capital. This provides them with a means of seeing the world differently, and of playing according to a different set of rules to everyone else (Bourdieu, 1984: 254–5).

Lifestyle practices form around shared tastes. Taste is 'the product of the conditionings associated with a particular class of conditions of existence [and so] unites all those who are the product of similar conditions while distinguishing them from all others' (Bourdieu, 1984: 56). Those with approximately equivalent levels of cultural and economic capital share a habitus, which is productive of values, tastes and practices cohering into a distinctive lifestyle (Bourdieu, 1984: 260). For me, one of the great achievements of Bourdieu's work, *Distinction*, is the way it so persuasively demonstrates that lifestyle, 'a systematic commitment which orients and organizes the most diverse practices' (1984: 55–6, 172–4), is inherently cultural. In other words, particular lifestyles depend for their organization on specific spaces, times, and—the focus here—materialities.

Environmental activists lead distinctive ways of life. Typically, activists practise vegetarianism, favour organic and locally-grown foods (often growing it themselves), and move around locally on foot or by bicycle; they also tend to live without either a car or television, and they strive to reduce their dependence on 'wage labour'. In some of the ethnographic descriptions which pepper *Distinction* Bourdieu could be talking about contemporary British environmental activists. Activists' 'leisure pursuits' are oriented to the 'culturally most legitimate and economically cheapest practices' (Bourdieu, 1984: 267), such as walking and cycling, and a taste for 'natural, wild nature' (Bourdieu, 1984: 220). Activists values, tastes and practices cohere into what might be called 'ascetic lifestyles' (Savage *et al.*, 1992: ch 6).

Identity performance and the assemblage of green lifestyle

Without strong ascribed identities, individuals must make choices about the kind of person they will become (Melucci, 1996a). With evermore 'options' for the investment of identity, people must learn to belong to a culture; the active construction of lifestyle becomes a personal responsibility. Like the ethnographer approaching the culture as an object of study, would-be environmentalists enter, negotiate and develop competence within an initially strange cultural world. Over time, immersion within a shared world produces appropriate forms of performance and competence in culturally specific behaviours and understandings, what Melucci (1996b) calls 'cultural codes' and what Bourdieu (1984) terms 'a scheme of perception and appreciation'. Gradually the person learns to belong, to feel 'at home' (on the progressive internalization of the forces structuring any field of action, and the consequent development of the accomplished actor, or 'player', see Bourdieu, 1990, 1998).

The green cultural world, or habitus, is productive of green performances. These green performances are enacted according to a continuously made and remade set of green cultural codes, which regulate 'appropriate' behaviour. These codes, similar to norms, are the encapsulation of behaviours appropriate to the green cultural world. They are neither so rigid, mechanical and determining as rules, nor so free and voluntaristic as options.

Here, it might be helpful to distinguish between what I am calling 'green codes' on the one hand, and 'green scripts' on the other. Scripts are more settled narratives to which activists must conform, whereas codes are specific behaviours which can be breached so long as they are made to fit a relevant script. Put differently, green scripts are comprised of green codes which are widely and routinely recognized, if not always faithfully adhered to. Thus, for example, shopping in a supermarket is a breach of green cultural codes, but by placing this behaviour in context, and appealing to mitigating circumstances, such as 'lack of time', the 'need for economy', or 'the requirements of non-green others (children, guests)', supermarket shopping can still conform to a green script. Here, supermarket shopping is done 'guiltily', with the appropriate awareness that it is not 'good, green' practice. Similarly, 'moving to the country', in order to lead a 'greener' lifestyle involving greater self-sufficiency in food and more intimate, embodied contact with 'the natural world' is a green script to which many activists aspire; it is also one which, it is commonly recognized, almost inevitably leads to the breaking of the green code of carlessness. The breaking of green cultural codes depletes green capital, but the deviation from green scripts spoils green identity. Thus, provided performances conform to a settled green cultural script, they are able to negotiate and manipulate specific green cultural codes.

Operating ordinarily as implicit and embodied principles, green cultural codes are most noticeable when broken (see Butler, 1990; 1993). For example, arriving at a green meeting by car and dressed in business attire would constitute a 'misperformance' of appropriate green cultural codes. As a breach of the expected performance script of arrival on foot or by bicycle, in casual (even 'scruffy') dress, it would be highly conspicuous. The boundaries of the green cultural world are also transgressed and rendered visible through 'overperformances' of appropriate behaviour. For example, to scold someone for using a disposable tissue rather than a washable handkerchief constitutes, for the major-

© The Editorial Board of the Sociological Review 2003

ity of activists, an overperformance of green cultural codes. Such a rebuke treats a code as a rule, and stretches too far both the appropriate 'purity' of a green identity and the appropriate external monitoring of 'personal' practices.

Reiterative performance of distinctive cultural practices, emanating from a particular habitus, produces hexis, an embodied orientation to the world which is visible to the eye: a certain gait and bodily disposition above and beyond particular styles of dress, modes of mobility, and forms of speech. Here performance has become unconscious, behaviour learned to the point that it takes on an inevitability. That 'radical' and 'reformist' environmentalists ordinarily occupy different habitus, which converge only occasionally, becomes evident in the discomfort that each sometimes feels in the others' cultural spaces. At such times, ordinarily unconscious performance is rendered conscious, as the activist becomes aware of their inability to know 'how to proceed'. Self-consciousness and discomfort emerges with the awareness that one does not know the cultural codes, and thus does not know how to perform appropriately in the setting. This results in the feeling of clumsiness, the opposite of the hexis of Bourdieu's accomplished player, in command of the rules of the game.

Discomfort can emerge over something so seemingly trivial as 'milk'. Faced with a choice of 'milk', whether at a green meeting or when shopping, the activist confronts a choice of identity. There is no one 'right milk', and 'milk' correspondingly becomes a site around which identities are distinguished and performed. How should one buy one's milk? Should it be delivered to the door, lugged home from the supermarket, or fetched from the corner-shop? From where can organic milk be bought? Is the best milk container made of glass, plastic or reinforced cardboard? How can one best ensure one's milk is produced locally? Ought one to abstain from the consumption of animal milk entirely, and choose soya 'milk' instead? What if the only soya 'milk' available is non-organic, and potentially genetically modified? Given the impossibility of satisfying all these criteria simultaneously, which ones ought to be privileged when making milk-drinking decisions? Which elements of the diverse 'milk economy' should be supported, and why? Through their choice of 'milk' activists perform and are performed by their positioning within green networks.

Different kinds of relationship to milk are appropriate in different green networks. However trivial the dilemmas surrounding milk consumption might seem, minor differences in favoured milk-purchasing behaviour signal important differences in activist lifestyle; like many other mundane elements of daily life, milk preference performs the cultural affiliations of its drinker. Committed vegans might buy soya milk irrespective of its geographical origins (and even its genetic 'contamination'); devout localists might privilege geographical origin above all else; activists seeking to support organic production sometimes buy milk from supermarkets, where other activists would not tread. Many activists perform concern for all these positions, and either shift preferences across contexts, or remain ambivalent.

Here, it is precisely that elevation to a political status of mundane lifestyle practices among activists which increases their symbolic power and importance

© The Editorial Board of the Sociological Review 2003

as indicators of belonging to different habitus, as markers of inter-cultural and intra-cultural boundaries, and as performances of identity. The remainder of this chapter demonstrates the significance of materialities to the performance of green identity and the earning of green distinction more generally. What, in other words, is the role of material culture in the performance of activists' identities and their green distinction?

The role of materialities in the performance of identity

Recent years have witnessed increasing possibilities for performing green cultural codes, and therefore assembling a green lifestyle, whilst shopping. It is within the realm of 'routine provisioning' (Miller, 1998), and especially food shopping, that such greening processes are most advanced. The range of 'environmentally-friendly' food products available in the market-place has expanded enormously; indeed, more generally, a 'pre-fix' dominated food culture is on the rise. With evermore 'fairly-traded' and 'organic' goods to choose from, 'green shopping' has never been easier. Food is hugely important to the performance of green identity among environmental activists. Whether through its display on open kitchen shelving or through its sharing with other activists in green times and places, food is a significant ingredient of green distinction.

The undisputed site for 'green shopping' in Lancaster is the city's wholefood workers' co-op. As a co-operatively run, small-scale retailer, sensitive to issues of social and environmental justice, this shop fits with, and is constitutive of, green cultural codes. Places of consumption are part of the act of consumption. Not merely sites where shopping takes place, they are an integral part of the shopping experience (Shields, 1992; Uusitalo, 1998). The shop embodies the values, tastes and practices of the city's green networks; its interior is dominated by wood, and signs of the co-op's politics are evident in the contents of the magazine racks, and the posters, leaflets and notices adorning its walls. The strict ethical screening procedures enforced by the co-op ensure that purchases made there conform to green cultural codes. Shopping here, and only here, therefore eliminates the possibility of transgressing from a green lifestyle. This is a shop where impulse-buying can be conducted, safe in the knowledge that everything sold fits with (heterogeneous and contested, but nevertheless bounded) green cultural codes; food is organic and ethically-sourced, ethically suspect brands are absent and packaging is minimal. In this shop, then, people buy their way into green identities; their purchases form part of the assemblage of a distinctive green lifestyle.

Of course, activists do not always want to be restricted to 'the wholesome', and they sometimes shop elsewhere. Perhaps increasingly, given the proliferation of 'the exotic' (Bell and Valentine, 1997), activists must negotiate the constant possibility of slipping into 'ordinary shopping' practices. Although the absence of the car from everyday life puts some temptations out of reach, many of Lancaster's activists find the allure of supermarket shopping difficult to resist.

70 © The Editorial Board of the Sociological Review 2003

During the period of my research one activist made a 'new year's resolution' not to shop at supermarkets, which three years later he says he has kept to. Other activists, though, must live uncomfortably with the signs of their 'green infringements', their kitchen shelves revealing their seductions to fellow green cultural members. This exposes the precarious nature of a green identity, which needs constantly to be remade through appropriate performance in order to maintain its credibility to both self and others.

People literally eat their way into identity positions. Like food shopping, the eating of some foods and the refusal of others powerfully communicates lifestyle (Beardsworth and Keil, 1997; Gronow, 1997; Warde, 1997). Green cultural codes surrounding food are especially important, not only because green food choices are proliferating but also because green socialities often include food. Food and sociality come together particularly forcefully, to produce distinctively green performances of identity, in Lancaster's two key green 'meeting and eating' places, the vegetarian café and the green-inclined community centre. These places are where activists most often meet to perform and re-create their green selves, and provide sites for the earning of green capital.[4] Because of the centrality of eating and drinking to green encounters in these places, food values are often made explicit and centred in conversations taking place there.

Green distinctions and identities are also routinely performed outside these 'sites of social centrality' (Hetherington, 1998), during less public food events. Here, green cultural codes are assembled into particular styles of cooking and dining. The form of a 'Jacob's Join', for example, in which each diner provides a dish to be shared amongst the others, is a ritual re-enactment of the collective, participatory and democratic principles favoured within green networks. Also at such occasions, raw ingredients, preferably home-grown and organic, are concocted into a vegetarian dish. In this way, the dietary boundaries, cooking styles and gustatory preferences which flow from the codes implicit in the green networks are produced, recognized and reinforced. Diners are bound together into a symbolic community with shared values at its heart.

The 'Jacob's Join' is the ordinary form of food event within Lancaster's green networks but on one social occasion, a 'harvest supper' which brought together local activists from different environmental groups, the green cultural codes surrounding food were rendered particularly explicit. Everyone contributed a dish towards the communal meal, and had been told by the organizer beforehand that at least one ingredient of their offering should be home-grown. Before the meal began, each person briefly introduced, and recounted the history of, their contribution. The comfort of diners whose dishes conformed closely to the relevant green codes was matched by the awkwardness and apologising of diners who had less successfully incorporated home-grown or local organic food into their contributions.

The distinctive materialities of environmental activists extend beyond the realm of food, and two objects play particularly important roles in producing activists' green lifestyles. Especially within high consumption societies, but increasingly globally, the spectacular rise of car and television ownership since the end of the second world war has had a revolutionary impact on people's daily lives. Indeed, possession and use of the TV and car has become constitutive of a meaningful sense of civic participation, of what it means to be a modern subject (Urry, 2000). But it is the very absence of the car and TV from activists' everyday lives which facilitates their performance of appropriate green identities, and their assemblage of distinctively green lifestyles. The maintenance of a spatially close world of interaction is hugely enabled by the absence of the car and TV. The absence of TV from the everyday lives of environmental activists ensures the release of leisure time for the multiple socialities characteristic of close-knit green networks. The absence of the car is similarly massively consequential, and it is the car's absence on which I want now to focus.[5]

The car is important as a conspicuous object of non-consumption among environmental activists. Its absence demonstrates belonging to the elective green lifestyle community. Nearly all of Lancaster's activists live without a car; as one prominent activist in the local Green Party bluntly put it, 'I've never owned a car and I never will' (fieldnotes, May 2000). These activists move around by bike, on foot and—for longer journeys—by train and, less frequently, bus. Under exceptional circumstances some might take a taxi, but in the normal course of everyday life, at the local level, core activists rely almost exclusively on cycling and walking.

Among environmental activists in green places, talk often turns to the politics of transport, and the car is a common target of anger. Sometimes this distaste is general, with activists expressing hostility to the social and environmental effects of 'car culture'. At other times talk is much more personal, based on activists' direct and negative experiences as pedestrians and cyclists. Such talk continuously constructs car driving as a polluting practice, and thus maintains the status of the car as a pollutant of green lifestyles. It produces car ownership and use as one of the most powerful markers of the boundary between 'green' and 'ungreen'. It is the absence of car ownership among activists which makes this talk possible.

Absence of the car produces effects across the entirety of everyday life, and leads to distinctive socialities, spatialities and temporalities. Carlessness promotes spatially constrained socialities, ensuring that a handful of green meeting places are frequented by almost all activists. The performance of walking and cycling, the mobility practices considered typical of, and so constitutive of, activists' green lifestyles, is promoted by carlessness. The spatialities imposed by these 'green mobilities' promotes the face-to-face interactions of 'chance encounters', which keep activists in 'the thick of things'. Carless activists tend to produce, through their everyday geographies, a spatially tight sense of 'the local'. This 'local' encompasses residential locations relatively close to city centre amenities (including the hubs of public transport, and especially the train station); and it includes the close-to-home 'natural world'. Put briefly, in keeping life local the car's absence promotes the continued performance of green cultural codes.

An activists' credibility is jeopardized, and their level of green capital eroded, by car ownership. Failing to conform to one of the strongest green cultural

© The Editorial Board of the Sociological Review 2003

codes, and with green identity consequently threatened, activists need to justify their car use. One participant in a focus group of Green Party activists said:

> 'I really worry that people think I'm a hypocrite for having a car, but I always consider whether I need to travel and if I do, the best way to do it. And so I can justify myself having a car . . . And in your own life you can do trade-offs . . . say you use your car, it's more convenient to use your car but you could have used the train, so as a trade-off, instead of changing your bed whenever you change it, just say for argument's sake once a week, then you change it once a fortnight, so that you save on your washing, your energy use. So you can do trade-offs in your own life, to try and make yourself feel less guilty'.

Here, although the green cultural code of carlessness is broken, an acceptably green cultural script is followed—the person appeals to responsible use, and a willingness to 'trade-off' their car use against enlightened ecological practice in other spheres of everyday life. Other activists recognize their increasing seduction by the car, and are aware of the potential consequences. During a focus group comprised of 'radical activists', for example, one person said:

> 'I used to be really adamantly against car use, but occasionally now for work I need a car and I've got access to a car, which I never used to have, so I find myself occasionally using it when I don't really have to, I could cycle to Morecambe in the rain if I really wanted to, but sometimes I take the car . . . so I do feel like I'm becoming less radical, or less consistent'.

Given the symbolic significance of abstinence from the car to activists' own understandings of a green lifestyle, and given the vital role of such absence in performing activists' everyday geographies, increasing car use is interpreted, by both self and others, as signalling lapsed cultural membership. Activists who are in the process of leaving central locations within green networks tend to search out compromise positions, between their previously complete renunciation of the car and their drift towards absolutely non-green car ownership. As the structuring force of the cultural codes operative within green networks diminishes, people become more inclined to borrow or hire cars, to organize car-sharing arrangements, or to buy a (small, second-hand, fuel-efficient) car and then—perhaps in a final salve to their green conscience—convert it to run on liquified petroleum gas. The green cultural codes are successively broken, and the green cultural script of attention to 'sustainable mobility' stretched to its limit. If this limit is finally breached, the 'unapologetically ungreen' motorist, underperforming a symbolically central green cultural code, departs the green world; their performances are no longer structured by the activists' habitus, and from a green scheme of perception and appreciation, they become inept.

Although environmental activists shun the car, an important distinction emerges around their favourite vehicles. For some, the bicycle is the vehicle of choice, whilst for others it is the van. The bicycle is homologous with an orientation to, and concern for, 'the local', and also with the desire to get out into, but ultimately move through, 'the natural world'. As a relatively simple, cheap and non-polluting technology, it is deeply symbolic of the search for sustain-ability. Locally, activists use their bicycles to sustain spatially close-knit net-works; extra-locally their bicycles are an important resource in the performance of active, distinctive leisure identities. In conjunction with the train and ferry (and sometimes the plane), the bicycle enables the performance of 'green holi-days'. The van is homologous with a more nomadic way of life; it is simultane-ously visibly distinctive and provides a degree of privacy and security; and it is a vehicle which permits the combination and blurring of mobility and dwelling; here the quest is less for environmental sustainability, more the living out of an alternative and at times politically antagonistic and controversial way of life (see Hetherington, 2000).

Conclusions

Environmental activists distinguish themselves by the distinctions they make between themselves and non-activists. Activists also make distinctions between their own lifestyles and the lifestyles of other activists. These distinctions are performed. And these performances produce and reproduce the boundaries of, and within, the green cultural world. In this chapter I have specifically tried to show that distinctive green cultural codes, and the environmental identities they produce and reproduce, are performed materially. Through their distinctive materialities, environmental activists continuously perform their adherence to, and are enabled to maintain participation in, the green cultural world. Materi-alities are crucially involved in shaping the everyday lives of environmental activists. More generally, particular objects and the material assemblages of which they form part are crucial to the performance of identity.

Performances of green identity do not, of course, remain static over time. At a general level, new forms of distinction emerge. New kinds of food become avail-able in organic and fairly-traded varieties; sometimes such food is found more cheaply in places which generate dilemmas of identity, such as supermarkets. The production of fresh controversies politicizes new realms of everyday life, so that, for example, a growing awareness of the potentially harmful effects of carpets on health prompts the decision to expel them from the house. At the individual level, the everyday lives of activists are not static, and their commitments and convic-tions tend inevitably to shift over time. Initial hostility to the computer, internet and email gradually gives way to a recognition of their usefulness to a political life, and a process of incorporation into a green lifestyle. Changes in personal cir-cumstance which tend often to mark movement across the lifecourse, such as the demands of parenthood and career, can 'squeeze out' commitments to environ-mental activism, if not to a green lifestyle. Although many activists maintain lifestyles which juggle activism with other commitments, activists' environmen-tal identities can also fade, or become 'professionalized'.

Do the distinctive lifestyles developed among environmental activists have broader relevance to the search for sustainability? Activists' green lifestyles tend to be highly participatory and locally-based, and to involve a different, and I think more environmentally sensitive, orientation to the material world. These lifestyles are enabled by the absence of key material objects, such as the TV and car, together with the presence of other material goods, such as the bicycle and computer. They are also enabled by places such as vegetarian cafes, wholefood co-operatives and community centres where activists can act out their green identities. And these lifestyles are enabled by occasions, whether a monthly green group meeting, an annual green festival, a collective meal, or a sporadic 'day of action', when performing a green identity becomes particularly appropriate.

So what precisely can the lives of environmental activists tell us about routes to the greening of behaviour more generally? I think one implication of this research is particularly important for debates around the making of a 'sustainable culture'. Until now, policies aiming to promote sustainability have tended to rely on the provision of information and education, with the goal of producing 'green citizens'. But this research suggests that it is perhaps the materialities, as well as the spatialities and temporalities, upon which the lifestyle performances of environmental activists depend which ought to be extended in the search for sustainability.

Correspondingly, we need to devise what might be called a 'new, green architecture'. This architecture would be assembled from multiple materialities, times and spaces which call forth green practices. It would be an architecture productive of the performance of green cultural codes and broader green cultural scripts. Although each component of such a green architecture might by itself seem rather insignificant, as a whole such an architecture could enable the assemblage of a specifically green identity, which could be carried with the person and which would result in the production of a coherent green lifestyle. Rather than aiming to produce 'sustainable citizens', therefore, it is perhaps the making of 'sustainable performances' which should take centre-stage.

Identities cannot be 'grounded' but the conditions for their performance can be instituted. A green identity is not an essence, and owes its appearance of solidity to the regular, routine performance of green cultural practice. The most centrally involved environmental activists are continuously constituted and reconstituted as green subjects; they reiteratively perform green identity and internalize the resources necessary for the assemblage of green lifestyles. So I am arguing that we ought to think more about the provision of materials, times and spaces which might afford the performance of a green identity. And I am also arguing that we need a new green architecture. The wider adoption of green lifestyles depends on the extension of the green architecture on which the green performances of environmental activists currently depend.

Notes

1 Many thanks to Wallace Heim, Sue Holden and Bronislaw Szerszynski for their invaluable help with this chapter.

© The Editorial Board of the Sociological Review 2003

2 I take the concept of 'habitus' from the work of Pierre Bourdieu, who uses it to explain class reproduction in his epic ethnography of twentieth century French society (see Bourdieu, 1984: 101, 172–3). By speaking of 'the habitus of environmental activists' I mean the cultural space within which activists' green codes are produced and developed, where those codes become habitual and embodied, and where activists' green scripts are established and sedimented. This habitus is where specifically green kinds of performance become taken-for-granted, and out of which distinctively green lifestyles emerge.

3 How typical is the strength of 'the environmental movement' in Lancaster? Within Britain, Lancaster's relatively small size, combined with its geographical location and the presence of a large population of students and, more especially, ex-students, has undoubtedly contributed to its relative 'greening'. But environmentalism is thriving in many other places, from big cities (such as Manchester) to smaller cities (such as Oxford and Brighton) to small towns (such as Totnes, Devon). Presumably, throughout high consumption societies a generally dispersed environmentalism tends to establish strongholds in particular places, which become known as green centres of 'alternative living'.

4 Another important type of site for the performance of green identity is represented by places for the performance of highly valued green practices, such as tending the allotment and garden, and moving through 'the great outdoors'; here activists engage in what John Urry terms 'face-to-place' interactions, and variously dig, pedal, climb and walk their way into green identities (Urry, 2002).

5 In Britain, the car and the infrastructures co-constituted with the car have been the focus of much recent environmental protest. Protest events such as Reclaim the Streets and Critical Mass have sought to bring the system of automobility temporarily to a halt (Carlsson, 2002; Jordan, 1998); a whole series of longer-term, site-based road protests has attempted to obstruct state road building programmes (Merrick, 1996; Wall, 1999; Welsh and McLeish, 1996); and direct action against major transnational corporations, such as Shell and Esso, aims to challenge practices of the oil industry perceived as ecologically devastating and socially immoral. This recent phase of environmental politics has elevated the car's status, in Britain at least, to the most highly contested object of contemporary material culture.

References

Bagguley, P., J. Mark-Lawson, D. Shapiro, J. Urry, S. Walby and A. Warde (1990), *Restructuring: Place, Class and Gender*, London: Sage.

Barry, A. (1999), 'Demonstrations: Sights and Sites of Direct Action', *Economy and Society*, 28(1): 75–94.

Bauman, Z. (1993), *Postmodern Ethics*, London: Blackwell.

Bauman, Z. (1995), *Life in Fragments: Essays in Postmodern Morality*, Oxford: Blackwell.

Beardsworth, A. and T. Keil (1997), *Sociology on the Menu: An Invitation to the Study of Food and Society*, London: Routledge.

Bell, D. and G. Valentine (1997), *Consuming Geographies: We Are Where We Eat*, London: Routledge.

Berglund, E. (1998), *Knowing Nature, Knowing Science: An Ethnography of Environmental Activism*, Cambridge: White Horse Press.

Bourdieu, P. (1984), *Distinction: A Social Critique of the Judgement of Taste*, tr. R. Nice, London: Routledge and Kegan Paul.

Bourdieu, P. (1990), *In Other Words: Essays Towards a Reflexive Sociology*, tr. M. Adamson, Cambridge: Polity.

Bourdieu, P. (1998), *Practical Reason: On the Theory of Action*, Cambridge: Polity.

Butler, J. (1990), *Gender Trouble: Feminism and the Subversion of Identity*, London: Routledge.

Butler, J. (1993), *Bodies that Matter: On the Discursive Limits of 'Sex'*, London: Routledge.

Butler, T. and M. Savage (eds) (1995), *Social Change and the Middle Classes*, London: University College of London Press.

© The Editorial Board of the Sociological Review 2003

Carlsson, C. (ed.) (2002), *Critical Mass: Bicycling's Defiant Celebration*, Oakland, Ca.: AK Press.

Cotgrove, S. and A. Duff (1980), 'Environmentalism, Middle-Class Radicalism and Politics', *Sociological Review*, 28(2): 333–351.

Eckersley, R. (1989), 'Green Politics and the New Class: Selfishness or Virtue?', *Political Studies*, 37(2): 205–223.

Gronow, J. (1997), *The Sociology of Taste*, London: Routledge.

Hetherington, K. (1998), *Expressions of Identity: Space, Performance, Politics*, London: Sage.

Hetherington, K. (2000), *New Age Travellers: Vanloads of Uproarious Humanity*, London: Cassell.

Jasper, J. (1997), *The Art of Moral Protest: Culture, Biography and Creativity in Social Movements*, Chicago: University of Chicago Press.

Jordan, J. (1998), 'The Art of Necessity: The Subversive Imagination of Anti-Road Protest and Reclaim the Streets', in G. McKay (ed.), *DiY Culture: Party and Protest in Nineties Britain*, London: Verso, pp. 129–151.

Klatch, R. (2000), 'The Contradictory Effects of Work and Family on Political Activism', *Qualitative Sociology*, 23(4): 505–519.

Lichterman, P. (1996), *The Search for Political Community: American Activists Reinventing Commitment*, Cambridge: Cambridge University Press.

Maffesoli, M. (1996), *The Time of the Tribes: The Decline of Individualism in Mass Society*, tr. D. Smith, London: Sage.

Melucci, A. (1985), 'The Symbolic Challenge of Contemporary Movements', in *Social Research*, 52(4): 789–816.

Melucci, A. (1989), *Nomads of the Present: Social Movements and Individual Needs in Contemporary Society*, in J. Keane and P. Mier (eds), London: Hutchinson Radius.

Melucci, A. (1996a), *The Playing Self: Person and Meaning in the Planetary Society*, Cambridge: Cambridge University Press.

Melucci, A. (1996b), *Challenging Codes: Collective Action in the Information Age*, Cambridge: Cambridge University Press.

Merrick (1996), *Battle for the Trees: Three Months of Responsible Ancestry*, Leeds: Godhaven Ink.

Miller, D. (1998), *A Theory of Shopping*, Cambridge: Polity.

Offe, C. (1985), 'Challenging the Boundaries of Traditional Politics: The Contemporary Challenge of Social Movements', *Social Research*, 52(4): 817–868.

Savage, M., J. Barlow, P. Dickens and T. Fielding (1992), *Property, Bureaucracy and Culture: Middle-Class Formation in Contemporary Britain*, London: Routledge.

Shields, R. (ed.) (1992), *Lifestyle Shopping: The Subject of Consumption*, London: Routledge.

Urry, J. (2000), *Sociology Beyond Societies: Mobilities for the Twenty-First Century*, London: Routledge.

Urry, J. (2002), 'Mobility and Proximity', *Sociology*, 36: 255–274.

Uusitalo, L. (1998), 'Consumption in Postmodernity: Social Structuration and the Construction of the Self', in M. Bianchi (ed.), *The Active Consumer: Novelty and Surprise in Consumer Choice*, London: Routledge, pp. 215–235.

Wall, D. (1999), *Earth First! and the Anti-Roads Movement: Environmentalism and Comparative Social Movements*, London: Routledge.

Warde, A. (1997), *Consumption, Food and Taste: Culinary Antinomies and Commodity Culture*, London: Sage.

Welsh, I. and P. McLeish (1996), 'The European Road to Nowhere: Anarchism and Direct Action against the UK Roads Programme', *Anarchist Studies*, 4(1): 27–44.

Performing safety in faulty environments

Peter Simmons

This chapter, in contrast to others in the book, is concerned with the urban environment and, more particularly, an environment made 'faulty' by the presence of stigmatized industrial activities which may be harmful. Across Britain, as in other parts of the industrialized world, many thousands of people live with large chemical plants on their doorsteps. Despite local awareness of the potential dangers from such plants and the way in which their presence can contribute to a sense of living in a 'faulty' environment, in the majority of these neighbourhoods everyday life goes on, for the most part, without protest or opposition. Rather than take this apparent acceptance for granted, we need to ask how this state of affairs is produced. In this chapter I approach this question in terms of the notion of 'performance' developed in the work of sociologist Erving Goffman.

Goffman is well-known for his use of the metaphor of performance in his studies of the 'interaction order' (Drew and Wooton, 1988). I shall show, however, that Goffman himself was ambivalent about the 'dramaturgical' metaphor and its implications and point to a very different and rather contemporary sense in which his work leads us to think about the notion of performance. The way in which I use Goffman's ideas in the chapter, applying them to the activities of organizations, extends them beyond their original domain of interpersonal interaction. I begin with a discussion of Goffman's work before turning to the role of the production of safety in the normalization of danger in situations such as those where people live with the dangers of hazardous industries. I explore this process with reference to a specific case study, briefly describing the site and its relationship with the community before examining the ways in which the 'performance of safety' is interpreted by local residents. I conclude by reflecting on the way in which using a conception of performance based on Goffman's work can help us to better understand the responses of local people to such situations.[1]

Goffman, performance and performativity

Erving Goffman devoted his career to analysing the processes of interpersonal interaction, illuminating the ways in which they contribute to the re/production

© The Editorial Board of the Sociological Review 2003. Published by Blackwell Publishing Ltd,
9600 Garsington Road, Oxford OX4 2DQ, UK and 350 Main Street, Malden, MA 02148, USA

of social order. He employed a variety of metaphors in his analyses, most notably those of theatre and ritual. In some of his earlier work, he proposed what he termed a 'dramaturgical' perspective, a metaphor from which a range of loosely connected concepts were derived.[2] Goffman described how individuals in social encounters engage in *performances* that construct a public self in order to regulate the way that others will perceive and behave towards them. This *presentation of self*, with its interactive modulation of language and bodily deportment, is therefore a means of *impression management* (Goffman, 1969 [1959]). This appeared to depict individuals as cynical actors engaged in manipulative behaviour while hiding their 'true' selves behind a succession of masks.

Yet Goffman himself was ambivalent about the implications of this metaphor and in revisions made for the second edition of his book on the presentation of self he quietly undermines it (Branaman, 1997). In later work he played down the theatrical metaphor and emphasized the importance of the interpretative *frames* by which situations, performances and events acquire meaning (Goffman, 1975 [1974]).[3] In making this retreat from the implications of his earlier account of the human actor, Goffman adopts what seems an overly restricted notion of performance as relating only to those circumstances when an individual's behaviour is overtly enacted for an 'audience' and may legitimately be watched without offence. It may be premature to abandon his earlier conception of performance, however, as actors certainly do act strategically in some contexts and, as we shall see, it has relevance in relation to the activities of organizations.

Nevertheless, Goffman's view of performance is often contrasted to recent theorizing of performance and performativity. Gregson and Rose have criticized what they characterize as the 'Goffmanian' perspective on performance, arguing that Goffman implies in his performance metaphor 'an active, prior, conscious, and performing self' (Gregson and Rose, 2000: 433). They contrast this notion of subjectivity with a view of the self as social construction. For them, 'performance—what individual subjects do, say, 'act—and performativity—the citational practices which reproduce and/or subvert discourse and which enable and discipline subjects and their performances—are intrinsically connected, through the saturation of performers with power' (Gregson and Rose, 2000: 434).[4] There is a greater affinity, however, between Goffman's analysis and performativity theories than Gregson and Rose's characterization suggests. Goffman (1975 [1974]) cites W. I. Thomas's dictum that 'if men define situations as real, they are real in their consequences' but goes on to point out that those engaging in a situation ordinarily do not create this definition; rather it is defined by pre-existing social practices and norms (Goffman, 1975 [1974], p. 1). In a much earlier work he glosses this view: 'Instead, then, of starting with the notion of a definition of the situation we must start with the idea that a particular definition is *in charge of the situation*, and that as long as this control is not overtly threatened or blatantly rejected, much counter-activity will be possible' (Goffman, 1972 [1961], p. 132, emphasis in original). Elsewhere, he proposes an explicitly constructionist account of the subject in which the discourses and practices by which the situation is defined constitute roles and identities which those who participate perform and through repeated performance of which the definition itself is reiterated (Goffman, 1972 [1967]).

Although they do not possess the powers of definition, those who participate in a situation are still required to produce performances that instantiate that definition. Actors, however, are still capable of performing well, badly or even subversively the roles they have been given. What Goffman terms 'counter-activity' suggests the possibility of some kind assertion of individual agency but he also points out that this counter-activity may take place without fundamentally disrupting or challenging the order of the situation (Goffman, 1972 [1961], p. 77).[5] His discussions of the internalization of control by the (self-) disciplined individual seem to describe what Gregson and Rose refer to as 'the saturation of performers with power', a theme implicit in his references to the definitions that control situations and constitute human beings. In this reading of Goffman's work (and notwithstanding his own later efforts to restrict the application of the metaphor to a particular usage of the theatrical frame), performance takes on a rather different significance. Framed not by the metaphor of theatre but by that of ritual, it presents us with a view that has striking affinities to that advanced by Gregson and Rose. Viewed in terms of ritual, we have a more conditioned notion of performance as, to use current terminology, citing an inscribed discourse (Howe, 2000).

Although developed for the analysis of interpersonal encounters and relations, several studies have applied Goffman's earlier dramaturgical concepts to the behaviour of organizations, particularly those experiencing some kind of crisis or facing controversy or hostility (eg. Allen and Caillouet, 1994; Elsbach, 1994; Futrell, 1999). This work examines the use of impression management strategies intended to influence the way in which an organization is perceived by other actors but does not consider the ritual aspects of organizational behaviour. As I indicated at the outset, my interest here is in the production of a definition of the situation in which the presence of danger from industrial activities is normalized. A key device for achieving this state of 'normality' is the discourse and practice of 'safety'. 'Safety' is typically constructed within a technical discursive frame but it is not simply the product of 'technical' activity; at a 'local' level it must be socially constructed through interaction between the actors involved (Spencer and Tiche, 1994; Simpson, 1996; Rochlin, 1999) as they perform the ordering operations of discourse and practice.

Based on the preceding discussion of Goffman, I suggest that normalizing a potentially dangerous situation as safe therefore involves a particular definition of the situation, one that encodes particular roles, norms and behaviours which in turn must be enacted by participants. The local enactment of this hegemonic definition requires the production of a tacit negotiated order among the chemical company, government regulators, local government officials, local politicians, other local interests and members of the community. This negotiated order instantiates not only the discourse and practice of 'safety' but a configuration of socio-political processes and a disposition of power that constitute

© The Editorial Board of the Sociological Review 2003

the subject positions and roles which are enacted in separate but interrelated performances by the different actors. Lest this seem like an idiosyncratic reading of Goffman in the light of his well-known actor-centred work, I should note that he has been criticized for presenting far too deterministic a view of this process:

> The normalization process is a much more purposeful affair than it appears to be from [Goffman's] account, and in some ways a more conscious one. It originates in the fairly explicit, short-term, visible goals of those who benefit from it. And the principal beneficiaries are obviously the people who are at the head of large organisations—governmental, business, and service organisations (Burns, 1992: 377).

Burns' point is well taken but we can see that although such a situation may involve purposive organizational performances, it also implies ritualized performance that cites the hegemonic definition of the situation; indeed the purposive actions of organizational actors themselves cite pre-existing discourses and definitions. As I shall show, however, the meaning of such performances is not necessarily stable and they are vulnerable to contingencies, making them susceptible to conflicting interpretations, disruptions and failures. Even where routinized and repeated, their effects are always in some sense indeterminate, which might be expected to have implications for the role of purposive action in the normalization of danger. These issues may best be examined by turning now to our case study.[6]

Chemicals and the community: the corporate performance of safety

The presence of a major chemical production facility in a neighbourhood carries with it the potential for undesirable impacts on those living nearby. These sites often have associated with them the threat of environmental pollution or of harmful physical consequences arising from major accidents, such as explosions, fires or releases of toxic substances. Such neighbourhoods might be said to constitute 'faulty environments' for local residents (Irwin *et al.*, 1999).[7] As domestic environments, they are faulty in the physical sense that they are potentially dangerous but, being therefore inimical to constructions of place and home in terms of values such as security and well-being, they are also faulty in a normative sense. Hence the juxtaposition of domestic and industrial practices creates a conflict between different constructions and moral orders of place. This can be experienced by local residents in terms of compromised place values, leading to a spoiled sense of place, which in turn impinges on their quality of life (Simmons and Walker, 2004). This situation, however, also has implications for industry.

The proximity of a residential population has practical consequences for the operators of a large chemical production site. All chemical industry sites are subject to government controls to ensure compliance with health and safety and environmental standards. In addition, in the European Union all sites that store and use significant quantities of specified hazardous substances which might present a danger to people beyond the boundary of site are also required to inform the local population about the presence of the hazard and about what they should do in the case of an emergency.[8] Even where the distribution of information ensures local awareness of the danger, however, most host communities are not characterized by protest or opposition. Situations where local communities mobilize against an industrial or other hazardous site have been frequently studied (eg. Berry, 2003). Rather less attention has been paid to those more typical situations where, despite the presence of hazards and even the occurrence of events that contribute to the sense of living in a faulty environment, the community is apparently tolerant of the danger.

Longfield is part of a region of England with a long industrial history which has included chemical production, heavy engineering, iron founding and coal mining, although many of these traditional industries have long since declined or disappeared.[9] Despite being now part of an industrial conurbation, Longfield retains a strong sense of local identity. Local officials and company managers described the area to me as having a relatively cohesive community and inhabitants frequently referred to it as having a 'village' culture.[10] The company, which I shall refer to as Foschem, was established in 1851. It was originally a local, family-run firm but is now a multinational company, which has been briefly in and out of US ownership, and has its head office about three miles from Longfield. The site covers 55 acres and employs approximately 600 people. In the past, many of these lived in the immediate vicinity of the Foschem site; now far fewer of the workforce live close by. At the time of the research, the zone around the site that was identified by regulators as being potentially at risk should a major accident happen included a residential population of nearly 8,000 people. Although this population was demographically mixed, many households were headed by manual workers and the overall level of prosperity was relatively low, with unemployment levels above the national average. Many of these potentially 'at risk' homes are a just few streets from Foschem while others look onto the site.

Foschem engages in a number of risk management and communication activities that might be seen as performing, in various ways, a definition of the situation as safe. Whether practical or symbolic, these activities all entail an element of impression management in that they are performed in relation to a segmented 'audience' of regulators, local politicians and institutions, interest groups and residents.

A number of hazardous chemicals, including chlorine, phosphine and phosphorous, are used at the Longfield site which bring it under the highest level of regulatory control. There have been various small fires, explosions and releases of gas over the years. None have had off-site consequences but many have come to public attention as a result of the attendance of the fire service or of local media coverage. The principal hazard to the local community is associated with the chlorine stored and used at the site. The conflict between safety concerns and pressures for local regeneration eventually led the local Development Corporation to loan money to Foschem to help finance the introduction of a 'just-in-time' delivery system that reduced chlorine storage at the site, thereby reducing the extent of the zone covered by planning controls and minimizing the constraints on local redevelopment. This organizational and technological change enabled the safety regulator to redesignate a large area around the site as 'safe'.

The company is an active member of the Chemical Industries Association, which promotes a programme called Responsible Care aimed at demonstrating high standards of health, safety and environmental management and of community relations. Impression management is at the heart of Responsible Care, which is a package of voluntary mechanisms designed to produce public trust in chemical companies and to secure the legitimacy of their operations (Simmons and Wynne, 1993). Some observers have expressed the view that Responsible Care is less about 'caring' and more about pre-empting complaints and heading off opposition that might pose a threat to industrial operations, to the detriment of affected local communities (Moberg, 2002). Others, equally sceptical of the industry's motives, see these developments as creating a space for oppositional struggle (Pearce and Tombs, 1998). Many of the practices at the Longfield site pre-date the introduction of Responsible Care but amount to the same kind of exercise. For example, Foschem has held a number of site open days, arranged regular opportunities for tours of the plant and public talks, and periodically distributes a newsletter to all of the local households and business premises within the zone identified as being 'at risk'. The company also supports a variety of community activities such as tree planting and environmental improvement schemes. In 1975, following a period of difficult relations with local residents over safety issues, Foschem established a community liaison committee. The committee meets 3–4 times a year and is usually attended by 10–12 local residents, along with local councillors and representatives of a number of local organizations. The number of complaints from the public logged by the company, many of them concerning odours perceived to emanate from the site, fell steadily during the 1990s to only one or two a year and few complaints were received by the local office of the environmental regulator.

All of this paints a very positive picture of the situation in Longfield; the company's safety performances seem to have had the desired effect and achieved an environment in which it is 'safe' for the company to operate. To rework a point made by Kroll-Smith (1995), the repetition of these performances—and of the public's deference to their authority—may been seen as reaffirming the safety of the place and defining the moral order of the situation, creating in the process a 'pacified social space'. However, the processes by which pacification is achieved are ambivalent and may as readily be forces for disruption (Burkitt, 1996). Indeed, neither the enactment of nor the response to these authoritative performances of safety is as straightforward as the account given above suggests. The outcome of performances may be indeterminate in at least two, often connected ways: (a) the meaning of the performance may be semantically unstable and (b) the success or effectiveness of the performance itself may not be assured, particularly if participating actors do not perform their roles according to the 'script'. I want to turn first to the problem of semantic instability before returning to the problems of co-ordinating performances.

The semantic instability of performances

The success of a performance, whether in a dramatic or a ritual context, is dependent upon setting aside other framings and available discourses for interpreting the activity that is taking place. However, there are always other ways in which a performance may be viewed and there are situations when something may provoke a different interpretation of the performance that is taking place.

In Longfield, the interpretation of the company's performance of safety was influenced by the context in which it took place. For example, a key factor identified in the risk perception literature as supporting public trust in those responsible for managing risk is whether or not they are perceived to care about those whose wellbeing and lives are dependent upon them. Invoking the ethos of the company's Victorian founders, who were important local benefactors, Foschem emphasizes its contribution to the local community. It is closely identified with the history of the area and hitherto employed many people who lived locally. People whose family had roots in the area frequently drew comparisons with how unsafe or offensive activities at the plant used to be a generation or more ago, noting how much things had improved. Perceived economic benefits also influenced the way in which some people viewed the site, with several long-standing residents commenting on the company's contribution to the area. However, Foschem's perceived failure to recruit new workers from Longfield, where the emergence of a low-wage economy of retail superstores and warehousing was causing local concern, was construed by others as demonstrating a lack of commitment to the community. We can also see this semantic instability in the heavily publicized redesignation of a large area of Longfield as safe for new residential development, which was presented as unequivocal 'good news'. The series of impression management performances by company and institutional actors involved in this process unintentionally highlighted the fact that the remaining area immediately adjacent to the plant—and the 8,000 people living in it—were still considered to be 'at risk'. This instability inheres in all of the company's efforts to reinforce a definition of the situation that affirms the safety of its operations and presents a potential threat to the local negotiated order.

A tactic that Foschem, like many other chemical companies, has adopted to reinforce the hegemonic definition of the situation and to counter perceptions of danger and community concern is that of holding site open days for local residents. Following Zonabend (1993), we can see the open day as a social ritual intended to reassure. It was apparent from comments made in some of the groups that the open days, by emphasizing the familiar and reiterating the performance of safety, could be an effective way of influencing people's perceptions of the plant:

   © The Editorial Board of the Sociological Review 2003

Anne: Yeah. I must say before I went around there I thought it was all radioactive sort of stuff you know. [laughter] And top secret and that. But it's not at all. You know I'm really glad I went around there because it's just generally household things.

The quote is also interesting for the rather anxious and sinister image of the company, indicated by the references to 'top secret' and 'radioactive', that the speaker professes to have held before visiting the site, an image echoed by other participants. Zonabend (1993) describes the site open day as an exorcism ritual designed to dispel from the minds of the locals the haunting presence of the plant. The experience of that ritual, however, may also establish quite negative impressions. Some residents were very conscious of the impression management function of the events and had their scepticism reinforced. Others were quick to point out that there were parts of the plant where visitors were not allowed to go, firm in the conviction that there were processes which were so hazardous that no-one was allowed to know of their existence, as the following passage from one lifelong resident illustrates:

Brian: I have worked in Foschem but only in a building capacity. But they have got very, very stringent rules and regulations in there. A lot of places where you just can't go unless you've got the right calling card on your, your jacket. But if anything does go up it's going to be catastrophic. It is a living time bomb there.

One might argue that the examples given all relate to activities that had a clear public relations (PR) function. We also find this semantic instability, however, at the heart of the company's performance of ritualized safety practices. In conformance with regulatory requirements, every two years Foschem distributes emergency information, in the form of a laminated card illustrated with simple pictograms, advising residents of the nature of the hazardous substances on the site and telling them what to do in the case of emergency. The distribution of the card may be seen as performing two functions from the point of view of the company and the public authorities. First, the card implicitly signals that even contingent events are 'under control' by established procedures although sustaining this assertion is itself contingent upon how that control is performed in an emergency. Second, it explicitly attempts to enrol the audience of local residents as participants in a performance in which they are required, in the event of a chemical emergency, to enact prescribed safety rituals. The capacity to elicit an appropriate performance from local residents becomes less certain, however, if the status of the instructions is in question or the cue for action is not agreed.

The distribution of the emergency information card is accompanied by a company newsletter, which informs readers about consumer products made with chemicals from Foschem, broadcasts good news about developments at the site and about the company's work in the community, gives details of open day events, and reproduces the same emergency instructions that are on the card. This exercise conforms to research findings that have become received wisdom in risk management; that familiarity with a source of hazard, recognition of benefits of the activity and a perception that those responsible for managing the hazard have a caring stance towards those at risk all tend to increase public acceptance.

Although distributing the newsletter together with the card was in line with 'good practice', it also had unintended consequences for the way in which that information was perceived. Many (although not all) residents recalled receiving the card but because it had arrived with the company's self-promotional material some treated the whole package as 'PR' from the company and disposed of it without reading it, while others were sceptical of the veracity and value of the information it contained. The narrative of reassurance (Phillimore, 1998) encoded in the way in which the Foschem emergency information was packaged was undermined by the semantic instability of the message, not only because of the mixed message communicated by the presence of promotional material but because the narrative was susceptible to alternative framings from different standpoints, which led some to read the 'safety' information as an indicator of how dangerous the site was:

> Carol: And they, and they just give you erm a safety guide
> Diane: Yeah.
> Carole: [telling you what to do] if something happens.
> Diane: But it shows how bad it can be.

And if the idealized, well-managed scenario implied by the cards was an indication of 'how bad it could be', what if that scenario proved a poor reflection of reality? In the next section I consider the contingencies that may undermine performances of safety.

Cues, contingencies and co-ordination: performing the emergency

Despite the company's reiterated performance of the discourse and practice of safety, things periodically go wrong, as they do at any complex chemical production site. As the emergency instructions to local residents indicate, these contingent events are prepared for and the appropriate response scripted by the site management and the emergency services, with the allocation of roles and routines. Although the occurrence of incidents and accidents is uncontrolled, the response is planned to ensure that control is quickly re-established. The handling of high profile incidents also reasserts the definition of the situation as 'safe'; it is simultaneously a performance of 'the emergency' as a managed event and a performance of 'safety'. We therefore need to examine the performance of such events, the contingencies that unavoidably occur and local people's readings of the performance in order to establish their consequences for the definition of the situation.

Until 1995, the most recent incident of any note at the Foschem site was a phosphorous fire in 1990 but this had taken place late one cold, wet night when most local residents were indoors and had attracted relatively little attention. Then, in August 1995, about seven months before I conducted interviews in the

 © The Editorial Board of the Sociological Review 2003

area, a phosphorous pentoxide plant exploded.[11] The company informed the local press that the plant was old and had been due for decommissioning just a week later. It was used in the production of phosphoric acid, an ingredient manufactured by the company for use in cola drinks. The incident took place on a hot summer's evening when many local people were out in their gardens enjoying the good weather. The loud explosion was clearly audible and the plume of smoke visible to those living near to the plant. For some, the event had been an inconvenience or even a spectacle, whereas for others it had been alarming and unsettling and had shaken their confidence in the company and the emergency services. In other words, local people did not share a common experience of the incident; the experience was contextualized and the performance of the key actors interpreted in different ways.

One encountered very different accounts of the incident and its aftermath. Events were constructed and reconstructed in the light of different concerns and contexts and similar stories told to make very different points. Several people acknowledged that the company had dealt positively with local concerns raised after the explosion, sending out senior members of staff to reassure residents. For instance, Foschem received a number of complaints that a sticky deposit had been left on the cars of people downwind of the plant at the time of the accident. The company responded by offering to clean or, where paintwork was damaged by the deposit, to pay for respraying the vehicles. Accounts of the company's response were presented both as illustrations of the company's responsiveness to local concerns and as an example of a cynical PR exercise which did nothing to mitigate the risks to which the speakers felt themselves to be exposed. This illustrates the way in which explicit impression management may result in a 'failed' performance by evoking a negative response (Crant, 1996). More than that, it illustrates that impression management can never be fully under the control of the organizations engaged in such performances because it is a reciprocal influence process that entails cycles of negotiation in which the 'audience' plays a crucial role (Ginzel *et al.*, 1992). An audience's awareness of the impression management dimension of corporate 'behaviour' will condition its response to the performance. Hence, the situation we find is typically not one of simple corporate persuasion but of the organization needing to enrol other actors in a 'negotiated order' that is consonant with a particular definition of the situation. Recalling Goffman's observation that we should think in terms of a definition which is in charge of the situation, we are not referring here simply to a definition produced and imposed by company managers but a hegemonic definition that naturalizes current socio-economic relations, and which ascribes roles and identities to the various actors and inscribes itself through reiteration and routinization.

The Foschem emergency information card tells people that 'in the event of detection or notification of a major emergency' they should follow a series of prescribed actions; taking cover inside their homes, making the place safe and waiting for further information or the all clear from the emergency services. Many people recalled, if rather vaguely, the basic instructions:

© The Editorial Board of the Sociological Review 2003

Betty: You get a leaflet, what to do if you erm, you know, 'Close all your windows, etcetera.'

For the institutional actors—the emergency planners, the site managers and the emergency services—the local populace is expected to recognize the appropriate cue ('detection or notification') to assume the role of rational, self-protective subjects in the ritual of emergency response. A paragraph at the bottom of the card elaborates on the term 'emergency notification'. It advises that if a 'major emergency' were to occur the police would issue information and advice via the local TV and radio stations and by 'any other means deemed appropriate'. It also advises that anyone close to the works should be able to hear sirens on the site and gives the time at which they are tested each week. These on-site sirens, however, were not designed for alerting the local population and so are not audible over the whole of the affected area. In case these notification measures should fail to warn anyone, the characteristic odours of the main hazardous chemicals are described to aid detection. The company newsletters repeat the basic contents of the card and include supplementary information; for example, residents are informed that the police will announce the all clear using loudspeakers and/or local radio stations.

Following the explosion at Longfield, however, local people were not clear whether a cue had been given but, confronted by evidence that something uncontrolled was happening at the site, made their own diverse interpretations of the situation. In the absence of a siren, many took the explosion itself as the cue and enacted their ritual roles:

Elsie: But when that explosion went off before, there was no siren. There was no siren or nothing so I automatically shut the doors.

Some were simply confused by the lack of a recognizable cue when something had clearly gone very wrong. In the initial uncertainty about the nature of the incident and any threat that it might present, the emergency services warned people close to the plant to go into their houses and to close doors and windows, performing their role as though a major emergency had occurred although, in the terms of the advice given to residents, this was 'merely' an accident. Many others, however, whether due do the absence of a cue or not, abandoned the ritually prescribed behaviour altogether and treated the accident as spectacle. One couple living adjacent to the Longfield site, having told how, on hearing the explosion and seeing the smoke, they had followed in detail the emergency procedure, recounted what they saw:

Frances: I mean even that [pause] you get that card telling you what to do. 'Go in'. If anything happens there, 'go in and close the windows', you know, 'and stay inside until an all clear'. Now we [pause] looking out of our window it was like a street party ... People just standing there looking at it.
Carl: We didn't believe it. Running towards it.

Another individual described hearing, twenty minutes after the blast, police loudhailers warning residents to go inside and close doors and windows but

 © The Editorial Board of the Sociological Review 2003

receiving no subsequent 'all clear'. What we see, then, are multiple interpretations of the expected cue and different perceptions of the performance that was required.

Despite the fact that the explosion did not constitute a threat to local residents, the response to this accident may be viewed as a failed performance or, more specifically, multiple failures. The everyday presence of the dangers associated with these sites is normalized through official discourse and practice by an ideological framing in terms of 'safety' and routinized in the behavioural ritual prescribed in the emergency instructions. What took place, however, was not simply a failure of many of the actors to perform the ritual but a failure of the ritual itself to produce disciplined performances.[12] The compliant, unencumbered actor implied by the emergency instruction card bears little resemblance to the complex, critical and even contradictory individuals that it attempts to enrol in the safety ritual.[13] Instead of a reassuring performance that enacted and legitimated hegemonic discourses and practices of 'safety', there was a confusing and ultimately subversive melee of improvisations. In the concluding section of the chapter, I consider the implications of this contingent failure and of the problem of semantic instability outlined earlier for the relevance of the concept of performance to our understanding of faulty environments.

Conclusion

I began this chapter with a discussion of Goffman's work and argued, contra Gregson and Rose (2000), that far from focusing on the purposive performances of actors he generally emphasizes the ways in which actors' performances instantiate the definition that is 'in charge' of the situation. The metaphor that most closely informs this interpretation of performance is not the dramaturgical metaphor that shapes his analyses of impression management but the metaphor of ritual. I suggested that his work in fact bears comparison to recent theories that emphasize the role of performativity. However, I also noted Burns' criticism of Goffman's account of normalization and his argument that such processes may be traced to the purposive action of relatively powerful organizational actors. In the subsequent description of the performance of safety and the normalization of risk at Longfield, which focused on the activities of Foschem, there was certainly evidence of the kind of purposive organizational activity to which Burns points. Nevertheless, the discussion of semantic instability and contingency in the performances of the company and of other organizational actors highlighted the extent to which the effects of these purposive performances are indeterminate and in themselves would not seem to guarantee the maintenance of the negotiated order that cites the definition of the situation as 'safe'. Indeed, one conclusion from the discussion is that the performance of 'safety' is simultaneously the performance of risk/danger, despite this being played down in the hegemonic definition of the situation; the

© The Editorial Board of the Sociological Review 2003

attempt to enact a safe, 'normal' environment' cannot, therefore, avoid enacting a risky, 'faulty' environment.

Is there any evidence, however, that this semantic instability and consequent 'misreading' of the performance by local residents affects the hegemonic defini- tion of the situation or undermines the local negotiated order that the official performance attempts to enact? Despite their expressions of distrust and dis- quiet, their criticism and concern, one must conclude that local residents did not challenge this definition. Neither did the coordination failures of the orga- nizational actors in practice undermine the local negotiated order. One possible explanation is that the event that took place in Longfield, while a cause of alarm and anxiety, was not serious enough in its consequences to challenge that defi- nition. One can point to other situations, however, where more serious accidents have taken place without significant disruption to the status quo.[14]

An alternative explanation is that the definition of the situation as safe is maintained by more than organizational performances, which may be seen at times to fail; crucially it is internalized by individuals themselves. Despite their expressions of complaint and concern, a certain degree of variation in perfor- mance, as Goffman notes in his comments on counter-activity, is possible without challenging the definition of the situation. This internalization can be seen as part of the coping strategies that individuals adopt in response to the presence of industrial hazards. Giddens (1990, p. 134–137) identifies four adap- tive responses that individuals adopt towards ubiquitous risk: pragmatic accep- tance, sustained optimism, cynical pessimism and radical engagement. These accord with reported responses to the presence of hazardous sites (Walker *et al.*, 1998; Wakefield and Elliott, 2000).[15] People rationalize such coping responses in a variety of ways that are frequently related to local contexts. For example, expressions of faith in the regulators and emergency services to protect them have been found to be associated with sites where no major incidents have taken place to disturb such confidence, while arguments for the benefits to be gained or for the competence and trustworthiness of the company have been associated with some kind of links to the industry (Simmons and Walker, 1999).

As noted earlier, the response of radical engagement is rarely found and usually short-lived, as with the brief episode at Longfield during the 1970s. This episode, in which newcomers to the area who had not internalized the defini- tion of the situation played a leading role, was subsequently dissipated by the company's agreement to establish a community liaison committee, an action which only marginally reconfigured the local negotiated order and ultimately reaffirmed the definition of the situation. Yet the most widespread disposition observed in affected communities such as Longfield, where there is a conspicu- ous and obtrusive source of risk, seems to be one which combines a sense of distrust, powerlessness and vulnerability (Simmons and Walker, 1999). This does not suggest that local people's apparent toleration of such sites reflects a genuine lack of concern about the dangers; rather that, in the absence of a viable alter- native definition of the situation, it reflects a feeling of being unable to influ- ence the circumstances. It therefore appears that although local people's

© The Editorial Board of the Sociological Review 2003

day-to-day practices instantiate the hegemonic definition of the situation, both because of and despite the performances of the company and the authorites they simultaneously enact the situation as safe and as a faulty environment.

Notes

1 I should like to acknowledge the financial support given by The Leverhulme Trust to the Programme on Understanding Risk, which partly supported the writing of this chapter. My thanks also to my colleagues in the original project, Alan Irwin, Gordon Walker and Brian Wynne.

2 Goffman produced over his career an eclectic body of work that was unified by certain core concerns rather than by an overarching theoretical framework. Typically taking the form of essays, his writings were unconventional and drew upon literature and reflection as much as empirical social science, employing a variety of metaphors to generate acutely observed analyses that categorized the micro-ordering practices of US society. In this chapter I make rather liberal use of some of his concepts but do not attempt to summarize his work. For discussions of his work, see Ditton (1980), Drew and Wooton (1988) and Burns (1992).

3 For discussions of this shift, see Manning (1992) and Branaman (1997).

4 I should in fairness note that Gregson and Rose's paper is not primarily a critique of Goffman but uses their characterization of 'Goffmanian' approaches as a foil against which to counterpose their own perspective. However, their account typifies a perception of Goffman's work and its relation to recent work in a performative vein which this chapter attempts to correct.

5 This is not to say that Goffman denies the possibility of resistance; for example, he reflects on the radical use of 'frame breaking' tactics to challenge 'from below' hegemonic definitions and practices, citing examples from radical theatre and theatrical political radicalism (Goffman, 1975 [1974]: 425–438).

6 The case study material is drawn from a project funded by the Health and Safety Executive (Walker *et al.*, 1998). The HSE bears no responsibility for the content of this chapter or the views expressed. The quotations given in the following sections are taken from focus group discussions with local residents. All names have been changed.

7 The presence of industrial hazards described here is not, of course, the only factor contributing to the sense of a 'faulty' environment; others might include the physical effects of socio-economic deprivation or the air pollution associated with a busy motorway traversing the neighbourhood, as was the case in Longfield.

8 Currently set out in *The Control of Major Accident Hazards Regulations 1999*, London: The Stationery Office.

9 Longfield and Foschem are pseudonyms.

10 There was certainly evidence of a residual sense of 'community' and of attempts to defend Longfield's identity against assimilation into that of the larger administrative unit to which it belonged. However, there were observable differences between the way the area was perceived by lifelong 'locals', many of whom had a sense of place attachment and extensive social networks in the neighbourhood, and by more recent arrivals who, typically, did not.

11 The site was not chosen because the explosion had occurred; rather ironically it was selected about one year earlier because it was a non-controversial site that appeared to have been free of major accidents.

12 That is not to say that the Foschem response or that of the emergency services was less than competent in their handling of the physical hazard rather that, taken together, they failed in their social performance in a way that undermined the definition of the situation as safe.

13 Commenting on the way in which disaster management plans are often out of touch with organizational and social realities, Clarke (1999) has described them as 'fantasy documents'.

14 For example, an explosion in a chemical works in West Yorkshire in 1992 resulted in the death of five people and considerable damage to buildings, yet the situation returned to 'normal' after

© The Editorial Board of the Sociological Review 2003

a brief period of disquiet and scrutiny. The incident is described in Health and Safety Executive (1994).

15 Wakefield and Elliott (2000) have related the four responses identified by Giddens to different psychological styles of coping.

References

Allen, M. W. and Caillouet, R. H. (1994), 'Legitimation endeavors: impression management strategies used by an organization in crisis', *Communication Monographs*, 61: 44–62.

Berry, G. R. (2003), 'Organizing against multinational corporate power in Cancer Alley—The activist community as primary stakeholder', *Organization & Environment*, 16(1): 3–33.

Branaman, A. (1997), 'Goffman's Social Theory', in C. Lemert and A. Branaman (eds), *The Goffman Reader*, Malden, MT: Blackwell, pp. xlv–lxxxii.

Burkitt, I. (1996), 'Civilization and ambivalence', *British Journal of Sociology*, 47(1): 135–150.

Burns, T. (1992), *Erving Goffman*, London: Routledge.

Clarke, L. (1999), *Mission Improbable: The Use of Fantasy Documents to Tame Disaster*, Chicago: University of Chicago Press.

Coleman, J. S. (1982), *The Asymmetric Society*, Syracuse, N.Y.: Syracuse University Press.

Ditton, J. (1980), *The View from Goffman*, London: Macmillan.

Drew, P. and Wooton, A. (1988), *Erving Goffman: Exploring the Interaction Order*, Cambridge: Polity Press.

Elsbach, K. D. (1994), 'Managing organizational legitimacy in the California cattle industry: the construction and effectiveness of verbal accounts', *Administrative Science Quarterly*, 39(1): 57–88.

Futrell, R. (1998), 'Performative governance: impression management, teamwork, and conflict containment in city commission proceedings', *Journal of Contemporary Ethnography*, 27(4): 494–529.

Giddens, A. (1990), *The Consequences of Modernity*, Cambridge: Polity.

Goffman, E. (1969 [1959]), *The Presentation of Self in Everyday Life*, London: Penguin Books.

Goffman, E. (1972 [1961]), *Encounters: Two Studies in the Sociology of Interaction*, London: Penguin Books.

Goffman, E. (1972 [1967]), *Interaction Ritual: Essays on Face-to-Face Behaviour*, London: Penguin Books.

Goffman, E. (1975 [1974]), *Frame Analysis: an Essay on the Organization of Experience*, Harmondsworth: Penguin Books.

Gregson, N. and Rose, G. (2000), 'Taking Butler elsewhere: performativites, spatialities and subjectivities', *Environment and Planning D: Society and Space*, 18: 433–452.

Health and Safety Executive (1994) *'The Fire at Hickson & Welch Limited. A report of the investigation by the Health and Safety Executive into the fatal fire at Hickson & Welch Limited, Castleford on 21 September 1992'*, London: Health and Safety Executive.

Howe, L. (2000), 'Risk, ritual and performance', *Journal of the Royal Anthropological Institute*, 6(1): 63–79.

Irwin, A., Simmons, P. and Walker, G. (1999), 'Faulty environments and risk reasoning: the local understanding of industrial hazards', *Environment and Planning A*, 31: 1311–1326.

Kroll-Smith, S. (1995), 'Toxic contamination and the loss of civility', *Sociological Spectrum*, 15: 377–396.

Moberg, M. (2002), 'Erin Brockovich doesn't live here: Environmental politics and "Responsible Care" in Mobile County, Alabama', *Human Organization*, 61(4): 377–389.

Pearce, F. and Tombs, S. (1998), *Toxic Capitalism: Corporate Crime and the Chemical Industry*, Aldershot: Dartmouth.

Phillimore, P. (1998), 'Uncertainty, reassurance and pollution: the politics of epidemiology in Teesside', *Health and Place*, 4(3): 203–212.

Rochlin, G. (1999), 'Safe operation as a social construct', *Ergonomics*, 42(11): 1549–1560.

© The Editorial Board of the Sociological Review 2003

Simmons, P. and Walker, G. (1999), 'Tolerating risk: policy principles and public perceptions', *Risk Decision and Policy*, 43: 179–190.

Simmons, P. and Walker, G. (2004), 'Technological risk and sense of place: industrial encroachment on place values', in Å. Boholm and R. Löfstedt (eds), *Contesting Local Environments*, London: Earthscan.

Simmons, P. and Wynne, B. (1993), 'Responsible Care: trust, credibility and environmental management, in J. Schot and K. Fischer (eds), *Environmental Strategies for Industry*, Washington, D.C.: Island Press, pp. 201–226.

Simpson, R. (1996), 'Neither clear nor present: the social construction of safety and danger', *Sociological Forum*, 11(3): 549–562.

Wakefield, S. and S. J. Elliott (2000), 'Environmental risk perception and well-being: effects of the landfill siting process in two southern Ontario communities,' *Social Science & Medicine*, 50(7–8): 1139–1154.

Walker, G., P. Simmons, Irwin, A. and Wynne, B. (1998), *Public Perception of Risks Associated with Major Accident Hazards*, Sudbury: HSE Books.

Zonabend, F. (1993), *The Nuclear Peninsula*, Cambridge: Cambridge University Press.

© The Editorial Board of the Sociological Review 2003

Public participation as the performance of nature

Stephen Healy

Introduction

Bruno Latour (1993) contends that contemporary environmental problems, such as climate change and ozone depletion, are 'hybrid' because they involve an intimacy between 'nature' and 'culture' obscured by prevailing thinking. He further argues that this tendency, exemplified by the segregation of the non-human from the human manifest in the divide between the natural and social sciences, facilitates the proliferation of such problems (Latour, 1993). One response to the challenges, complexities and risks posed by these matters has been a turn toward greater public participation in environmental policy and decision-making. This chapter is focused by an analysis of how one example of local public participation engaged with this 'hybridity'. It is argued that the environmental outcome achieved by this process, characterized in this chapter as a performance of nature, required significant engagement across and between the material and social domains, and that analogous approaches may be of relevance for our collective responses to these matters at the larger scale.

The access to public knowledge and values granted by public participation is widely regarded as having the potential to enhance the management of risk and complexity (Beck, 1992; Irwin, 1995; Irwin, 2001; Irwin and Wynne, 1996) and reinforce the legitimacy of decisions and decision-makers. However, public participation, while conceived as a practice to bring diverse knowledges to bear upon specified problems, is commonly constrained by the notions of 'rational decision-making' that routinely dominate policy procedures and are informed and shaped by scientific conceptions of knowledge (Irwin, 1995). Indeed, participation commonly takes the form of a procedure or mechanism devised so as to grant existing 'rational decision-making' arrangements access to public knowledge and values. While this 'access' is frequently compromised with, for example, adversarial notions of argumentation in which the 'best' (read scientific) argument wins, central to these arrangements, of more fundamental interest, is the view of knowledge—the epistemology—underpinning them. Reflecting the disciplinary divide discussed above this embraces the ontological distinction between an 'external' material world and 'internal' human world and conceives of knowledge as representations of these worlds.[1] As a result, public

© The Editorial Board of the Sociological Review 2003. Published by Blackwell Publishing Ltd, 9600 Garsington Road, Oxford OX4 2DQ, UK and 350 Main Street, Malden, MA 02148, USA

participation is largely understood and structured as a process enabling the transmission or flow of representational information. This reduces the effectiveness of the resultant procedures and mechanisms in a number of ways.

Two of these constraints are of particular concern to this chapter. Firstly, lay understandings are commonly highly contextualized and combine an embrace of both the social and material domains difficult for representational under- standings to grasp (Irwin, 2001), and so tend to be systematically marginalized. Secondly, and following on from this, representational understandings can obscure how everyday practices and behaviours affect the non-human environ- ment with which they engage and, as a result, act to change or (re)perform that environment. This focus upon not only understandings but also the behaviours and material practices to which these give rise, and thus the environment they enact, is central to the case study of this chapter. This describes a local envi- ronmental project designed to empower a community to improve the quality of its local environment. Central to this project was an intensive, ongoing process focused on developing both: a) contextualized community understandings and behaviours; and, b) a context that might allow these to be articulated and put to effect. In other words in addition to facilitating the development and articu- lation of community understandings (a), there were at the same time many, what are below characterized as, 'stage-setting' activities (b), designed to ensure that these community understandings could become manifest in (re)performing the local environment.

These two concerns, and the intimate intertwining of 'nature' and 'culture' they involve, are further reflected in the two different yet interlocking ways in which notions of performance are used in this chapter. Actor Network Theory (ANT) is drawn upon to describe how collective practices and behaviours engage with and act to (re)perform the local environment, while the development of the understandings informing these practices and behaviours are characterized using cultural notions of performance. These latter illuminate a performative style of deliberation that, transcending the strictures of represenationalist think- ing, facilitates the collective understandings primed to inform these (re)perfor- mances of 'nature'.

Participation—background and context

Contemporary ideas about public participation emerged in the 1960s in tandem with developing notions of 'participatory democracy' (Kaufmann, 1960) and were reflected from the late 1960s in legislation and many fields such as plan- ning (Arnstein, 1969). As this interest matured, the potential benefits of expos- ing decision-making to a diversity of public values diverted attention from *democratic* toward *deliberative* dimensions of participation. Jurgen Habermas (1984, 1987) has been particularly influential to this 'deliberative turn' (see Dryzek, 2000 for a contemporary overview). Habermas argues that rational, scientific, *instrumental-technical reasoning* has been allowed to crowd out *moral* and *emotive-aesthetic reasoning* that more typically characterize the lifeworld of personal existence, impoverishing both our lifeworld and economic and political life. The theory of communicative action advanced by Habermas advocates fair, free and open forms of debate and communication as the means to transcend the dominance of one form of reasoning over others. Habermas' advocacy of 'the power of the better argument' (1984), however, has paradoxically resulted in the practical application of these ideas supporting adversarial forms of deliberation that reinforce the dominance of *instrumental-technical reasoning*.[2] An example illustrating this is outlined below.

Interest in the potential for public contributions to enhance decision-making has been particularly influential in the environmental domain. Environmental problems are commonly complex, controversial and thoroughly scientized (Beck, 1992). Participation in environmental decision-making is seen as a way of bringing to bear a broader, more representative range of knowledge and values to help manage the complexity and uncertainty of these problems, as well as reinforcing the legitimacy of, and thereby sustaining, the decisions arrived at. Ensuring that public concerns and insights are considered and deployed not only makes successful outcomes more likely but also encourages consensus and trust, helping to ensure the viability of future problem solving efforts (Irwin, 1995). This interest further reflects a widespread contemporary concern, over and above well established theoretical critiques such as that of Ulrich Beck (1992; 1995a&b; 1999) and others, that the scale and frequency of major problems is escalating and signals a breakdown in established processes of 'rational decision-making'. Matters such as BSE (Seguin, 2000) and the controversy over genetically manipulated crops and foods (Healy, 2001) have been argued to demonstrate the limitations of expertise and decision-making predicated upon a narrow rational/technical definition of the problems at stake. This point is often reinforced by a growing awareness of how, as Beck (1992; 1995a&b) points out, public trust and the legitimacy of the institutions perceived responsible for these problems including science, governments and business appears to be at an unprecedented low.

However, while greater public involvement is now promoted at the highest levels (eg. HMSO, 2000) public contributions are still commonly marginalized in practice. Les Levidow and Claire Marris (2001) argue, for example, that the recent openness to public involvement is largely motivated by a desire to legitimate conventional expert-determined decisions rather than by any imperative to open them to public dialogue. While the devaluation of lay involvement has been widely discussed, if not effectively addressed, broader, particularly epistemological, dimensions of public participation have gained far less attention. As outlined above, effective engagement with public concerns and environmental matters is significantly inhibited by the hegemony of representational conceptions of knowledge and the ways in which these tend to configure participation in terms of information flow. This reinforces an institutional inertia described

© The Editorial Board of the Sociological Review 2003

by Robert Hoppe (1999) who notes that while 'new post-positivist epistemological assumptions may be considered in place . . . the new institutional arrangements for developing and implementing them in practice have not yet arrived'. Reflecting this the institutional context of the project described in the case study below was the focus of particular attention.

The notion of 'cooperative discourse' developed by Ortwin Renn and colleagues (Renn *et al.*, 1997; Renn, 1998) exemplifies many of these concerns. Nominally predicated on the Habermasian ideal this approach involves 'three steps' in which experts, stakeholder groups and the public are all allocated separate and distinct roles. Lay input is diminished by reduction to scientific terms and subordinate to that of expertise until the final step, at which point it becomes an evaluation of the options emerging from a well-bounded and controlled expert led process. So rather than a creative interchange of views, ideas and understandings, the process locks the different groups into reified and differentiated perspectives. As a result 'cooperative discourse', informed and structured by representational scientific rationality, controls and circumscribes public involvement, ultimately reflecting rather than transcending *instrumental-technical reasoning*.[3]

To summarize, while public participation is increasingly regarded as a legitimate, and even necessary, way of tackling the challenges and risks of complex contemporary problems, the practice of participation is severely hampered by the hegemony of traditional conceptions of knowledge and rationality. Two particularly challenging issues are: a) the established difficulties of integrating lay and expert perspectives equitably (see Irwin, 1995, 2001; Irwin & Wynne, 1996); and, b) the less widely discussed matter of how to engage the outcomes of participation with decision-making and material realities. Equitably to integrate lay and expert perspectives, rather than police their partition as in 'cooperative discourse' or similar approaches, and then engage the outcome with external realities, requires processes able to creatively combine divergent perspectives as well as transcend the broader constraints of representational thinking. This analysis thus highlights the processes of public participation—that is, their structure, quality and context—as matters of fundamental significance in contrast to the representationalist emphasis on the sources or forms of knowledge. With this change in emphasis, the conception and design of participatory processes may then focus on the facilitation of a creative interchange of views and ideas between all, and on ensuring that the resulting outcomes can engage the broader, including material, context.

Performing participation that performs nature

The notion of 'performing nature' articulated in this chapter was drawn from actor network theory (ANT), which describes the world in terms of 'ensembles' of humans and non-humans.[4] Rather than the enduring backdrop to human activities implied by representational thinking, ANT depicts reality as something fundamentally shaped by the performance of human/non-human relations, one of the two major features of ANT distinguished by John Law (1999). The first of these, *relational materiality*, refers to how entities both '. . . take their form and acquire their attributes as a result of their relations with other entities' (Law, 1999: 3), and the second, *performativity*, to how entities are 'performed in, by, and through those relations' (Law, 1999: 4). In ANT, the distinctions between nature and culture underpinning representational perspectives are understood to result from the relations between entities rather than to reflect the order of things. Reality, then, is not 'out there' or in our heads but is rather a complex, many-layered performance, constituted by the multiple performances of the relationships between both people and the things that go to make it up.

Performance in this ANT sense involves conceding the multiplicity of forms that reality may take and understanding how our performances involve choices over which of these we wish to bring into being—something described by Anne-Marie Mol (1999) as 'ontological politics'. This involves acknowledging reality as something open, dynamic and contestable and reveals a potential role for participation in shaping it. Mol (1999: 86) discusses the choices implicit in our performances of the world in terms of individual choice. Applied to public participation, however, these choices are more usefully interpreted in collective terms. Participation, conceived as the articulation of collective understandings giving rise to practices and behaviours that shape the form and content of a local environment, may then be interpreted as collective choice over the form or state of local reality. Understanding the world as something performed in relationships underlines the flexibility and impermanence of any state of reality, and how work over time and space is necessary to maintain it.

This flexibility and impermanence requires public participation to attend to the production and maintenance of the contexts, both human and non-human, supporting the sets of relationships underpinning the performance of nature intended, something described in this chapter by the term 'stage-setting'.[5] Law (2001) describes two ways in which human/non-human 'ensembles' can be maintained: firstly, by ensuring the durability of their constitution; and secondly, by way of diverse and multiple relationships. Extended to participation, durability can be interpreted as referring to a requirement that both the participatory process and the social and material 'stage-setting' supporting the outcomes of deliberation are sufficiently robust. Law further suggests that such durability is grounded by embedding human designs and intentions into material form. The emphasis on diversity and multiplicity rather stresses how effective participation may require numerous, overlapping, 'stage-setting' strategies across both human and non-human elements of the requisite context. The case study below, for example, required particular attention to the organizational context, to many sets of stakeholders and to their, often overlapping, material impacts.

ANT cannot, however, explain the forms of deliberation that might facilitate such performances of nature,[6] and for this another source of theoretical work

© The Editorial Board of the Sociological Review 2003

deploying a different notion of performance proved particularly helpful. Richard Schechner's performance theory (Schechner, 1988; 1993) illuminates a performatively facilitated form of deliberation whose outcomes embody and reflect mutual learning, rather than reflecting the perspectives some participants commenced with and more forcefully argued. Schechner describes a 'collective reflexivity' (Schechner, 1993: 83) facilitated when a group's collective resources are freely and creatively harnessed to the generation of collective responses. Under such conditions participants not only clarify the understandings that they bring with them, but also the assumptions and preconceptions these embody, for all to understand or potentially contest and reshape. Processes of this kind, able to facilitate innovative solutions distinct from those which some participants originally put forward—an impossibility in 'cooperative discourse' or similar processes—are detailed by Judith Innes and David Booher (1999).

Innes and Booher (1999) describe processes of 'role playing and bricolage' that exemplify a 'collective reflexivity' of this form. They found that intractable policy conflicts were resolvable when participants in stakeholder-based consensus building exercises played out scenarios and took on different roles enabling the transformation of assumptions and preconceptions, and facilitating the creation of new strategies, options and ideas. Describing this, Innes and Booher (1999: 12) note:

'In many of their most productive moments, participants . . . engage not only in playing out scenarios, but also in . . . collective, speculative tinkering, or bricolage . . . That is, they play with heterogeneous concepts, strategies, and actions with which various individuals in the group have experience, and try combining them until they create a new scenario that they collectively believe will work. This . . . is a type of reasoning and collective creativity fundamentally different from the more familiar types, argumentation and tradeoffs . . . produc[ing], rather than a solution to a known problem, a new way of framing the situation and of developing unanticipated combinations of actions that are qualitatively different from the options on the table at the outset. The result is . . . learning and change among the players, and growth in their sophistication about each other, about the issues, and about the futures they could seek'.

Innes and Booher (1999: 12) further underline the creative possibilities unleashed by transcending conventional strictures and assumptions. Performance theory (Schechner, 1988; 1993) helps to clarify this transformative potential by emphasizing the creative nature of performance, its contestatory and anti-structural nature and its indebtedness to play, something Innes and Booher reflect in the analogy they stress between their analysis and popular interactive role playing games.

Innes and Booher's observations and Schechner's performance theory shed light on a form of deliberation able to combine divergent perspectives and transcend the assumptions underpinning representational thinking and, therefore, engage socio-material concerns, practices and behaviours. Innes and Booher

© The Editorial Board of the Sociological Review 2003

specifically note how such deliberation can remove 'actual and assumed constraints' and so result in 'unanticipated combinations of actions' and the creation of 'new conditions and possibilities' (1999: 12). Both Innes and Booher and Schechner underscore how deliberation of this form can facilitate the scrutiny of commonly 'taken-for-granted' notions and, as a consequence, result in the articulation of relations between people and things that, in ANT terms, perform the environment along changed lines. In addition to indicating the creative, contestatory and anti-structural nature of such deliberation, Schechner (1993) stresses how performance enables the valuation, articulation and embrace of ambiguity, ambivalence and paradox, all anathema to representational thinking. Deliberation of this form does not of itself deny conventional rationality, but rather enables it to be held in creative tension with other insights and ways of understanding, facilitating the production of collective insights which transcend conventional strictures. Innes and Booher further note longer term and more intangible benefits including '. . . personal and professional relations, joint learning, agreement on databases and political influence' (1999: 11) demonstrating the way in which deliberation of this form powerfully engages broader reality, matters variously reflected in the case study below.

In summary, this account has drawn upon different notions of performance to describe a form of participation that facilitates both collective understandings, embodying a diversity of insights, and the translation of these, via changes in practices and behaviours, into a changed state of nature. In order to arrive at mutual collective understandings, participants must be willing to relinquish conventional notions of knowledge and argumentation, engage with others on all levels and to expose the assumptions underlying their own position to critical scrutiny. Under these conditions reality might then be understood as dynamic, contestable and open to human influence rather than enduring and open only to scientific intervention. This view of participation thus encompasses a range of interrelated elements, key among which are: a pluralist, non-representational view of knowledge; participation as process; deliberation as the performance of collective meaning; participation that articulates collective rather than individual choice; and participation that facilitates the manifestation of this collective choice in the performance of nature.

A particular contribution of ANT in this context is to highlight the work involved in the 'stage-setting' necessary for these kind of processes to have purchase and resilience outside of their immediate context. ANT suggests that the world, made up of human/non-human networks or ensembles, requires considerable maintenance in order to keep it in a desired state. These ensembles can be maintained by ensuring the durability of their constitution and by way of diverse and multiple relationships. Both of these maintenance requirements suggest that the work that is done to achieve them cannot be taken for granted. From an ANT perspective, a process designed to have material and non-material effects on the human and non-human world, such as that described below, must attend not only to the human processes of dialogue and delibera-

© The Editorial Board of the Sociological Review 2003

tion but also to the institutional, physical and infrastructural relationships around which those processes are focussed. In other words, the human/nonhuman network itself needs attention and work. In the case study below this kind of work is highlighted as an essential element of the deliberative process.

Performing local participatory stormwater management

The Bronte Catchment Project (BCP) ran from November 2000 to November 2001 and was designed to facilitate a community-based participatory process to enhance stormwater quality within the micro-catchment of Bronte, in Sydney, Australia that drains into Bronte Beach. The project specifically '. . . aimed to support, develop and evaluate inclusive community and organizational processes to improve water quality at Bronte Beach' (Ryan *et al.*, 2001: 3) and was funded by the Stormwater Trust established under the aegis of the NSW Environment Protection Authority with a mandate to encourage and support improved urban stormwater quality management practices. A notable feature of the project was 'its developmental and iterative nature' (Ryan *et al.*, 2001: 3). This facilitated project learning and reflection with an increasing understanding of local conditions and issues feeding into the development of conceptual insights deployed during the project. Roberta Ryan of *Elton and Associates*, a local consultancy, managed BCP as a non-profit project.[7]

Centred on Bronte's popular beach in Sydney's Eastern Suburbs, the catchment of approximately 135 hectares is highly urbanized and affected by stormwater pollution, the majority of which originates with residents and visitors (eg. litter, garden waste, etc.) and which drains onto the beach.[8] Current approaches to stormwater management centre on 'end of pipe' Gross Pollutant Traps that remove solid debris from stormwater on the one hand, and controlled or 'top down' community education initiatives on the other. Both approaches are problematic: traditional 'end of pipe' approaches disregard the potential for community preventative action and soluble stormwater contaminants (eg. pesticides and detergents), while 'top down' educational initiatives are limited in effect. By addressing social behaviours as matters for control rather than dialogue such 'top-down' initiatives commonly serve to alienate rather than engage local communities. While the Bronte community had had no prior opportunity to participate in managing stormwater pollution, previous work had demonstrated a significant level of community concern about environmental issues and a willingness to address them.[9]

The BCP '. . . assumed that meaningful democratic participation entails a deliberative process in which citizens can collectively assess arguments and form judgements around the common good' (Ryan *et al.*, 2001: 17). However the citizen's jury process embodying these ideas, described below, was envisaged as the culmination of an extended and comprehensive process of community engagement, with 'stage-setting' activities regarded as pivotal to securing the viability and success of the jury process itself. Conventional community development work played a large part in these activities with a residential education campaign involving over 3000 households supplemented by displays across the catchment 'including community centres, the Council, the library, shops and the surf club' (Ryan *et al.*, 2001: 41). Business and non-resident stakeholders, including visitors and the traditional owners of the Bronte catchment, were also the focus of specific targeted strategies.

A significant further element in this 'stage-setting' was detailed social and ethnographic research on and in the community. In addition to tracking the knowledge, attitudes and motivations of the community at large, key individuals and community groups were analysed and tracked, particularly with regard to their potential to influence decision-making. Reflecting the 'socio-materiality' of ANT these 'stage-setting' activities also explicitly addressed matters of material concern to stormwater outcomes. So, for example, local schools and resident volunteers were recruited to establish preliminary participatory stormwater quality monitoring. Many other material practices were also addressed including: resident practices regarding car washing; rainwater collection; the collection and disposal of garden litter; garden chemical use; and the waste disposal practices of tradespeople with whom residents interacted.

The local council, a crucial overarching stakeholder, was the focus of particular attention. As part of these pre-jury 'stage-setting' activities, the Bronte project carried out 'regular presentations and discussions with the Executive Team; interviews with 36 staff . . . and with Councillors; a written survey of 51 staff . . . and five focus groups' (Ryan *et al.*, 2001: 10). The outcomes from this fed into an organizational review (affecting many issues other than stormwater), the development of a Stormwater Working Party, an Integrated Stormwater Management Plan, and the establishment of a full time Council position focused upon stormwater management. These council-focused strategies also encompassed numerous matters directly concerned with material stormwater outcomes including: issues of urban design and planning; council street cleaning and waste collection practices; council grass verge mowing practices; and the practices of local Park Rangers. Specific attention was also directed toward cultivating awareness of and openness to community initiatives throughout the Council.

Much of the comprehensive nature of this 'stage-setting' process is encapsulated by the project's conception of participation which '. . . include[d] individual thoughts and actions, shared reflection and discussion and collective catchment initiatives . . . applied across community concerns, institutional relationships and governance processes' (Ryan *et al.*, 2001: 7). This also conveys the sense of place and locality that pervaded the BCP. Photographs, for example, played a significant role, with resident volunteers being given disposable cameras so that they could monitor stormwater quality. Information packs used in the project also featured photographs and these were later used to inform and facilitate deliberation during the citizen's jury. In terms of 'stage-setting' this sense of place and locality acted to bind and integrate various elements of the project together and was probably also important in bridging the social and material domains.

© The Editorial Board of the Sociological Review 2003

With the 'stage set', the project settled, in September 2001, upon a citizen's jury of 15 randomly recruited residents as the vehicle for focussed deliberation. In order to make the 'depth' of deliberation more broadly accountable, the jury was preceded by a tele-poll of 358 residents, which fed into and informed the jury process. This was held over three days preceded by a half-day pre-jury forum at Bronte Beach.

The jury process

The sense of place and locality pervading BCP was brought into the jury process by various means. The half-day pre-jury forum at Bronte Beach, for example, was designed to be specifically 'experiential' and reinforce a sense of place and stewardship. This half-day, spent on the beach itself, centred around '. . . experiential catchment-based activities designed to explore environmental and coastal issues related to the focus of deliberation' (Ryan *et al.*, 2001: 22). Designed to reinforce the collective identification with locality and place '[t]he insights gained . . . were revisited by Jurors at key points throughout deliberations, and acted as reference points that both reinforced and enhanced collective experience' (Ryan *et al.*, 2001: 28). Photographs also played a significant role and were used to inform and facilitate deliberation throughout the three-day process.

The three-day jury process was 'intensive, in-depth and creative' (Ryan *et al.*, 2001: 29) and involved the consideration of specialist briefing material and expert testimony followed by sustained deliberation over a day and a half. The deliberation was:

'. . . a wide ranging and fluid process . . . focused on small group and whole group deliberation . . . a workshop style of discussion . . . a series of exercises, based on photographs. . . . small group exercises, whole group brainstorms, focused daily ice-breakers and closing processes, and visioning tasks . . . critically enhanced by . . . clearly expressed preferences and ideas offered by Jurors' (Ryan *et al.*, 2001: 29).

It was notable that although a broadly informed effort had been made to arrive at questions for the jury that facilitated but did not unduly determine the outcome of deliberation, these 'proposed 'working' questions' soon played a limited role, with '[p]articipants report[ing] they did not feel the need to refer to them, as the deliberations themselves defined the issues for consideration'(Ryan *et al.*, 2001: 32). This counter representational emphasis on process was facilitated by how '. . . the project team felt that the process itself—the act and experience of deliberation informed by accountable and transparent approaches, quality information, and opportunities to test the evidence—formed the essence of the outcomes' (Ryan *et al.*, 2001: 31).

The over fifty recommendations arrived at by the jury surprised many of the non-jurors present by their sophistication, breadth, and practicality.[10] These

© The Editorial Board of the Sociological Review 2003

emphasized integrated approaches to stormwater pollution encompassing all stakeholders, source control measures involving community education and participation, and complex matters of urban design and statutory planning controls. In addition to these broad-scale recommendations there were many more local, place-based recommendations including: an interactive and guided eco-walk at Bronte Gully; a community mulching station; a free public car washing space; an annual 'Water Festival'; and the use of film canisters by beach-goers to 'put their butts in'.

The completion of the jury process did not mean that 'stage-setting' ceased but rather placed new demands for such activities tailored to help ensure that the both the recommendations themselves and the community capacity for innovation and change engendered by the project, were carried forward. This process is ongoing. In October 2001, members of the jury presented to the local Council a report which received unanimous support and praise across party political divisions, from senior Council Officers and from state government agencies. Since then the jury's recommendations have been deployed in the new Waverley Council Integrated Stormwater Management Plan 2001–2006[11] and a community consultation forum has been established to review the implementation of initiatives resulting from BCP.

Performance and 'capacity building'

BCP both gives substance to the view of participation developed in the previous section and provides an indication of its significance. The collective vision of improvements to local environmental quality represented by BCP was facilitated by way of a comprehensive and extended process of community engagement and broader 'stage-setting'. Central to this was the facilitation of community, organizational and governance capacity able to underwrite change and the continuation of project objectives over time. The citizen's jury facilitated the integration of external, including expert, contributions with local concerns and insights by way of inclusive, creative and reflective processes. Crucially, the complex range of interrelated activities that BCP encompassed were driven not by a narrow pre-determined agenda but by a focus upon the nature, quality and contexts of these activities and the processes they embraced. A key project insight being that it was these, and not the sources and forms of information and knowledge, that were crucial to underwriting the quality of the outcomes achieved. Furthermore these outcomes were not conceived in terms of disembodied representational knowledge but in terms of insights and understandings concerning practices and behaviours and their reflection in material realities.

The BCP's success in this regard is reflected in a change among residents from a conventional view of nature as something external to them and unaffected by their behaviour to one cognizant of how their behaviours may act to shape it. The BCP Final Report (5) notes:

 © The Editorial Board of the Sociological Review 2003

'A positive shift in environmental attitudes and values among residents, away from 'externalized' notions of environmental responsibility (typically expressed by agreement with the statements 'I believe that technology will solve any environmental problems' and 'my lifestyle has very little impact on the environment') . . . towards 'internalized' notions of environmental responsibility (as expressed in agreement with statements 'Individuals should be responsible for the environment' and 'I am prepared to change my lifestyle for cleaner Bronte waterways')'.

This shift in resident attitudes toward views implicitly reflecting what ANT terms *relational materiality* is necessary, if project outcomes are to (re)perform the Bronte environment, and flags the success, if only partial, of the project's 'stage-setting' activities. Equally necessary, however, is that this 'stage-setting' facilitates alignments of people and things able to support the changed behaviours arising from this shift in attitudes and values. This more institutional and infrastructural dimension to 'stage-setting' is reflected by the project's emphasis on 'capacity' and 'capacity-building'.[12] Widely used but ill-defined, 'capacity building' takes on a variety of meanings but is generally used to indicate an enrichment or expansion of collective possibilities enabled by a range of means—organizational, institutional, and intellectual. The BCP final report under the heading of one of the eight project outcomes ('Establishment of self-governing sustainable participatory processes [strengthening relational networks]') notes (Ryan *et al.*, 2001: 7):

'Our conception of participation did not simply apply to environmental issues and stormwater pollution, but across all dimensions of institutional and democratic capacity-building to that end. Participation enhances the development of sustainable institutional relationships, capable of being integrated across and within a range of policy and practice frameworks that in the longer term will lead to improved stormwater outcomes'.

These ideas—central to BCP—can be interpreted in terms of the development and maintenance of an ANT ensemble. Encompassing both human and non-human entities 'improved stormwater outcomes' requires both durable participatory processes involving: 'institutional and democratic capacity-building'; 'sustainable institutional relationships'; 'policy and practice frameworks', and the maintenance of their diversity and multiplicity. This ANT interpretation helps us, then, to understand both the socio-material engagement at the core of BCP and the complex 'stage-setting' this necessitated, pointing perhaps to a new, broader notion of 'capacity'.

Conclusion—building 'performative capacity'

The BCP's illumination of how a community might match, or even outdo, more conventional approaches to environmental management directs attention to new ways of thinking about the achievement of collective goals. Both the sophistication of the jury's recommendations and their ongoing institutional uptake supports the arguments presented above, highlighting the potential benefits of not only well-executed discursively facilitated deliberative processes but also the 'stage-setting' work necessary to underpin them. In the case of BCP this work in tandem with the jury process acted to change the local environment by way of altered collective actions and behaviours and so can be understood, in this sense, to effect a (re)performance of that environment. This performed world, however, is one in which humans are intimately embedded rather than detached from, as representational thinking implies. BCP does not, though, suggest that this embeddedness is easy to engage with.

The BCP identification with place and locality probably motivated collective deliberation and helped cement the understandings generated to changed behaviours and actions, suggesting a potential difficulty in transferring these ideas beyond a local setting. In addition, the extensive nature of the project encompassing both the deliberative process and comprehensive 'stage-setting' activities were very demanding and resource intensive. BCP was also marked by its 'iterative and developmental' nature that allowed project practices to be intimately tailored to context. While it would therefore be unwise to consider the achievement of larger scale collective goals in terms directly analogous to those used to describe BCP here, it is worth examining what larger scale lessons might be drawn.

BCP suggests that outcomes are determined not by knowledge, conceived in narrowly representational terms, but rather by the contexts and processes in and by which knowledge is generated, articulated and deployed. In other words the configuration and quality of knowledge producing and decision-making processes should be significant at all scales, with analogous processes drawing upon performative forms of discourse and deliberation similarly valuable at the larger scale. The particular value of these processes resides in how they facilitate the interrogation and integration of conventional knowledge with more contextualized understandings. While the 'stage-setting' involved in BCP paid particular attention to the organizational context, it also specifically targeted socio-material practices. In the end it is these matters—where and how residents wash their cars and how the council mows grass verges, etc.—that determines improved stormwater outcomes. This requirement to maintain over time and space the alignments of people and things underpinning certain performances of nature, rather than others, is something particularly opaque to representational understandings but particularly critical at the larger scale. Effectively drawing the many elements underpinning these performances together is a substantial challenge. A notion of 'meta-capacity', encompassing not only the social categories of conventional concern—community, organizational, and deliberative capacities etc.—but also the non-human aspects of the context of interest, might provide a vehicle for this. Termed 'performative capacity', this could convey both the potential of the ensemble of interest to (re)perform the environment of concern, as well as how a performative style of deliberation might facilitate this.

106

© The Editorial Board of the Sociological Review 2003

Acknowledgements

Thanks for their valuable comments and feedback on earlier versions of this chapter are due to Catherina Landstrom and the editors of this volume, particularly Claire Waterton. I also gratefully acknowledge my fellow members of the Bronte Catchment Project 'Working Group', in particular Roberta Ryan and Susan Rudland.

Notes

1 See Ch.1 'Varieties of Epistemology' in Tanesini (1999) for a discussion of traditional epistemologies of this form and of an alternative epistemology predicated upon practical engagement with the world that resonates with the analysis of this chapter.
2 'Difference Democrats' (Dryzek, 2000) attribute this to Habermas' 'foundationalism' (subsumed here by 'representational thinking'). See Squires (1998) for a good account.
3 This critique of 'cooperative discourse' is further detailed in Healy (2003).
4 I choose to use 'ensemble' (Healy, 2003) rather than the more common ANT terms 'hybrid' or 'collective' because I find it more semiologically neutral.
5 While sounding similar to Kothari's (2001) application of Goffman's notions of 'front-stage' and 'back-stage' to Participatory Rural Appraisal, 'stage-setting' is, in socio-material terms, more a matter of bringing 'front-stage' and 'back-stage' together. It is thus very much a matter of collective 'ontological politics' (Mol, 1999) and differs from 'framing' (Callon, 1999) in being less targeted, more open and indeterminate.
6 Reflecting Martin's (1998: 30) observation that '. . . culture [is] the missing term in ANT'.
7 This account draws upon my involvement as a member of BCP's 'Project Working Group', as observer on BCP's 'Deliberative Processes Planning Group', and membership of sundry other ad hoc groups convened to discuss matters of conceptual concern to the project. All quotes are taken from Ryan et al., (2001), the final report of the project.
8 In Australia stormwater systems are separate from the sewage system, unlike in other countries such as Britain where they run together.
9 The BCP was a *Stormwater Trust* Round 3 Project that built upon the 'Effective Environmental Education Project—working with the community and small business', a Stormwater Trust Round 2 Project, and an earlier *Australian Research Council* funded 'Community Indicators and Local Democracy Project'.
10 This is a personal observation of the general response of the project team, expert witnesses to the jury and of council staff and councillors.
11 Available online at http://www.waverley.nsw.gov.au/council/enviro/stormwaterbak.htm.
12 Reflected in the sub-title of the projects final report 'Improving stormwater outcomes while strengthening democratic capacity' (Ryan et al., 2001: 1).

Bibliography

Arnstein, S. R. (1969), 'A Ladder of Citizen Participation', *AIP Journal*, (July): 216–224.
Beck, U. (1992), *Risk Society—Towards a New Modernity*, London, Thousand Oaks & New Delhi: Sage.
Beck, U. (1995a), *Ecological Enlightenment: essays on the politics of the risk society*, New Jersey: Humanities Press.
Beck, U. (1995b), *Ecological Politics in an Age of Risk*, Cambridge: Polity Press.
Beck, U. (1999), *World Risk Society*, Cambridge: Polity Press.

Callon, M. (1999), 'Actor-network theory—the market test', in J. Law and J. Hassard (eds), *Actor Network Theory and After*, Oxford: Blackwell Publishers/The Sociological Review.

Dryzek, J. S. (2000), *Deliberative democracy and beyond: liberals, critics, contestations*, Oxford: Oxford University Press.

Kaufmann, A. S. (1960), 'Human Nature and Participatory Democracy', in C. J. Friedrich (ed.), *Responsibility: NOMOS III*, New York: The Liberal Arts Press.

Habermas, J. (1984), *The Theory of Communicative Action: Vol. 1: Reason and the Rationalisation of Society*, London: Polity Press.

Habermas, J. (1987), *The Philosophical Discourse of Modernity*, Cambridge: Polity Press.

Healy, S. (2001), 'Risk as Social Process: the end of 'the age of appealing to the facts'?', *The Journal of Hazardous Materials*, 86(1–3): 39–53.

Healy, S. (2003), 'A 'Post-Foundational' Interpretation of Risk—Risk as 'Performance', *Journal of Risk Research*, in press.

Hoppe, R. (1999), 'Policy analysis, science and politics: from 'speaking truth to power' to 'making sense together'', *Science and Public Policy*, 26(3): 201–210, endnote 1.

Innes, J. E. and D. E. Booher (1999), 'Consensus Building as Role Playing and Bricolage—Toward a Theory of Collaborative Planning', *Journal of the American Planning Association*, 65(1): 9–26.

Irwin, A. (1995), *Citizen Science: A Study of People, Expertise and Sustainable Development*, London: Routledge.

Irwin, A. (2001), *Sociology and the Environment—A Critical Introduction to Society, Nature and Knowledge*, Cambridge: Polity.

Irwin, A. and B. Wynne (1996), *Misunderstanding Science? The Public Reconstruction of Science and Technology*, Cambridge: Cambridge University Press.

Kothari, U. (2001), 'Power, Knowledge and Social Control in Participatory Development', in B. Cooke and U. Kothari (eds), *Participation: the new tyranny?*, London and New York: Zed Books.

Latour, B. (1993), *We Have Never Been Modern*, Hemel Hempstead: Harvester Wheatsheaf.

Law, J. (1999), 'After ANT: complexity, naming and topology', in J. Law and J. Hassard (eds), *Actor Network Theory and After*, Oxford: Blackwell Publishers/The Sociological Review.

HMSO (2000), *Science and Society*, Report of the House of Lords Select Committee on Science and Technology (Lord Jenkin, Chair), London: HMSO.

Law, J. (2001), 'Ordering and Obduracy', Lancaster: the Centre for Science Studies and the Department of Sociology, Lancaster University [http://www.comp.lancs.ac.uk/sociology/soc068jl.html (version: obduracy4.doc; 3rd January)].

Levidow, L. and C. Marris (2001), 'Science and governance in Europe: lessons from the case of agricultural biotechnology', *Science and Public Policy*, 28(5): 345–360.

Martin, A. (1998), 'Anthropology and the Cultural Study of Science', *Science, Technology and Human Values*, 23(1): 24–44.

Mol, A. (1999), 'Ontological Politics. A word and some questions', in J. Law and J. Hassard (eds), *Actor Network Theory and After*, Oxford: Blackwell Publishers/The Sociological Review.

Renn, O., B. Blättel-Mink and H. Kastenholz (1997), 'Discursive Methods in Environmental Decision Making', *Business Strategy and the Environment*, 6: 218–231.

Renn, O. (1998), 'The role of risk communication and public dialogue for improving risk management', *Risk Decision and Policy*, 3(1), 5–30.

Ryan, R., S. Rudland and A. Phelps (2001), *Enhanced Stormwater Management in Bronte Catchment Through Local Community Participation—Improving stormwater outcomes while improving democratic capacity: Final Report*, Sydney: Brian Elton and Associates Pty Ltd.

Schechner, R. (1988), *Performance Theory*, New York and London: Routledge.

Schechner, R. (1993), *The future of ritual: writings on culture and performance*, New York and London: Routledge.

Seguin, E. (2000), 'The UK BSE crisis: strengths and weaknesses of existing conceptual approaches', *Science and Public Policy*, 27(4): 293–301.

Squires, J. (1998), 'In different voices: deliberative democracy and aestheticist politics' in J. Good and I. Velody (eds), *The Politics of Postmodernity*, Cambridge: Cambridge University Press.

Tanesini, A. (1999), *An Introduction to Feminist Epistemologies*, Oxford: Blackwell.

© The Editorial Board of the Sociological Review 2003

Part III
Embodying abstraction

Performing the classification of nature

Claire Waterton

Introduction

In an enthusiastic moment, Michael Lynch and John Law (1999: 336)[1] urged scholars within science studies to experiment in the field with ways of 'nature study' both alone and with other people. This, they assured, would only require the use of a pair of binoculars and a field guide. Their zeal derived from their own experiences of making field observations of birds which, they suggest, had provided an easily accessible entry, not into the world of bird watching *per se* (for this was not their primary interest), but rather into epistemological debates of interest to philosophy, history and sociology of science. Lynch and Law were particularly interested in processes of observing, describing and categorizing in specific geographical and cultural situations. One of the general insights from their work concerns the way in which orderings in nature are discovered and organized through the use of texts. 'Natural kinds' (birds), they argued, are not simply representations of what the eye (or the mind's eye) can see. Rather, they can be related to situated practices of reading and writing carried out in the field (1999: 320).

In a variation on their chosen theme of bird watching, this chapter narrates an attempt to experiment and think about ways in which we come to observe and describe the natural world, using prior orderings, or classifications[2], with which to do so. The chapter recounts an experiment carried out in the field by myself and my colleague, Nigel Stewart, a dance artist and lecturer in Theatre Studies at Lancaster University in the UK. Our experimental 'field trip' put to work, in the course of one day, two different ways of classifying the plant life which made up a particular kind of agricultural grassland found in north Lancashire. In the chapter I describe the way in which we each instructed one another as we applied our respective classifying practices to a selected patch of grassland. Throughout the day we attended to our own and one another's classifications, paying particular attention to the implicit or tacit qualities of classifying activities and hoping to make many of the latter explicit through the act of instructing the other—an approach often used in ethnomethodological, sociological and anthropological studies of knowledge systems (see Garfinkel, 1967; Suchman, 1987; Goodwin, 1994).

© The Editorial Board of the Sociological Review 2003. Published by Blackwell Publishing Ltd, 9600 Garsington Road, Oxford OX4 2DQ, UK and 350 Main Street, Malden, MA 02148, USA

This chapter has a broader scope of interest, however, as I use the field experiment to explore ways in which classifications of natural/cultural worlds are 'performative'.[3] Performance as a quality attributed to classifications is not singular. I try to bring out, through the field experiment, two contrasting ways in which classifications might be analysed as performance.[4] Social science literatures have brought to our attention the tension between two such interpretations: performance, on the one hand, that implies a concept of *accurate replication*; and on the other hand, performance which entails a never-ending *improvisation and adaptation* to local contingencies, unexpected events or terrain (Bell, 1998). Such a tension is an integral part of classifying and has been described by sociologists and others interested in how classifications themselves work (see Foucault, 1970; Richards, 1993; Bowker and Star, 1999).

The third part of the chapter describes the field experiment: part of the experiment entailed explaining one's own tacitly understood classification to the other person, who was a novice in that particular scheme. Here attention is drawn to the ways in which this kind of instructive situation may afford insight into the contingent nature of some of the taken-for-granted assumptions and actions that are part of classifying grassland—assumptions that may be 'served back' (iteratively, and in other times and spaces) as unproblematic 'naturalized' representations of the grassland after the classifying event.

Of particular interest in the chapter overall is the observation that daily or frequent users of accepted classificatory systems often fail to 'see' the ways in which such systems can be said to 'perform'. The different kinds of performances that are enacted through the constant use of a classificatory scheme are implicit, hidden or masked—they are simply 'done'. The idea that the orderings that we make to interpret the world, including the classifications we invent, can also be seen to 'perform' that very same world has been extensively studied in anthropology and the social sciences. The chapter aims to highlight the difficulty of our knowing this in the context of our being enmeshed within systems of knowing that are, to some extent, 'naturalized' within the cultures to which we belong. The replications of our classificatory practices are, however, always situated, never wholly replicating, and always containing elements of improvisation, contingency and surprise. A performative look at classifications entails, therefore, not only unraveling tacit assumptions with the aim of making them explicit, but also in understanding how, *in situ*, such assumptions and 'givens' are adapted and re-appropriated for specific context-dependent use. As I shall suggest at the end of the chapter, such contexts often promote the concealment of the very contingencies and improvisations that our field exercise attempted to expose.

How classifications work

Classifications have long been the object of fascination and focus of study by anthropologists and other social scientists because of their central role in

© The Editorial Board of the Sociological Review 2003

making sense of the complex phenomena of the world. As Geoffrey Bowker and Susan Leigh Star note, 'to classify is human' (1999: 1–32). Classifications, they remind us, are all around us, and vary from the simple ways in which we order information on our own computer desktops to the elaborate conceptual schemes aimed at ordering concepts of illness, madness, intelligence, race, as well as the living organisms of the natural world famously described by Karl Linnaeus in the 18th Century. Studies of classifications, carried out from the early 20th century onwards by anthropologists in 'exotic', far-away (from the western and scientific contexts of their initiation) lands, have historically debated the relationship between classifications and culture, looking at the classifications inherent in the lives of 'primitive' tribes people (Durkheim and Mauss, 1970 [1903]) or more recently, through the cultural milieu of a particular profession (Goodwin, 1994). Classifications have largely been studied as being analytically inseparable from the historical social, cultural and political contexts in which they take place (Douglas, 1992; Foucault, 1970; Ellen and Reason, 1979) and have afforded many insights about the relationship of formalized knowledges, such as our modern day 'science', to concepts of everyday culture (Dean, 1979; Nicholson, 1989; Ritvo, 1997; Schiebinger, 1996).

An important contribution of such studies derives from the idea that humans and human societies tend to project their own values upon the natural world through the very process of the construction of the discontinuous categories and classes that make up a classification (Douglas, 1975: 285; Sahlins, 1976: 101). These classes are then 'served back', to use Keith Thomas' phrase, 'as a critique or reinforcement of the human order, justifying some particular social or political arrangement on the grounds that it is somehow more 'natural' than any alternative' (Thomas, 1984: 61). Classifications are described, by those that analyse them, as having powerful naturalizing tendencies: they are not only descriptive of the world, they have consequences in the world and are 'operative'—defining the possibilities for action (Bowker and Star, 1999: 326) and bounding one's sense of agency. In important senses, then, classifications are seen to be 'performative' of natural, social and moral orderings. Thus Thomas recalls that ants, in the early modern period, were supposed to be living in a 'tightly governed commonwealth'; rooks had their own parliament and bees exemplified impressive monarchical structures. The historical viewpoint has often illustrated how hierarchies in nature were invoked to defend hierarchies in human societies (see also Ritvo, 1997). However the contemporary user or creator of classificatory schemes is often blind to such relationships, encultured as they are within the symbolic and material orderings implied within a particular scheme (Bowker and Star, 1999).

The 'invisibility' that pervades classifications makes it difficult to see how they work. Like the awkward questions young children often ask, it is hard for us to encounter questions as to why we order things in particular ways, and not others; how we draw the line between categories; and what the criteria are that allow for the definition of such boundaries. As a way of trying to understand how humans make discreet classes in relation to the myriad things around them,

© The Editorial Board of the Sociological Review 2003

attention has historically been focused, in the field of cognitive anthropology and related areas, on the 'mind' as the main organizing driver (Tyler, 1969: 1–23). More recently however, anthropologists and sociologists have begun to focus on ways in which ordering takes place within 'situated communities of practice' (Lave and Wenger, 1991), 'social worlds' (Strauss, 1978) and 'cultural models' (Quinn and Holland, 1987), often in the setting of a work-place (Cicourel, 1964; Suchman, 1987; Goodwin, 1994). Accordingly, anthropologists, sociologists and historians have turned to the 'construction sites' of classifications, to the actual times and places where new categories were, or are, being made in order to understand the tacit understandings, conceptual frameworks, and inclusions and exclusions that underpin a classificatory scheme. As many anthropologists, historians and sociologists of science have noted, it is at the site of construction, particularly when troublesome categories arise, or when the classifying activity is being described to a relative novice in the particular community of practice in question, that what are to *become* invisible and naturalized boundaries are questioned and made explicit (Secord, 1986; Suchman, 1987).

Key influences on such work were the 'practice theorists', among them Marshall Sahlins, Sherry B. Ortner and Pierre Bourdieu. As Catherine Bell notes, metaphors of performance began to be used by such authors[5] in liberating new ways—by explicitly moving away form the notion that a performance implied a repeatable execution of a 'script' or the enactment of a particular set of hierarchies or ideologies.[6] The emphasis markedly shifted, as Bell neatly notes, from seeing 'action as a kind of text' (implying the possibility of action as a reproducible ritual) to seeing 'text as a type of activity' (Bell, 1998: 206) where such activity is interpreted as variable according to context and contingencies operating in particular, situated cultural settings and according to the particular logic of human agents in such settings. When texts (including classificatory texts) are interpreted as a type of activity, in other words, human agents are seen not as passive inheritors of a system conditioned to replicate it (Bell, 1998: 209) but rather as 'unrecognized producers' (de Certeau, 1984), silent and invisible re-workers, with individual agency, who re-fashion in their own ways and according to their own logic, the orderings that shape and discipline their world. In this context performances are improvisatory, situated, and, importantly, embodied, encompassing much more than cognition and intellect, thus attributing creativity to what may appear simply to be acts of replication and tradition.

Studies of classifications illustrate both of the two contrasting tendencies that I have rather artificially separated for the moment—of *accurate replication* on the one hand, and *creative improvisation and adaptation* on the other. Classifications of race in the South African apartheid regime, for example, have been described as underpinning a cultural template for the *replication* of certain kinds of social and moral order (Bowker and Star, 1999: 201). Attention to the *practice of classifying*, in contrast, has ensured that the more emergent, *improvisatory and adaptive* qualities inherent in the on-going performance of classifications have come to the fore.

© The Editorial Board of the Sociological Review 2003

Classifications as disciplinarily-based practice

This section introduces the short 'experiment' that I carried out with my colleague, Nigel Stewart, in July 1998. The two classifications that were part of this experiment were unconnected by aim, method of construction, or disciplinary basis. What they had in common, albeit temporarily, was the fact that we were able to apply them simultaneously to the same environment—a piece of grassland in north Lancashire. Each classification was, in some sense, the product of what Geerz has called 'métier-formed minds' (Geertz, 1973: 155). That is, each classification was carried out by a different person with an associated disciplinary background—myself in the natural and social sciences (having been a student, rather than a practitioner, of one of the classifications) and Nigel Stewart in dance and performance studies. Geertz suggests that:

> [T]he various disciplines (or disciplinary matrices), humanities, natural scientific, social scientific alike, that make up the scattered discourse of modern scholarship are more than intellectual coins of vantage but are ways of being in the world, to invoke a Heideggerian formula, forms of life, to use a Wittgensteinian, or varieties of noetic experience to use a Jamesian . . . Those roles we think we occupy turn out to be minds we find ourselves to have (Geertz, 1973a: 155).

As practitioners of one or another discipline, we find it difficult to displace the familiarity of our own 'ways of seeing' (Geertz, 1973b: 14) and hence to understand the assumptions and preconceptions inherent in our own systems of knowledge and world-making. The experiment I recount below was an attempt to shed this familiarity and to expose some of the hidden characteristics of the classifications which we have come to know, to use and through which we play perhaps a small part in ordering experiences of the world. Since each classification was only familiar to one of us, what the experiment set up was a situation in which each one of us was a 'first time user' of (Suchman, 1987: 114), or illegitimate stranger to (Bowker and Star, 1999: 295), the other's classificatory frame of reference. The advantages of this for the aims of our experiment—to shed the familiarity of our own classificatory frames—are spelt out by Lucy Suchman:

> . . . [T]he troubles encountered by first time users of a system are valuable in that they disclose work required to understand the system's behaviour that, for various reasons, is masked by the proficient user (Suchman, 1987:114–5).

So, the first aim of the experiment was somehow, through instructing one another in our respective methods, to render ourselves strange to the practices and institutionalized norms that we had come to take for granted, and hence to give ourselves the opportunity of interrogating those practices as kinds of 'performances' that we had learnt (and learnt, at the same time, *not* to interrogate).[7]

I would also highlight that the first classificatory performance I am about to describe (that relating to the National Vegetation Classification) is part of a wider system belonging to specific communities, and replicated in other far-away contexts in a way that allows something ('nature' or 'a grassland' in this case) to be seen and understood in a particular way. This is a performance that is handed down, institutionalized, cultural (in Thomas Kuhn's 'paradigmatic' sense), a performance which adds up, through processes of apprenticeship, repeated practice and professionalization to a 'professional vision'—a way of seeing the world entrenched in a particular disciplinary or professional culture (Goodwin, 1994). Such a sense of performance is typical of the carrying out of scientific experiments, which may be interpreted, for example, as performances which are:

> . . . unique events in the world undertaken for the purpose of allowing something to be *seen*. What comes to be seen is not something unique and peculiar to that event, but something that can also be seen in other contexts. . . . (Crease, 1993: 96, quoted in States, 1996: 21).

Much recent work within sociology of science has tried to characterize the mobility of this kind of professional vision, how particular versions of the natural are represented and re-performed in multiple and far-away contexts, and what is needed for this 'action-at-a-distance'. Such studies have successfully held in tension the ways in which, at the very same time, such universalizing scientific performances are simultaneously 'situated practice' (Latour and Woolgar, 1979; Latour, 1995; Lynch and Law, 1999: 337; Suchman, 1987; see also Watson, this volume; and Lorimer and Lund, this volume).

The grassland

The first classification which Nigel Stewart and I used to understand the agricultural grassland was a classification of vegetation communities. This classification, called the 'National Vegetation Classification', incorporates, like many classifications, *both* a textual canon—a more or less stable reference system for relating any observed vegetation type in the UK to a recognized ordering of vegetation communities (Rodwell, 1991)—*and* a methodology usually employed by 'phytosociologists' (the community of vegetation scientists who adhere to the theoretical viewpoint that plants can be recognized to belong to assemblages of 'plant communities').

The second classification which we applied to the same grassland setting was derived from a phenomenological approach to understanding movements of the body. This classification is a 'categorization' in David Reason's terms (see note 2). It is based upon an analysis of the 'components of virtual force' by Maxine Sheets-Johnstone (1979) and is an ordering device of another kind, a system of phenomenologically-based nomenclature used by movement analysts and dance theorists to understand and represent variations and sensations of movement.[8] Nigel Stewart had previously used this classification to derive an understanding of the movement and spatio-temporal attributes of a barley field in Kent. In his work he used the phenomenological classification of the components of virtual

© The Editorial Board of the Sociological Review 2003

force (which can relate to both human and non-human (plant, or other) bodies) to interpret the variation of movement in plant bodies. Later, he used his observations to choreograph a dance relating to the barley field.[9]

In our own one-day experiment, the first classification (the National Vegetation Classification (NVC)) was put to use to try and understand what vegetation community (relative to a national median type as established by the NVC) the grassland exemplified. The second classification, on the other hand, was employed in order to derive and understand the spatialization, movements and textures of the same piece of grassland. The account that follows highlights the main elements of the proceedings of the day that was spent carrying out this experimental 'field-work'. Our experience in carrying out our respective classificatory practices bore similarities to that of Lynch and Law (1999) as they studied the situated practices of consulting texts and identifying species in the field. In both cases Nigel and I were trying to derive accurate observations of the qualities of the grassland by using predetermined ordering devices which gave us clues as to what we were looking for. In both cases we experienced the struggle of using such prior orderings *in situ*, in the bumpiness of the field, taking account of unexpected events (including rain), and using our own bodies, various bits of equipment, and sensory faculties. It soon became apparent, especially for the relative 'novice' in each case, that neither exercise was a question of reading instructions or guides and then simply making observations. In both cases, the actual practices of deriving and recording the appropriate attributes of the grassland demanded a reinterpretation of what needed to be done by the more experienced practitioner and a kind of concentrated field-apprenticeship for the relative novice.

A stranger to grassland

Our piece of field work took place in a small field on a north-facing hillside just four miles from the campus of Lancaster University. We had driven to a farm, Little Crag, where I had in 1996 been taken as a student to learn how to 'do' the National Vegetation Classification (NVC). Nigel and I asked at the farmhouse whether we might be able to look at the vegetation on a field adjacent to the farm buildings. The farmer gave us permission and we walked over to a small rocky outcrop which overlooked the field to begin our day's work. I remembered from my own tuition that the first thing we had to do was to find a 'homogeneous patch' of vegetation, in order that one's sample might be considered representative of the vegetation found in that area as a whole. Nigel was unsure as to what a 'homogeneous patch of vegetation' might be (just as I had been when I was first instructed), and asked what I meant by that phrase. I explained that it would be a small patch of the field, about 2×2 metres in size, that looked from this distance (about 10 metres from the edge of the field) to be one colour, one texture—one 'kind' of vegetation, rather than what phytosociologists call a 'mosaic' of vegetation communities. Nigel's question, and my own response,

© The Editorial Board of the Sociological Review 2003

indicated to me that our experiment was working: the very question that I had myself asked when first presented with the hillside and the task of identifying a homogeneous patch of vegetation (the first stage in the classification of a plant community) was brought to the fore by Nigel whilst I was tending to present the task as straightforward, in a 'taken-for-granted' manner. Further questions suggested a similar dynamic between me as 'tutor' and Nigel as 'student' when we walked down from the crag to the patch we eventually decided to demarcate. As other accounts relate (Suchman, 1987), whilst I (not without a certain amount of effort as a relative novice at these practices myself) was trying to ensure a relatively smooth performance of the practice of classifying a segment of vegetation, Nigel encountered several surprises and difficulties in carrying out these practices. His moments of surprise, his questions and the difficulties he encountered served as reminders to both him and me of the elements of contingency in the relevant classificatory procedures, and of the aspects of craft, embodied, situated and tacit knowledge involved in doing scientific fieldwork (Roth and Bowen, 1999; Law and Lynch, 1999; Latour, 1995).

Once off the raised crag and down in the grassy and boggy field, it became more, not less, difficult to find a homogeneous patch of vegetation. This seemed to be because the scale at which we were seeing variation in vegetation became much smaller: we were actually standing on and around the vegetation we were about to classify. At this scale, beneath and around our feet, the slightest hint of another colour, another texture, an emergent piece of rock, or a particularly long grass gave the impression of lack of homogeneity within a two metre square. I gave Nigel the task of choosing the homogeneous 2×2 metre area which we were to demarcate from the rest of the field using four tent pegs and eight metres of string, thus making what phytosociologists call a 'quadrat'. Although we had, from the craggy outcrop, decided to place our quadrat in a certain part of the field, once we were down in the field, choosing our field site took considerable time and was accompanied by considerable uncertainty as to whether the patch we eventually decided upon was representative of the grassland in the field as a whole. To both of us, but perhaps especially worrying to Nigel, it seemed almost impossible to tell.

Once, however, we had pegged our 2×2 metre 'quadrat' to the ground, Nigel and I began the next task of determining which vegetation community was to be found in this particular field. According to the standard NVC method, we had two tasks to perform: first, to identify, using the Linnaean classification system, all the individual plant species to be found within that two metre square. And second, to determine quantitatively the percentage amount of 'cover' that each individual plant species represented over the area which we had marked off. Both of these tasks required us to carry out scientific practices that I, alone, was used to. As a student of ecology in 1991–2, I had learnt how to identify plant species, using identification guides and keys. I had also become familiar with the accepted way of quantifying vegetation cover, using the Domin system.[10] To Nigel, however, both of these practices were strange and new.

© The Editorial Board of the Sociological Review 2003

The differences between total novice (Nigel) and instructor/relative novice (myself) were stark throughout the first half of the day. An indicator of such differences early on in the proceedings lay in our sense of anticipation. Whilst I was anticipating that the most difficult aspect for us both would be to identify the different grasses present in this 2 × 2 metre square of grassland, Nigel revealed to me that he had not realized that there would be *different* kinds of grasses on a grassland such as this. He had assumed that on a single example of grassland that there would be only one type of grass.

Anticipating this problem, I began furiously flicking through the classic grassland identification text, Hubbard's *Grasses: A guide to their Structure, Identification, Uses, and Distribution in the British Isles* (1954), looking up what I thought the three different grass species I saw before me in the quadrat might possibly be.[11] Whilst I was doing this Nigel was, a) initially blissfully unaware of the challenges I felt might be immediately facing us in providing an accurate identification of the individual grass species found on the site (a pre-requisite for correct identification of the plant communities therein), and b) once engaged with Hubbard's text, seemingly quite enchanted by the detail of the descriptions within it which serve to distinguish one grass from another.

As I read out bits of Hubbard's text in order to identify one or another grass that we had separated out from the sward as being 'different', the detail of Hubbard's text, the meticulous detail on visually discernable parts of the grasses, and the new vocabularies to which Nigel was introduced, struck him as somewhat 'exotic' (Geertz, 1973b: 14). The idea of identifying a grass species by peeling back its tiny ligules (the very small green ridge that occurs at the point where the leaf branches out from the stem) and assessing whether it is long or short, or whether it has hairs on it, was to Nigel both a fantastically *novel* idea belonging to the practice of identification, as well as being an incredibly *difficult* task to execute with any confidence in practice. The whole process of separating out individual grasses from the mass of grass and flowers (the 'sward'), of looking up possible likely species in the field guide, of isolating tiny parts of the plant and observing them with an eye for what seemed amazing detail, of coming to a conclusions that, yes, this grass was a certain species, was a 'performance' that Nigel had never come across before.

As well as Nigel, I also found these ways of sorting and identifying the grasses challenging, but somehow, on the other hand, I felt I *knew* the difference between Sheep's Fescue (*Festuca ovina*), Purple Moor Grass (*Molinia caerula*), Common Bent (*Agrostis tenuis*) and White Matt Grass (*Nardus stricta*) through some other means—although often I could not put a finger on what these means were in a way that was intelligible as an instruction to Nigel. (I was also still a little unsure and so carried out a common practice of taking a specimen of each different grass back with me to be later identified by a botanist, the late Professor Andrew Malloch.) I also somehow felt that I *knew* that a sheep-grazed specimen of *Festuca ovina* which was perhaps 2 cm high, wiry and compact looking, was the exact same species as a neighbouring specimen (that had not been grazed) that had soft, wavy leaves of some 20–30 cm in height. To Nigel

119

these two morphologically opposite specimens looked like utterly different grass species, given that we were establishing species difference on the basis of a combination of visually discernable differences. Experience, even of the modest kind which I was possessed, was obviously part of a smooth performance, one key to 'getting one's eye in' and to gaining the tacit knowledge that was needed to identify the different grasses on the hillside.

Performing in the field

The practice of identifying all the individual species within a quadrat placed upon the ground, of documenting these species in a list on a proforma designed for the purpose, and of estimating the 'cover' of each listed species in terms of the percentage of space it covered over the 2 × 2 metre quadrat is the phytosociological ritual of making a 'relevé'. This practice is a highly prized activity amongst phytosociologists. The records of such activities are species lists written on cards, with 'Domin values' corresponding to each identified species written adjacent to them. Such record cards (or simply 'relevés') are classic Latourian 'inscriptions' (Latour, 1987) and hold much value amongst phytosociologists, who use them as a kind of currency, trading them, borrowing them, and using them as a basis for establishing the legitimacy of one others' work. But how did Nigel's brief exposure to this 'cultural practice' belonging to the science of phytosociology illuminate it as a kind of 'performance'?

First, the kind of questions that Nigel asked me (What is a homogeneous patch of vegetation? Is this ligule hairy? How can this short, wiry specimen be the same species as that soft, wavy one? How can we estimate percentage cover for this plant that has very thin leaves, as opposed to this other plant that has very wide leaves?) made me realize that Hubbard's guide did not encompass a general theory relating to grasses and their classification. It was, like the field guides that Lynch and Law used in their bird watching exercise, more like a 'collection of instructions and tools associated with a particular craft like pottery or carpentry' (Lynch and Law, 1999: 326). In addition, Nigel's questions were sufficiently disarming to show me that what I was doing was handing down verbally a kind of received and distilled wisdom about how to classify plant communities that didn't encompass the 'whole' of what we were doing. The verbal instructions that I was giving were like a kind of script, comprising only the basic elements, of a much richer 'performance'. This performance contained the elements thought essential for this kind of practice but was also more complete than the instructions implied. Nigel's difficult questions made me try to account for the differences between the 'script' and the richer performance in which we were engaged—classifying the vegetation in a particular space, using particular tools, texts, and bringing to bear some received and tacit knowledges as far as we were able to do so.

Second, the utter unfamiliarity of the concept of a 'vegetation community' to Nigel had the effect of making me realize the amount of 'connecting' knowledge

© The Editorial Board of the Sociological Review 2003

that I could put to use in this context. This knowledge was not necessarily related to the identification and quantification of plants, but perhaps to a knowledge of seasonality (plants look different in the summer from in the winter), to a knowledge of farming practices and the effects of grazing (grazing affects the morphology of plants), to the theoretical ideas behind the concept of 'communities' of plants (as opposed to contrasting theories of plants being individually spatialized along 'gradients' thought to correlate to a combination of environmental factors (Gleason, 1926)). In placing a quadrat on the ground, and trying to establish what kind of plant community existed in a particular place, Nigel's unfamiliarity brought into relief the familiar yet largely tangential knowledges that I could bring to bear on the problems at hand. My lack of ability to articulate clearly some of these contributing bits of knowledge, and the putting all this knowledge into practice in the face of a set of instructions that did not necessarily call for them, had the effect of highlighting the whole activity as a kind of cumulative crafting of knowledges which was partially embodied in the memory and experience of the person who happened to be taking on the role of instructor. The performance was, in this sense, very much lodged within human capabilities—it would get cumulatively richer with time, reflection and experience.

Third, some of the difficulties we had in getting to grips with the grassland, especially the problem of where to place the quadrat, highlighted the making of the relevé as a practice that was highly embodied, highly specific and localized to our own positioning in the field. The sense of being part of an improvisation in an embodied, contingent and localized sense is often quite strong when one is out doing ecological work in the field (Roth and Bowen, 1999; Latour, 1995; Lynch and Law, 1999). In carrying out such an activity with someone who is less experienced this improvisation is often called into question and worried about—a matter of concern—whereas for the more experienced performer improvisation, according to the specificities of the place and the relationship to one's own knowledge, the tools to hand, and one's disposition in the field, is what makes the exercise creative and interesting. The worrying that Nigel and I exercised with respect to where to place our quadrat highlighted the sense that we were to a large extent both novices and did not have the experience automatically to gauge and calibrate bodily experiences with the immediate and surrounding environment: we had explicitly to think about it. Thinking back to previous field work with experts in the NVC, I remember observing the way that eyes, hands, movements and perhaps the body overall are, in a sense, calibrated to the landscape and the vegetation within it as an integral part of making relevés and classifying vegetation. The grassland, or vegetation in question, in a sense comes into being partly as a result of this finely tuned and improvised set of procedures contingent upon both human and non-human elements. At workshops with European phytosociologists near Rome, I had seen their scientific observations and brief field 'performances' in the countryside as incredibly improvisatory, imaginative, even playful—there was none of the bodily awkwardness that Nigel and I displayed so painfully as we went round and round in circles trying to find the best place to position our quadrat!

© The Editorial Board of the Sociological Review 2003

I have highlighted above just three ways in which our attempt to classify the grassland at Littledale can be seen as performative. First there was the sense of moving beyond a predetermined 'script' or instruction manual as we got down to the actual practices of interpreting the grassland according to the National Vegetation Classification. Performance, as Butler suggests, is always 'derivative', never strictly repetitious (Butler, 1995: 205). Second, there was a strong sense of the human-ness of the performance, the sense that what we were drawing upon was a cumulative set of experiences bearing upon many tangential and relatively unarticulated knowledges and remembered practices. These knowledges and practices were lodged within a person, rather than in any text or set of instructions and were drawn upon in relation to practice, and to the demands of attending to the details of that practice. This was, in other words a human performance (with all the limitations that a lack of experience of such performances entails) rather than a scientific methodology. Third, the somewhat awkward positioning of our own bodies in relation to the contingencies of the environment hinted paradoxically that it would be possible, given enough bodily experience of this type of situation, to carry off a 'smooth', creative and improvisatory performance that would be responsive to changes and contingencies in the conditions belonging to any one particular site. The bodily dis-ease of our efforts highlighted this very corporeal aspect of our classificatory exercise.

A stranger to Choreology

Once we had filled in the NVC proforma which established species presence and cover within it, Nigel began to carry out his own classificatory exercise. The aim, in this case, was not to characterize what kind of vegetation community was present but to derive accurate observations of the spatio-temporal and kinaesthetic qualities of grassland. Nigel, like me, was using predetermined ordering devices. Embedded within the schemes he was using was the concept that dance incorporated a qualitative structure, portrayable in terms of 'force', which could be broken down into two broad categories: temporalizaton of force and spatialization of force. These categories themselves were further broken down in a hierarchical fashion thus making up a classificatory scheme (Maxine Sheets-Johnstone, 1979). Focussing on the spatialization of force, Nigel interrogated the different species of grass that we had found in our quadrat in terms of the categorizations of 'force' within Sheets-Johnstone's classification.[12]

Standing over the 2×2 metre quadrat, and still looking carefully at individual plants within it, Nigel asked me a number of questions to help categorize the different types of 'force' displayed by the forms of the plants making up the grassland. Perhaps the first thing to say is that these questions were almost unintelligible to me, as a complete outsider to the world of dance and choreography, movement and space. However, to dancers and choreographers like Nigel they are meaningful and form the basis of a way of classifying movement in and through space.

122

Nigel asked me the following questions relating each to the different species of grass that we had earlier identified as being the dominant grasses in the quadrat:

1. What is the spatialization of force of this plant?
2. What is the amplitude of this plant as it appears within your consciousness?
3. What is the amplitude of space surrounding this plant?

These questions were, as I have said, almost unintelligible and actually somewhat shocking to me! I had no idea what they meant and had to ask repeatedly what Nigel meant by them. So for example, when Nigel asked me the first question—concerning the spatialization of force of a particular grass—I felt I did not understand what he was saying. When I asked him what he meant by the expression 'spatialization of force', he suggested I try to think about the linear patterns that the plant might make. Would they be 'curvilinear', or 'zig-zag', for example? My response was to try and answer as best as I could. Some of the plants seemed to have straight, direct leaves; a kind of 'vertical force' seemed perhaps to be operating. If a particular specimen had been grazed by sheep, however, this quality of straightness might be quite disrupted, the grass may instead display a kind of 'curvilinear' quality.

What was interesting here was that two such morphologically opposite grass specimens, according to my own classificatory practice, would end up, in effect, in the same class, a class relating to the species to which these two specimens belonged. However they would, in Nigel's classification, end up in different categories (vertical and curvilinear). Nigel was extracting information and collecting data about the linear and aerial qualities of the grasses making up the grassland, and the way in which the grasses appeared in space to him and to me. The way, however, that he 'limited and filtered the visible', to use Foucault's terms, was based on a classification in which 'force', detected in the body of the plant, could be seen to have varying spatial qualities. What was visible to Nigel, but relatively opaque to me, were precisely these directional and amplitudinal qualities. Whereas, what was visible to me were what botanists call the 'structure' of the plants, the 'composition and arrangement of pieces that make up its body' (Linnaeus, *Philosophie botanique*, section 299, quoted in Foucault, 1992: 34). Unlike natural scientists like Linnaeus, Nigel was not interested in the constant properties of a plant which can be identified *in spite of* its particular morphology. He was actually interested *in* morphology, and the variation of spatial forms and forces which collectively made up the grassland. Our classificatory practices and our ways of seeing the grassland were utterly different. Perhaps, as Helen Verran has described in her observations of natural scientists and aboriginal landowners, one can see each not just as embodying different ways of seeing, but as embodying a different metaphysics (Verran, 2002: 757).

When Nigel asked me the second question: what is the amplitude of this plant as it appears within your consciousness, again I had to ask Nigel what he meant. He replied that I should think of the 'virtual expansiveness' or 'virtual contractiveness' of a plant. This almost seemed to be an exercise in documenting what sort of impression a plant made upon one's mind. Again I tried to answer as best as I could. Some grasses perhaps seemed bolder, more expansive, and more strident, where as others had a more diminutive, delicate feel—were these the kind of qualities that Nigel was trying evoke?

The third question was again very difficult—I was asked to think about the amplitude of space surrounding the body of a plant. This, for my own purposes could have been infinite—how much space *is* there around a plant? But Nigel was trying to get at aspects of the relationship between the plant and the space around it in terms of two continua—'intensive' and 'extensive', and 'contained' and 'diffuse', concepts central to Sheets-Johnstone's scheme (Sheets-Johnstone, 1979) that are important to one's movement through space as a dancer.

I have highlighted in this part of the account the insecurity (documented in similar studies of novice-tutor relationships, eg. Lynch and Law, 1999: 319) that I felt in carrying out the classificatory performance that Nigel introduced me to. Despite my commitment to answering Nigel's questions as part of the exercise, I had the sense, even as I was doing it, that I had no foundation on which I could do so. I had no knowledge of movement, I had no real conception of how a plant might be thought to make a pattern in space—zig-zag, curvilinear, or otherwise. As we went through each question in relation to each species, I felt lost in a world of unfamiliar and strange concepts. Whilst I struggled to make some sense of and to answer Nigel's questions, at the same time I felt a fraud at the shallowness and lack of foundation of my answers. What Nigel was trying to get at, he explained, was a phenomenological understanding of the grassland, a kind of 'tending to' our consciousness of the grasses that, hours earlier, he had learnt to see as individual species.

For Nigel, the experience of having a novice fumble around using unfamiliar concepts and asking awkward questions, as I did in the second half of the day, was apparently not as obfuscating as it appeared from my point of view. Perhaps, in accordance with findings by Suchman (1984: 114–5), it was even illuminating. Nigel suggested that my answers to his questions were in some way refreshing, on account of my not knowing the taken-for-granted categories both explicitly and implicitly built into Sheets-Johnstone's classificatory scheme. My naïve experimentation with the vocabularies and concepts introduced to me in the field alerted Nigel to aspects of the grassland that he would not have noticed alone. At the same time, my faltering answers to his questions gave him an alternative perspective with which to interrogate and better understand the qualities of his own classificatory framework.

Conclusions: nature performed through two classifications of vegetation

Natural kinds, as Lynch and Law suggest, are evidently not simply representations of what the eye can see. Through this brief sketch of Nigel Stewart's and my field experiment, I hope to have highlighted some different ways in which classifying activities relating to the grassland can be seen as performances. The activities we carried out are evidently performances relating to very different disciplinary communities, métiers, or communities of practice. Within those communities the representations deemed 'natural' within them involve the ordering of raw nature (plants, vegetation, bodies). Such representations of the kind we were creating have particular meanings for those communities and are able to travel, keeping their meanings intact (see Watson, this volume; Waterton 2002). The results of the classifying performances we carried out however, also become performances in themselves. The day spent in the grassland, observing, reading texts, writing down notes, interrogating each other, gave Nigel, for example, specific descriptors of the movements of plants that he then explored through his own body in a performance with the company *Grace and Danger*, a collective dedicated to dance and music improvisation. His observations and his categorizations of the spatial qualities of the individual plants, had what Bowker and Star call 'consequences' (Bowker and Star, 1999: 319) in terms of the movements that he was able to produce, and the effects of the choreographed piece within the dance community to which he belongs.

As for the classification of plant communities, Nigel and I were able to establish, using the data from our quadrat, that the vegetation community on which we had spent the day was probably an example of what is known as U5—'*Nardus stricta-Galium saxatile grassland*'. This category of grassland is said to occur 'widely through the uplands of northern and western Britain in zonations and mosaics with a variety of other grasslands, heaths and mires' (Rodwell, 1992: 358). As such it is not of especially high conservation value, being an example of ordinary upland grassland, and so would not be valued as eligible for any particular kind of protection, conservation designation or other status. Again, *its* categorization might have certain 'consequences' (Bowker and Star, 1999: 319), or come to be performative in the way that Bowker has suggested in the context of biodiversity databases (Bowker, 2000: 675). Logged onto a planning database, and used as a basis for decision making, the class U5 would not signal that there should be any protection from impending development, in contrast to other less common classes of upland grassland. U5, as a representative category of the kind of grassland we observed, not only contains within it the performances we carried out to establish where in the national classification it belonged, but as that U5 category, can initiate certain performances: it has the ability, to use Thomas' phrase again, to 'serve back' the assumptions and dispositions entailed in its making.

Much of the 'invisible work' (Star, 1996; Bowker and Star, 1999: 249) entailed within our classifying practices and the subsequent representations of nature distilled from them was revealed through the methodology of having a 'stranger' try to perform classifications unknown within their own disciplinary practices. The performances we enacted on the Littledale hillside were more than a replication of a professional ritual, script or even scientific methodology. They *were* a replication, but attending to one another's norms and practices and answering one another's awkward questions revealed the contingencies, the awkwardnesses and the improvisations needed to 'pull off' such a replication in this particular context. As Bourdieu says, '[p]ractices always emerge as improvisations because situations and the people that participate in them are always only analogous to each other; they are never exactly the same (Bourdieu, 1977: 83 quoted in Schieffelin, 1998: 205).

The tension outlined in the first half of this chapter—between a conceptualization of classifications as either ordering the world in their own image, or, on the other hand, as flexible and adaptable to local situations—was inherent in the joint performances of the two classificatory schemes we carried out, and is implicit in the 'handing down' of such knowledge in the form of apprenticeships or the passing on of one's knowledge-making systems to others. Strangely enough, however, not only do we ourselves become increasingly blind to the performativity inherent within our own classificatory schemes, but as the anthropologist Frederik Barth notes, we also become increasingly good at disguising it. Carrying out disciplinary traditions, such as making a relevé, or categorizing the spatial properties of the world around us, can be seen as a hidden 'history of creativity' whereby practitioners adapt to their present circumstances the knowledge and skills passed onto them 'in such a way as to deny change and temporality and to fabricate timelessness' (Barth, 2002: 14–15). This itself, Barth suggests, is 'a performative illusion of considerable ingenuity and persuasive power' (Barth, 2002: 14–15). Our experiment aimed both to understand and to puncture this illusion, bringing to the fore a further tendency—that of reflexivity—important to studies of performance.

Acknowledgements

It would clearly not have been possible to write this chapter without the accompaniment of Nigel Stewart, who not only spiritedly experimented in the field with me, and later in the studio, but also gave very helpful comments on earlier drafts of the chapter. I am grateful to the Economic and Social Research Council (ESRC) who funded the project, 'Databases and Environmental Policy' (1994–1997) which supported much of the research represented in this chapter. Particular thanks are due to Professor John Rodwell and the late Professor Andrew Malloch who not only taught me the basics of how to 'do' the NVC, but much more about the fascinating world of phytosociology besides. Hearty thanks must go to the 'Between Nature' conference team for their encouragement with this experiment, including at various times, Robin Grove-White, Gabriella Gianacchi, Wallace Heim, Baz Kershaw and Bron Szerzynski. Especial thanks to Bron and Wallace who stayed with the chapter-writing from start to finish, and for the many great conversations and laughs we have had along the way. I have also benefited greatly from the insights and help of colleagues in my Institute and further afield, Rebecca Ellis, Mark Toogood and Brian

   © The Editorial Board of the Sociological Review 2003

Wynne, who have read drafts of this chapter and helped me understand what I wanted to say. All errors remain my own.

Notes

1 I refer here to a paper (Law and Lynch, 1999) that was reprinted from an original published in 1988 (Law and Lynch, 1988), and re-printed again in 1990 (Law and Lynch, 1990).

2 I use the term 'classification' here to include what David Reason calls 'categorization' as well as his 'stronger sense of classification' (Reason, 1979: 222). Categorization, Reason suggests, concerns acts of distinction and demarcation and 'solicits recognition of a kind which depends on no particular features of expression for its correct exercise', whereas 'classification is not only rule-governed (since it indicates a culture property), but these rules must be articulable in principle and constitute criteria of identity' (Reason, 1979: 222). One of the classifications I shall talk about, the National Vegetation Classification, falls fully into Reason's 'classification' category whereas the second classification (relating to 'force') that I shall talk about seems to be better described as a categorization.

3 I use the word 'performative' here as an adjective, and in the rather loose sense outlined by Richard Schechner (2000: 110) to mean 'something that is "like a performance" without actually being a performance in the orthodox or formal sense'.

4 Schechner's notion of 'as performance' as opposed to 'is performance' is also close to the way that I describe classifications 'as performance' here and later in the chapter (Schechner 2000: 32–35).

5 One can include here Victor Turner, J. L. Austin, Erving Goffman, Stanley Tambiah and Clifford Geertz. Bell's review of these contributions is comprehensive (Bell, 1998: 205–211) but we should also include more recent work in the field of Actor Network Theory that has developed ideas of performance (eg. Latour, B. and S. Woolgar (1979); Law, J. (1994); and several contributions in Law, J. and J. Hassard (1999)).

6 The notion of a 'script' is acknowledged as somewhat problematic here, however, since even a scripted performance (as opposed to free improvisation) contains within it the space for new interpretations.

7 Studies of 'instructed action' (Garfinkel (1967); Suchman (1987); Amerine and Bilmes (1988); Goodwin (1994) provide more examples of this kind of work and rationale.

8 Sheets-Johnstone's nomenclature, I was informed by Nigel, is too abstract a scheme for most working dancers and choreographers. Nigel described Sheets-Johnstone's categorization as a set of distinctions familiar to some dance scholars with a particular interest in movement analysis and continental philosophy.

9 Nigel Stewart's chapter about this performance will appear in the volume, *Performing Nature: Explorations in Ecology and the Arts*, Bern: Peter Lang, which is due to be published in 2005. See Stewart (1998) for a broader phenomenological exploration of his work.

10 Percentage cover is a record of the vertical projection of the living parts of a species on the ground. This is estimated by eye in the field and translated into a relative abundance scale from 1–10: the 'Domin scale'.

11 See Lynch and Law (1999: 323) for an account of different customary ways of looking up species in the field using field guides.

12 It is interesting that, once in the field, the way in which we began to look at the plants within it in the first half of the day (by individual species, within a quadrat) began to frame the way that we looked when we began to use Sheets-Johnstone's classificatory scheme. There was no reason, for example, why we could not have dispensed with the quadrat and any ideas of 'species' in the second half of the day. What actually happened was that we began to hybridize our two methodologies as Nigel continued to use the species focus as a way of interrogating the grassland in terms of 'force'.

© The Editorial Board of the Sociological Review 2003

References

Amerine, R. and J. Bilmes (1988), 'Following Instructions', *Human Studies* II (2/3): 327–339.

Barth, F. (2002), 'An Anthropology of Knowledge', *Current Anthropology*, 43(1): 1–18.

Bell, C. (1998), 'Performance' in M. Taylor (ed.), *Critical Terms for Religious Studies*, Chicago: University of Chicago Press, pp. 205–224.

Bowker, G. and S. L. Star (1999), *Sorting Things Out: Classification and Its Consequences*, Cambridge Mass.: MIT Press.

Butler, J. (1995), 'Burning Acts—Injurious Speech' in A. Parker and E. Kosofsky Sedgwick (eds), *Performativity and Performance*, New York and London: Routledge, pp. 197–227.

Cicourel, A. (1964), *Method and Measurement in Sociology*, New York: Free Press of Glencoe.

Crease, R. P. (1993), *The Play of Nature: Experimentation as Performance*, Bloomington: Indiana University Press.

Dean, J. (1979), 'Controversy over Classification: A Case Study from the History of Botany' in B. Barnes and S. Shapin (eds), *Natural Order: Historical Studies of Scientific Culture*, London: Sage, pp. 211–230.

De Certeau, M. (1984), *The Practice of Everyday Life*, tr. Steven Randall, Berkeley: University of California Press.

Douglas, M. (1975), *Implicit Meanings: Essays in Anthropology*, London: Routledge and Kegan Paul.

Douglas, M. and D. L. Hull (1992), *How Classifications Work: Nelson Goodman among the Social Sciences*, Edinburgh: Edinburgh University Press.

Durkheim, E. and M. Mauss (1970 [1903]), *Primitive Classification*, tr. R. Needham, London: Cohen and West.

Ellen, R. and D. Reason (1979), *Classifications in their Social Context*, London: Academic Press.

Foucault, M. (1992 [1970]), *The Order of Things: An Archaeology of the Human Sciences*, London: Routledge.

Garfinkel, H. (1967), *Studies in Ethnomethodology*, Englewood Cliffs, NJ: Prentice-Hall.

Geertz, C. (1973a), *The Interpretation of Cultures*, New York: Basic Books.

Geertz, C. (1973b), *Local Knowledge: Further Essays in Interpretative Anthropology*, New York: Basic Books.

Gleason, H. A. (1926), 'The Individualistic Concept of the Plant Association' *Bulletin of the Torrey Botanical Club*, 43: 463–481.

Goodwin, C. (1994), 'Professional Vision', *American Anthropologist*, 96(3): 606–633.

Hubbard, C. E. (1954), *Grasses: A Guide to their Structure, Identification, Uses, and Distribution in the British Isles*, London: Penguin.

Latour, B. and S. Woolgar (1979), *Laboratory Life: The Construction of Scientific Facts*, Thousand Oaks, CA: Sage.

Latour, B. (1987), *Science in Action: How to Follow Scientists and Engineers Through Society*, Milton Keynes: Open University Press.

Latour, B. (1995), 'The 'Pédofil' of Boa-Vista: A Photo-Philosophical Montage' tr. B. Simon and K. Verresen, *Common Knowledge*, 4: 144–187.

Law, J. (1994), *Organizing Modernity*, Oxford: Blackwell.

Law, J. and J. Hassard (1999), *Actor Network Theory and After*, Oxford: Blackwell/The Sociological Review.

Lave, J. and E. Wenger (1991), *Situated Learning: Legitimate Peripheral Participation*, Cambridge: Cambridge University Press.

Lynch, M. and J. Law (1988), 'Lists, Field Guides and the Descriptive Organization of Seeing: Bird Watching as an Exemplary Observational Activity', *Human Studies* II (2/3): 271–304.

Lynch, M. and J. Law (1990), 'Lists, Field Guides and the Descriptive Organization of Seeing: Bird Watching as an Exemplary Observational Activity' in M. Lynch and S. Woolgar (eds), *Representation in Scientific Practice*, Cambridge, Mass.: MIT Press, pp. 267–299.

© The Editorial Board of the Sociological Review 2003

Lynch, M. and J. Law (1999), 'Pictures, Texts and Objects: The Literary Language Game of Bird-watching', in M. Biagioli (ed.), *The Science Studies Reader*, London: Routledge, pp. 317–341.

Nicholson, M. (1989), 'National Styles, Divergent Classifications: A Comparative Case Study from the History of French and American Plant Ecology', *Knowledge and Society: Studies in the Sociology of Science Past and Present*, 8: 139–186.

Quinn, N. and D. Holland (1987), 'Culture and Cognition', in D. Holland and N. Quinn (eds), *Cultural Models in Language and Thought*, Cambridge: Cambridge University Press, pp. 3–40.

Reason, D. (1979), 'Classification, Time and the Organization of Production' in R. Ellen and D. Reason, *Classifications in their Social Context*, London: Academic Press, pp. 221–247.

Richards, T. (1993), *The Imperial Archive: Knowledge and the Fantasy of Empire*, London: Verso.

Ritvo, H. (1997), *The Platypus and the Mermaid and Other Figments of the Classifying Imagination*, Cambridge, Mass.: MIT Press.

Rodwell, J. S. (1991), *British Plant Communities: Volume 3: Grasslands and Montane Communities*, Cambridge: Cambridge University Press.

Roth, W-M. and G. M. Bowen (1999), 'Digitising Lizards: the Topology of Vision in Ecological Fieldwork', *Social Studies of Science*, 29(5): 719–764.

Sahlins, M. (1976), *Culture and Practical Reason*, Chicago: University of Chicago Press.

Schechner, R. (2000), *Performance Studies: An Introduction*, London: Routledge.

Schiebinger, L. (1996), 'Gender and Natural History' in N. Jardine, J. Secord and E. C. Spary (eds), *Cultures of Natural History*, Cambridge: Cambridge University Press, pp. 163–177.

Schieffelin, E. L. (1998), 'Problematising Performance' in Hughes-Freedland, F. (ed.), *Ritual, Performance, Media*, London: Routledge, pp. 194–207.

Sheets-Johnstone, M. (1979), *The Phenomenology of Dance*, London: Dance Books.

States, B. (1996), 'Performance as Metaphor', *Theatre Journal*, 48(1): 1–26.

Stewart, N. (1998), 'Relanguaging the Body: Phenomenological Descriptions of the Body Image', *Performance Research*, 3: 42–58.

Strauss, A. (1978), 'A Social World Perspective', *Studies in Symbolic Interaction*, 1: 119–128.

Suchman, L. (1987), *Plans and Situated Actions: The Problem of Human-Machine Communication*, Cambridge: Cambridge University Press.

Tyler, S. A. (1969), 'Introduction', in S. A. Tyler (ed.), *Cognitive Anthropology*, New York: Holt, Rinehart and Winston, pp. 1–23.

Secord, J. (1986), *Controversy in Victorian Science*, Cambridge: Cambridge University Press.

Thomas, K. (1984), *Man and the Natural World: Changing Attitudes in England 1500–1800*, London: Penguin.

Waterton, C. (2002), 'From Field to Fantasy: Classifying Nature: Constructing Europe', *Social Studies of Science*, 32(2): 177–204.

Verran, H. (2002), 'A Postcolonial Moment in Science Studies: Alternative Firing Regimes of Environmental Scientists and Aboriginal Landowners, *Social Studies of Science*, 32(5): 729–762.

© The Editorial Board of the Sociological Review 2003

Performing facts: finding a way over Scotland's mountains

Hayden Lorimer and Katrin Lund

In a letter dated 7th February 1895, Joseph Gibson Stott, first editor of the *Scottish Mountaineering Club Journal* and recent emigrant to New Zealand, offered his views on the quarterly's latest issue to William Douglas, his successor in the post:

> There is too much 'mountain timetable' these days . . . what I want is a paper—in which I can hear the roaring of the torrent, and see the snows and the brown heather and the clouds flying athwart the blue above the rocky peaks—something that will set my pulses beating; and conjure up dear old Scotland; and what is of no particular interest are some of these papers; all miles and fact and minutes, and endless dissection of the unhappy points of the compass. To me these are really little more interesting than an architect's specification for building a dry stane dyke.[1]

While readers might not necessarily share these views, amid the elegant protestations an intriguing line of argument emerges: one that sets up the aesthetic and sensual qualities of mountain walking in direct opposition to reductive and numerical abstractions of those same experiences on foot. For Gibson Stott, the familiar conventions of the romantic landscape canon were routed through a personal, emotional connection with nature's sublime qualities. However masterful, his mountaineer was also embodied: a sensing traveller attentive to feelings of freedom, awe and longing inspired by natural surroundings. It was with considerable regret that he noted efforts increasingly skewed towards a quantification of outdoor practice. His problem— perceived in bold relief—was a very different mode for registering outdoor experience: one based on objective measurement, cartographic knowledge and normative conduct. Numbers, facts and systems for order, it seems, were the province of an unpalatably rational frame of mind.

Introduction: the practice of abstraction

This century-old commentary marks the departure point for a chapter in which we consider various means by which 'hill-walking' is encoded, and enacted, as a popular leisure pursuit in the Scottish mountains. Drawing on findings from

© The Editorial Board of the Sociological Review 2003. Published by Blackwell Publishing Ltd, 9600 Garsington Road, Oxford OX4 2DQ, UK and 350 Main Street, Malden, MA 02148, USA

an ethnographic study we narrate, and critically analyse, a succession of meaningful phases from the prescription and performance of walking. Our ethnography was variously orientated: active and participative research in learning settings extended from hill-walking under both summer and winter conditions to the attendance of evening classes on mountain navigation skills and the prescribed study of technical instruction manuals detailing the lore of 'mountaincraft'. Evidence emerging from these activities is supported by material from interviews with members of hill-walking clubs and individual walkers.

The same archival commentary is a counterpoint to our arguments too. Unlike Gibson Stott, we do not want to isolate realms of objective and subjective expression, and thereby attribute to them a separate epistemological status. Instead, we want to draw attention to the complex nature, and function, of the 'objectifications' embedded *within*, and integral to, sensuous performances of nature. By doing so we caution against a disregard of quantitative measures as disembodied, and therefore unhelpful. By looking closely at the 'practical activity of objectification and abstraction itself' (Harvey, 1997: 10) we show how numbers, facts, rules and bearings are not mere abstractions but are themselves generated through certain kinds of embodied, emplaced and socially situated performance. Consequently, our comments explore the establishment, rehearsal and practice of systems of calculation and classification as negotiated acts, and as sensuous performances of nature. In sum, what we propose is an analysis of the relational interactions that create embodied subjectivities *and* standardized facts.

Given the suite of spatialized practices that concern us here—mapping, surveying, counting, navigating—and the instruments employed in them—compass, maps, lists, Global Positioning Satellites—we have found it helpful to extend our observations into cross-disciplinary debates on technology, materiality and skilled practice (Harvey, 1997; Graves-Brown, 2000). This field, fusing ideas from science studies and anthropology, suggests that transformations and continuities in technical capacity can be usefully confronted through an awareness of the social nature of material 'things' and practical tasks. Rather than being rendered inert, objects are then animated by intentions issued from the user in the context of a bodily engagement within an environment. What Ingold (1997: 112) says of the generation of artefacts is also, we argue, true of the generation of facts and numbers: they 'are not inscribed by the rational intellect upon the concrete surface of nature, but are rather generated in the course of the gradual unfolding of that field of forces and relations set up through the active and sensuous engagement of the practitioner and the material with which he or she works'. To draw these theoretical ideas into the grounded conditions of our own ethnographic research, is therefore to understand different embodied dispositions, technologies of walking and repeatable habits of use as co-constitutive and produced within generative fields of *doing*. If the self-conscious mobilization of ethnography—a mode of research that ordinarily involves site-based immersion—was partly intended as a practical means to cope with the continuous movement of our practising subjects, this methodological decision also provided the opportunity for an unhurried observation of the interplay between sensual and objectifying modes of performance as actual happenings on the mountainside. Ultimately, by moving and interacting with hill-walkers we ensured that our ideas emerged out of, and were re-worked and enriched through, direct embodied experience.

While these themes extend the reach of our notes on walking, we should also acknowledge that our observations are characterized simultaneously by certain particularities of place, and of performance. While cultures of walking in England have been subject to recent investigation (see Macnaghten and Urry, 1998; Matless, 1999; Edensor, 2000; Darby, 2000), we consider Scotland's mountains a distinctive (and under-researched) 'stage for action' (Edensor, 2002) that must be grounded in specific social and historical contexts. In this regard, we fall back on the notable contributions of pioneers from the modern history of hill-walking in Scotland to anchor the narrative and to allow us to track thematic trajectories of practice between past and present. Our ethnography of walking performances must then be understood according to localized formations, and customizations, of scientific knowledge, outdoor conduct and cartographic method. The identities of those contemporary hill-walkers encountered during the chapter in some measure reflect, but also creatively rework, a unique history of leisure practice in the Scottish mountains. We are careful to note how codifications of achievement, ability, risk and trust in hill-walking can be understood through a regulatory discourse promoted in guidebooks. However, when manifested as embodied practice they are, we argue, subject to improvisation and strategies of resistance.

The chapter sections that follow are structured around three pedestrian 'events', in each case founded on a mobile abstraction: first, tracing the trajectory, and performance, of the mountain as identifiable 'fact'; second, refining an equation for calculating speed of movement through a landscape; and third, mobilizing a geo-spatial abstraction with a pair of pacing legs and different navigational technologies. Taken in turn, each event oscillates between the geometrical spatialities of the mapped mountain and the sensed spatialities of the body. While by necessity our description and treatment of these events is separate, they should not be considered as discrete but, instead, understood as the connected elements of a process.

Creating the mountain as *fact*

Published in September 1891, the sixth issue of the *Scottish Mountaineering Club Journal*, included an inventory of all Scotland's mountains rising above a height of 3000ft. Divided into seventeen separate geographical sections, the 283 mountains were numbered, recorded by name, height, and grid reference number from available Ordnance Survey maps. Meticulously detailed, these classificatory 'Tables' were the end product of several years of surveying, measuring and mapping undertaken by Sir Hugh Thomas Munro, prodigious walker, cartographic critic, sportsman and Scottish landowner.

 © The Editorial Board of the Sociological Review 2003

Munro's labouring individualism is notable for having produced a localized enumerative solution to the ancient philosophical conundrum, 'What is a mountain?'. By treating mountains as identifiable *things* and establishing their status as recognized *facts*, his classification created an orderly idea of Scotland's highest topographical points. A great deal has since been written about this enigmatic project (Campbell, 1999; Dempster, 1995), but in the context of this chapter how might 'Munro's Tables' be understood? Mary Poovey's (1998) inquiry into the epistemological condition of the 'modern fact' offers some guidance. Tracing uncertain shifts in learned, and popular, opinion over what exactly should be counted, how material reality should be understood and how quantification might contribute to a systematic knowledge of the world, she outlines the status of the 'fact' as both ambiguous category and powerful epistemological unit. Poovey's choice of empirical study—the sciences of political economy and statistics—underscores a contention that for numbers to accumulate the social power necessary to secure the transformation into modern facts, their representation must suggest immunity to interpretation or theoretical analysis.

The numbers in 'Munro's Tables' certainly held an authoritative appeal for the élite, gentlemanly club of Victorian mountaineers among whom he was already a prominent and respected figure. Although arguably sanctioned as much by social status as by the probity of scientific method, his work was undoubtedly a key contribution to the geographical knowledge of Scotland. And yet, his numerical system transformed many 'mountains' into problematic abstractions. The criteria used for the award of 'mountain' status were far from transparent: while some peaks over 3000ft were indisputably 'mountains', other 'less shapely' summits were deemed otherwise. If the aneroid barometer and map were Munro's trusted companions, his judgements were also swayed by a visual and sensuous aesthetic. His original bundles of blue and white index cards confirm as much, recording an enthusiasm for numerical correction on the grounds of accuracy, but also hinting at decisions based on situated circumstance.

The legacy of these endeavours might best be understood as the topographical version of an unfinished symphony. During the past three decades his work, now recognized as 'The Munros', has been subject to ever more complex and arcane inspection and re-interpretation among mountaineering circles; on occasion culminating in organized programmes of revision, alteration and reformulation. As evidenced here, the trajectory of the classification can be traced through a conventional documentary archive. However, it is also possible to understand it as a schema that is choreographed through contemporary, and continuous, performance.

Performing mountain classification

The vocabulary of 'performance' can mask (sometimes sharply) contrasting interpretations of recent theories of performativity, which are themselves very different in orientation and agenda (Butler, 1990; Thrift, 1996). Our ambition here, informed by Nash (2000), is that the concept of performance be put to work in two ways: as a means better to understand material interactions at the level of body practice; and to consider the social conditions of identity formation that emerge through particular sets of relations with landscape. Performance as an intersection of the material and social prompts novel forms of analysis that can help to mobilize the otherwise static and inactive analysis of Scotland's mountains as a leisure resource among a practising outdoor community (see for example, Prentice and Guerin, 1998). By thinking 'performatively' we divert our course away from a conventional treatment of hill-walking as a behavioural procedure determined by crude cognitive choices. Instead we seek out the tensions and correspondences that exist—at different scales, and for individuals or collective groups—between formalized configurations of coded acts and an improvised realm of creative acts. These performative concerns extend directly into the various ways that people maintain and re-create the classification of 'mountain' as a matter of fact.

For many thousands of hill-walkers, the Munros provide a classificatory system around which everyday leisure practice can be organized. Collecting and ultimately completing an entire round of the mountain summits by independent ascent is a long-term objective recognized by many in this loose outdoor community. Such is the popularity of the pastime that a specialist terminology has entered the popular lexicon. Moreover as proof-positive of a significant social trend, associated stereotypes are widely referenced in the national media. Thus, 'Munro-bagging' is recognized as an activity indulged in by the 'Munro-bagger' who finds the habit of collection to have become an all-consuming one.

Greater sensitivity to the impulses that energize hill-walkers reveal very different, sometimes overlapping, leisure identities in which the underlying, or explicit, presence of this numerical classification unfolds into each personal account of performed practice. A commonly expressed theme, and one that holds potent appeal, is the sense of presence within a national space that hill-walking can engender (Withers, 2001: 236). To plot your own personal progress (Parks, 2001) through the Munros is a popular means to claim knowledge of Scotland's geography, while affording a grounded point of connection to historical events: 'I feel like this is a part of a tradition'. Patriotism and an awareness of the body politic can however, be surpassed by more visceral bodily expectations. Walkers clearly enjoy the motivation provided by a target that will spur them on to greater, possibly unexpected, physical efforts: 'I push myself to do it, I mean sometimes I don't find it easy'. However, recent converts can disturb romantic convention by choosing to understand, and articulate, acts of collection through a more modish body culture of 'empowerment' and 'goal-orientation'. To internalize the list, and sense it through a kinaesthetic 'burn', is a markedly different enterprise from one rooted in a national narrative.

Within each climb undertaken the existence of objective(s) can bring immediate physical satisfaction while also contributing to a longer trajectory of factual reward: 'Well firstly, I am touching the top to say I have got there and maybe that's another one ticked you know . . . the famous tick, you know'. With

© The Editorial Board of the Sociological Review 2003

continued walking experience, and the steady accumulation of 'ticked-off' summits, the appeals of a quantitative understanding of walking experience become more evident. For many individuals, the collection of facts is a healthy distraction within the greater physical challenge of what many acknowledge as 'a game'. For some, the importance of an exhaustive, internal order to things emerges as a more illicit pleasure: 'I think I must be in danger of *Munrosis hyperdocumentalis*. In addition to full records of the climbs, I have elaborate data sheets giving distances and heights, time taken, times between peaks and so on . . .'. This confessional mode, allied to a knowing reflexivity in self-description, is crucial to many walkers as a means to avoid the barbs and jibes attached to the label, 'Munro-bagger'. However avid their 'summiteering' might become, the function of any outing can still be reduced to that of a harmless diversion: 'I think one of the things that appeals to me the most about this is . . . that it is just ridiculous.' Those who contend that the essence of walking should be strictly processual and phenomenal, however, look disapprovingly on any element of competition and the urgent desire to secure just one more fact, en route to the ultimate conclusion: 'quite a lot of my friends have finished and they became sort of obsessive about you know—'must do this hill, must tick it off'—even if they saw nothing. I don't enjoy that at all, so I have kind of fallen behind'.

De Certeau (1984) alerts us to the mobile strategies of resistance that pedestrians deploy to (re)create the city streets. In similar measure, it is possible to unpack complex tactics for movement within the staged setting that Scottish hill-walking and the Munro classification offers. Gently subversive and playful types of performance act as important statements of intent, and as markers for an alternative sensibility, within the wider community of collectors. 'Anti-munroists' steadfastly refuse to count summits, or keep a list, and in the most extreme cases, even to climb mountains with Munro status. Walkers on the verge of completion elect not to complete the round, while some of those who do, decide not to have their name entered on the official, all-time list of 'Munroists'. For some, the visual imperative in hill-walking is taken to its logical extent by only counting those summits from which a clear view was visible. Others observe a puritanical adherence to the original classification by ignoring all subsequent changes, or customize the accepted standard: 'My own "rules" differ from the lists in the current Tables, but as the Tables in their entirety fall within my own tables, officialdom should be satisfied'.

Evidently, the classification of Scotland's 'mountains' as identifiable facts is manifested in a wide variety of performances of both personal and collective identities. Different enactments mobilize conflicting ideas over the authenticity of natural experience, create deliberate displays of national identity, reflect urges for bodily improvement, and more fully socialize the systematic abstractions of collection. When refracted through Poovey's aforementioned thesis for the modern fact—that power and status is founded on an apparent imperviousness to change—Munro's Tables do not seem to fit the mould. Arguably it is their inherently contestable and malleable nature, rather than any putative impunity, that has ensured an enduring appeal.

© The Editorial Board of the Sociological Review 2003

In the two sections that follow we focus our attention on different walking 'events' that spatialize the mobile sensing body, against the mountain as both mapped form and material terrain. By observing performed action at close quarters, we consider how different abstractions, quantitative measures and navigational technologies function within embodied movements as they are planned for in instruction classes, and as they then happen in the landscape.

Calculating a route on the map and visualizing an objective

The 'Notes and Queries' section of the *Scottish Mountaineering Club Journal* for December 1889 included a brief account of a day's outing in the Central Highlands written by one William Naismith, then a mountaineer of growing repute. Factual in tone and practical in intent, his entry closed thus:

> The east side of Stobinian . . . retained its ordinary Alpine appearance. Distance, ten miles; total climb, 6300ft; time, six and a half hours (including short halts). This tallies exactly with a simple formula, that may be found useful in estimating what time men in fair condition should allow for easy expeditions, namely, an hour for every three miles on the map, with an additional hour for every 2000ft of ascent. (Naismith, 1889)

Reported with the minimum of fuss this was, ostensibly, a modest contribution to the journal's statistical marginalia. There was certainly little to hint at a longer trajectory that would transform his humble formula into 'Naismith's Rule', a time-honoured artefact for determining speed of movement through a landscape. Tailored to suit the topography of Scotland's mountains, it is still judged in standard mountaincraft handbooks to be 'just as valid today as it ever was' (Langmuir, 1984: 14). A simple formula on paper, in practice it requires a form of 'cartographic literacy' in which calculations switch between the flat representational plane of the map and the anticipation of embodied movement through a landscape. These successive shifts from abstraction to experience require fuller consideration.

During research, we found that instruction classes on mountain navigation reveal much about the application, and refinement, of this specific technique. On every possible occasion, the importance of miles and minutes as basic controls in a hill-walking outing are impressed on the learning student, often in the form of rudimentary questions: 'where are you heading?', 'what is the objective of the walk?' and 'how long will it take to get there?'. Responses are steered by a mounting awareness of remoteness, long distances and the unpredictability of weather conditions. The precautionary register is captured in a recognized code for safe and responsible conduct founded on sound navigational training: it is incumbent on the walker to begin pedestrian practice prior to any actual movement on foot.

With a preparatory decision taken on a likely summit the walker's next move is to measure the length of the planned route, and estimate the time needed to meet the objective. The map surface is to be understood through contour mark-

© The Editorial Board of the Sociological Review 2003

ings, duly measured in accordance with Naismith's Rule. The instructions given by the mountaineering instructor are simple and concise: 'Take out a map and visualize where you are going'. The implication is clear, that the map will provide a 'visual reality to an invisible reality' (Jacob, 1999: 29). Yet, we are still left pondering how this activity actually occurs. Of specific interest are the walker's attempts to *see* and *feel* the route as it emerges through the map before any embodied action occurs *in* the landscape.

In later lessons on the use of Naismith's rule, the class instructor supplements the measurement of distance, height, gradient of ascent and descent with additional considerations: 'terrain, experience, fitness, rucksack weight, navigational confidence'. At the same time as attempting accurately to measure the proposed walk in terms of quantitative measurements on the map, the instructor readjusts these calculations by reading known bodily capacities *onto* the map. While the novice might look at the map from a position on high, and only see a confusion of lines, markings and numbers, the more experienced walker learns to use the map as a way of looking *into* the landscape, and seeing how the topography rises and falls. By steadily examining the route it is possible to visualize landscape and speculate about the types of terrain likely to be encountered. Thus the summit objective, when conceived of within an embodied context of ascending or descending, becomes 'a key point only through its location within a broader narrative' (Matless, 1999: 200). It is important to recognize this more complexly layered process of cartographic visualization, when the map becomes a medium between the anticipating body and the still distant landscape. In this mode, the act of measuring and judgement begins to exceed quantitative facts established from a simple currency of metres and contours. These preparatory abilities are succinctly described by one hill-walker: 'The skills you have are what control you, and what you do. And the skills you have make the objective the skill of knowing what you can do and what you are ready to do'.

While navigational instructions presuppose a pure and objective realm of cognitive decision-making, the sentient aspects of these preparatory activities are less readily acknowledged. Arguably, it is the instructional imperative of possible risk and individual responsibility in hill-walking that renders the core message as one of rational, calculated action. Nevertheless, the importance of Naismith's rule is diluted by practice. It recedes into the background, overcome by the complexity and intensity of a dialogue between walker and map. If afforded its simplest definition, such a rule creates an identifiable relation between two objective facts. It then offers a resource for action. When placed under scrutiny in a field of practice, Naismith's version functions with lesser claims to accuracy and more of the characteristics that Lucy Suchman (1987: 55) identifies in a 'rule-of-thumb'. Malleable and alterable, the numerical products are open to reconfiguration and do not comprehensively regulate action. This version of mountain performance is based around the variabilities that open up within the calculation. As a quantitative event, much rests on its adaptive character: a standardized formula that will have to bear the weight of a body moving along the course of the route. Here, the establishment of a code for safe conduct and mountain mobility draws on the geometric order of the map and the anticipated reactions of the body.

Moving, bearing, counting and pacing

For our third walking event, we want to consider relations between embodied performance and numerical abstraction, during phases of movement across the mountain landscape. Equipped with an objective and a planned route, for the hill-walker the inter-subjectivities of practice are no longer limited to sensed visualization and are further complicated by relations with underfoot conditions, the surrounding landscape and navigational technologies. Differently practised techniques are required—these prioritize an understanding of the body felt through the physical terrain. On this particular occasion, it is helpful to consider a narrated sequence of embodied actions in place.

Immediately on setting out, for the walker there is a marked shift in attention from the terrain of the map to the ground that is being passed over. During the earliest stages of the route, a path is often followed which clearly guides the way ahead. The walker takes care to step over stones and boggy areas, but can take advantage of the relatively accommodating terrain to enjoy the landscape, viewed in 'wide-screen'. While the map is occasionally consulted, for the moment this is simply for verification of route judgement, or path selection. As the maintained or marked route gradually peters out, the experience of more immediate surroundings becomes acute and the practice of walking alters. On encountering more challenging terrain movement inevitably slows, sometimes until 'every step . . . become[s] a separate decision about direction and safety, and the simplest act of walking is transformed into a specialized skill' (Solnit, 1999: 133–134).

The multi-dimensional movements now required of the hill-walker have been subject to bio-mechanical prescription. For J. E. B. Wright (1955: 46) moving through the mountains was to be most accurately understood as an art requiring the 'proper use of parts of the body'. Replicable anatomical practice required the hill-walker to concentrate on balance and maintaining equilibrium between the locomotive power of legs lifting and a straight back supporting. W. H. Murray (1955: 5) was similarly convinced that discipline was the means to experience ultimate liberation: '. . . we must . . . get for ourselves a real technical competence. When we have that we can walk safely; only then do we know freedom, and only in freedom can real joy be ours'. But in this science of bi-pedalism, actions tend to be isolated from context. A more persuasive explanation of this intimate phenomenology of a body's spatial realm is offered by Jan Hendrik van den Berg (1952: 170), who imagines traversing an irregular surface in the company of the mountaineer:

> . . . the body is realized as landscape: the length of the body is demonstrated by the insurmountable steep bits necessitating a roundabout way, the measure of his stride

© The Editorial Board of the Sociological Review 2003

by the nature of the gradient which it is just possible or just not possible for him to climb, the size of his foot is proved by the measurements of the projecting point that serve as footholds.

One hill-walker's description of grounded practice develops this relational theme, suggesting the scaled spatialities embedded in her own performance and a need to align different bodily capacities:

'For me walking is a physical activity, it is a demanding physical activity sometimes, it also requires that you think about it, thinking so your mind has to be engaged . . . so there is an acute awareness of the sort of micro-environment as well as the larger situation.'

For our own notional hill-walker a change in conditions can necessitate different technical proficiencies. Featureless terrain, the absence of a visible path or a deterioration in the weather, encountered in any combination, mean that the embodied, relational dialogue must once again assimilate navigational technologies. Safe passage is dependent on continued map consultation and, for the first time, compass use *in situ*. Until now only a background presence in the walking experience, the compass now becomes its controlling mechanism. A bearing must be taken between two different points on route, and any judgement made of distance covered is predicated on a precise count of walking steps that have been taken. Instruction manuals and mountain instructors are quick to stress the significance of this skill: '. . . a *sense of direction* is a myth. On mountains and in bad visibility it is dangerous myth'. The chief skills for the hill-walker to master are reading the compass and then placing trust in it as a responsible device. In some measure, control and responsibility shifts from the hill-walker to the compass, which incorporates the technical solution to any navigational difficulty and can displace personal anxieties about safety and the unpredictability of conditions.

However once again, intimate observation and experience reveal a more complex arrangement of networked actions, intentions and agencies. For one walker, following a bearing requires a carefully co-ordinated series of skilled actions:

'Your head is down, you don't want anyone talking to you and you're counting. It's just you, and a bearing. Line up the needle, your feet and the base-plate. Keep the needle over the base-plate. You're trying not to fall over and trying not to lose count.'

While the isolation of this calculated act seems to him like 'the ultimate abstraction of the hill-walking experience', it also requires a very intimate understanding of a body moving on the mountain. Starting with a baseline number of walking paces per 100 metres, a succession of quick and small adjustments are made to this figure according to the terrain underfoot and the purchase it offers. This process is explained by our walker as 'reading the ground through your body', where a tight focus must be maintained on only that which is immediate. Sensory feedback—'this is tough and it hurts', 'I'm on a roll'—is determined in response to the feeling of leg muscles moving and foot placement.

Aligned with this practised response the counting continues; fingers occasionally clicking on a knitting counter carried especially to help keep tally. A halt in progress presumably, (hopefully), means the target point has been reached. Here, the walker takes stock, using the map to determine a new target point. And so the same process begins over again, and if weather permits, until the summit is eventually attained. In skilled hands, the compass is incorporated into a processing loop of thought, judgement and action that allows the walker continuously and fluently to adjust movement through an on-going perceptual monitoring of the task as it unfolds.

Arguably, what has eventually come to represent the walker's objective is not the summit itself, but rather the process of getting there, and getting back, and being able to judge and examine skills and abilities in transit. As Ingold (2000: 239) asserts '. . . we know *as* we go, not *before* we go. Thus the operation is not complete until one has reached one's final destination: only then can the traveller truly claim to have found his way'. In combination, a situated and emergent alliance between numerical order and bodily improvisation seems to erode the assured tone of the navigational instruction manual in which actions are presented as the execution of pre-conceived, cognitive plans. The notion of a rational sequencing of thoughts and actions is belied by practice where 'discursivity and subjectivity are complicated by simultaneous pre-discursive encounters' (Crouch, 2001: 70). The bearing, counted and paced out, is a constant within the complexity and unpredictability of the practised task. As Lucy Suchman (1987) persuasively argues, what surrounds this navigational calculation is a context of action in relation to surrounding objects, phenomena and subjective practice. It is the complexly layered and continuous dialogue of modifications between hill-walker, compass, map, the ground passed over and prevailing weather conditions that dictate situated practice. This, then, is to mobilize a specific quantification through a sensual *process*, following the bearing requires our walker to take the abstraction and act it out through an orderly performance.

Encompassing new means to navigate

Hill-walkers carry a keen awareness of historical practice with them, and purposefully inscribe techniques into their own preparations and actions. The learning walker is encouraged to adopt an entire language of Scotland's mountains into their personal identity and then to find orientation through acts of planning, walking, counting and collecting. Regular and knowledgeable references are made to the quantitative systems for ordering or abstracting embodied experience devised by Munro and Naismith. That there is on-going and active social life for these traditional methods and techniques perhaps goes some way towards explaining the ambivalence (and sometimes outright resistance) shown to particular technological innovations in walking. Attitudes displayed towards the use of Global Positioning Satellite (GPS) receivers are a revealing case in point.

© The Editorial Board of the Sociological Review 2003

The recent advent of GPS devices as portable hand-held navigation instruments, and the rapid realization of their marketability for outdoor leisure practice, is based around the promise of immediate and precise locational data expressed as a set of geo-spatial co-ordinates (Parks, 2001). While this holds obvious appeal for mountain navigation, walkers often display a hesitancy or reluctance towards this technological innovation: 'I have got one and I have used it. I try not to rely on it, I use it as a last resort . . . when we seem to be lost'. This statement captures a particular ethic of traditionalism in respect to skilled navigational practice that prevails among many hill-walkers. It is a commonly held expectation that knowledge and competence are accrued through practical application and well-grooved technique. For one experienced mountain guide: 'the whole hill-walking experience is to do with making decisions on your own, or a group of people making decisions together'. To orient practice according to this 'moral compass' means that individual safety and responsibility are learned and, as a corollary, peer respect is earned. Such is the power of this code that one walker with an extensive tick-list of mountain summits still feels her achievements diminished for want of having taken on independent navigational responsibility. If for some practitioners an over-reliance on the act of following, rather than leading, is problematic, then GPS is further evidence of 'a great move at the moment for people to hand over the decision making as if it is an adjunct to the whole experience'. Here, the basis of critique is one that understands GPS as a navigational guide, promoting a counter-intuitive logic where (in effect) you can know the exact position at which you stand, without any idea of where you are in a sensed landscape. As such GPS *seems* to be founded on a Cartesian, disembodied understanding of landscape.

Other active walkers give off similarly mixed messages about GPS and its possible uses: it is variously understood as a marker of increasingly professionalized practice, a mechanism to reduce personal risk, a dangerous gadget likely to encourage acts of irresponsibility and an intrusive presence in the hill-walking experience. Our mountain instructor suggested a cautionary and partial process of assimilation, with no displacement of compass work. A careful balance was suggested on acceptable technology, and on what are safe or acceptable forms of use. Meanwhile, a fellow walker—increasingly conscious of his wider responsibilities to friends and family—found a regular partner unprepared to join him on future outings to the mountains because of his choice to use a GPS for security. In this particular case, GPS seemed to disrupt the more intimate experiences associated with hill-walking in Scotland, and the seductive wilderness ideal that demarcates a space for leisure practice clearly separated from modernity.

The adoption of new technology is already delineating new forms of relational practice, and is the cause of a rescheduling in the acknowledged code for responsible, navigational conduct. Arguably, rejection also requires the reconfiguration of that same code. Evidently, the hill-walker holding this bit of 'kit' does not move across an isotropic plain, but acts in a social space. A technology of totalizing vision and knowledge that threatens to subsume personal practice can be understood alternatively as a facility that usefully extends bodily capacities and re-works versions of the self in nature. We suggest that attention can most usefully focus on the complex social mechanisms—stories, actions, histories and memories—employed in the active negotiation of this technology and the abstract information it offers. It is in such material and meaningful relations that the performativity of social identity becomes most apparent. There are clear continuities here with our treatment of the classificatory list, the map and the compass: all are technologies founded on the practice of abstraction *and* on sensual engagement. In an evolving genealogy of navigational technology in hill-walking, GPS certainly disrupts established modes of interactivity and relational conduct, but clearly does not disallow them.

Conclusion

Our chosen approach in this chapter has been to create a cultural biography of mountain quantification that focuses on the continuous social circulation and performance of facts. Framed in this way, 'facts' can then be more accurately understood as incomplete abstractions, since each is mobilized by different pairs of hands and feet, situated in historical contexts, and embedded in certain landscapes. The personal paths that they follow reflect the interplay between technologies, human agency and spaces of practice. None of our three narrated walking events can therefore be treated as static entities. Successively re-calibrated through actions, they are bound to be always process *and* product. Consequently, we are not content to limit ourselves to the set of tropes currently employed in performative theories to explain elements of body movement and the experience of mobility: a smooth-textured, amorphous realm of fluids, flows, rhythms, contingencies and desires that does not seem to settle (Thrift, 1996; Urry, 2001). To these must be added, orderings, facts, classifications, formulae and quantitative abstractions which, while by no means fixed or permanent, are important presences and significations in the performance of nature. Perhaps we might consider them as friction points in the flow of fleeting improvisations that constitute our performances in, and of, these settings.

It is our hope that this chapter has begun to place numbers as social and performed entities, and has not simply played with them. In this we are conscious of how, for Trevor Barnes and Matthew Hannah (2001: 380), 'to demonstrate that numbers partly construct reality, rather than only representing it' requires work that explores 'how context enters into the very pores of numbers and statistical techniques'. Using qualitative methods to explore the embodied animation of quantitative abstractions means being sensitive to contrasting forms of knowledge production, but not definitive as to their relationship. We certainly want to displace any crude definition of binary epistemological opposites, and thereby avoid the implication of an 'either-or' decision. According to James Corner 'our knowledge and experience of space is more ontological or 'lived' than it is mathematical or Cartesian' (1999: 214). We would suggest that it is both at once, an alternative phenomenology dependent on the practice of

© The Editorial Board of the Sociological Review 2003

abstraction *in* sensual movement. Moreover, by examining quantitative knowledge production and negotiation as performed practice we have begun to attend to the recent assertion that '. . . statistics are much too important to be left only to the statisticians. How and why they are constructed, by whom and about whom, how they are used and publicised, and to what ends and for those interests, are critical social scientific questions for critical social scientists' (Barnes and Hannah, 2001: 379–380).

Having so consciously emphasized not just the situated and the sensed but the processual aspects of walking, in conclusion it is worth posing the question: 'are the chapter's three meaningful 'events' not then just a means to an end?'. If this *was* the case then abstraction and objectification would be always, *and only*, generative activities that achieve a desired result: fluent, safe walking. Here we might draw an illustrative comparison between the hill-walker and a musician carefully following a score comprised of close notation: once flow, order and rhythm are realized systematic practice dissolves into the full orchestral performance. We don't subscribe to this premise; nor we suspect would the many thousands of hill-walkers carefully plotting their own personal signature by name, date and number across Scotland's geography of mountains. As they themselves demonstrate, numbers, rules and bearings are emergent within the process of walking itself, and then in turn feed back into that process. Our intention has been to initiate a type of inquiry into pedestrian practice that scrutinizes the spatial orderings, localised identities and sentient improvisations that make facts and abstractions. That this has been possible through a palpable realm of gestures, movements, postures, protocols, actions and reactions might prompt comparative work in the continuing study of different performances of nature.

Acknowledgements

We would like to thank all the walkers who took part in the research project which was funded by an award from the Economic and Social Research Council (Ref: R000223603). Tim Ingold, Nick Spedding and the book editors offered helpful, insightful and critical comment which we hope is reflected here. Responsibility for the writing remains our own.

Notes

1 Extract from a letter held in archives at the National Library of Scotland: National Library of Scotland (NLS) Acc. 11538 Dep. 41.

References

Barnes, T. J. and M. Hannah (2001), 'The Place Of Numbers: Histories, Geographies and Theories Of Quantification', *Environment and Planning D: Society and Space*, 19(4): 379–383.

© The Editorial Board of the Sociological Review 2003   143

Butler, J. (1990), *Gender Trouble and the Subversion of Identity*, London: Routledge.

Campbell, R. (ed.) (1999), *The Munroist's Companion*, Edinburgh: Scottish Mountaineering Trust.

Corner, J. (1999), 'The Agency of Mapping: Speculation, Critique and Invention', in D. Cosgrove (ed.), *Mappings*, London: Reaktion, pp. 213–252.

Crouch, D. (2001), 'Spatialities and the Feeling of Doing', *Social and Cultural Geography*, 2(1): 61–75.

De Certeau, M. (1984), *The Practice of Everyday Life*, tr. S. Rendall, Berkeley and London: University of California Press.

Dempster, A. (1995), *The Munro Phenomenon*, Edinburgh: Mainstream.

Darby, W. (2000), *Landscape and Identity: Geographies of Nation and Class in England*, London: Berg.

Edensor, T. (2000), 'Walking through the British Countryside: Reflexivity, Embodied Practices and Ways to Escape', *Body and Society*, 6(3): 81–106.

Edensor, T. (2002), 'Performing Tourism, Staging Tourism: (Re)Producing Tourist Space and Practice', *Tourist Studies*, 1(1): 59–81.

Graves-Brown, P. M. (ed.) (2000), *Matter, Materiality and Modern Culture*, London: Routledge.

Harvey, P. (1997), 'Introduction: Technology as Skilled Practice' *Social Analysis: Journal of Cultural and Social Practice*, 41(1): 3–14.

Ingold, T. (1997), 'Eight Themes in the Anthropology of Technology' *Social Analysis: Journal of Cultural and Social Practice*, 41(1): 106–138.

Ingold, T. (2000), *The Perception of the Environment: Essays in Livelihood, Dwelling and Skill*, London: Routledge.

Jacob, C. (1999), 'Mapping in the Mind: the Earth from Ancient Alexandria' in D. Cosgrove (ed) *Mappings*, London: Reaktion pp. 24–49.

Langmuir, E. (1984), *Mountaincraft and Leadership*, Glasgow: Scottish Sports Council.

Macnaghten, P. and J. Urry (1998), *Contested Natures*, London: Sage.

Matless, D. (1999), 'The Uses of Cartographic Literacy: Mapping, Survey and Citizenship in Twentieth-century Britain' in D. Cosgrove (ed.), *Mappings*, London: Reaktion, pp. 193–212.

Murray, W. H. (1955), 'Foreword' in J. E. B. Wright, *The Technique of Mountaineering: A Handbook of Established Methods*, London: Nicholas Kaye.

Naismith, W. (1889), 'Notes and Queries', *Scottish Mountaineering Club Journal*, 2(3): 133.

Nash, C. (2000), 'Performativity in Practice: Some Recent Work in Cultural Geography', *Progress in Human Geography*, 24(4): 653–664.

Parks, L. (2001), 'Plotting the Personal: Global Positioning Satellite and Interactive Media', *Ecumene*, 8(2): 209–222.

Prentice, R. and S. Guerin (1998), 'The Romantic Walker? A Case Study of Users of Iconic Scottish Landscape', *Scottish Geographical Magazine*, 15: 713–756.

Poovey, M. (1998), *A History of the Modern Fact: Problems of Knowledge in the Sciences of Wealth and Society*, Chicago: University of Chicago Press.

Solnit, R. (2000), *Wanderlust: A History of Walking*, London: Penguin.

Suchman, L. A. (1987), *Plans and Situated Actions: The Problem of Human Machine Communication*, Cambridge: Cambridge University Press.

Thrift, N. (1996), *Spatial Formations*, London: Sage.

Urry, J. (1999), *Sociology Beyond Societies: Mobilities for the Twenty-First Century*, London: Routledge.

van den Berg, J. H. (1952), 'The Human Body and the Significance of Human Movement: A Phenomenological Study', *Philosophy and Phenomenological Research*, XIII: 159–183.

Withers, C. W. J. (2001), *Geography, Science And National Identity: Scotland Since 1520*, Cambridge: Cambridge University Press.

Wright, J. E. B. (1955), *The Technique of Mountaineering: A Handbook of Established Methods*, London: Nicholas Kaye.

© The Editorial Board of the Sociological Review 2003

Performing place in nature reserves

Matthew Watson

The concept of place has had a difficult time over the last two decades. In previous incarnations, it has been a defining concept in traditions of geography. Conventional academic conceptualizations of place, however, have become moribund, tending to be blind to trans-local processes and the inequalities that result from them. Place as it has been dominantly formulated in academic discourse has recently been judged as too sedentary, static and parochial for social sciences that are increasingly concerned with tracing the flows, processes and hybridity of subjects, identities and spaces (see, for example, Doel, 1999). This chapter grapples with changing notions of place, arguing that place, if it is seen as *relationally performed*, can enjoy a revitalization that incorporates suggestions of flows, mobility, and hybridity of meaning. Using the vocabulary of performance enables an alternative notion of place—as an emergent effect of a complex mix of relations incorporating human subjects and agential non-human nature.

There have been various attempts to revive place as an analytical approach. Doreen Massey (1991; 1993) made an influential contribution, through her articulation of an outward looking 'progressive sense of place', which recognizes the contingency and porosity of the boundaries of places, and the networks of social relations in which they exist. From perspectives focusing more upon the hybridity and relationality of place, theorists including Nigel Thrift (1999) and Kevin Hetherington (1997) have made their own contributions to re-invigorated discussion of place. My engagement with the process of revitalizing the concept is through an exploration of place as an emergent effect of heterogeneous relationships, distributed across conventional boundaries between entities as well as through space and time. I develop this account through an exploration of some of the diverse ways in which place is performed in the distinctive context of nature reserves.

Nature reserves can appear as very 'local' spaces. The particular mix of animals and plants that characterize a reserve are a specific effect of the interplay of complex physical processes in a locality. These of course include ecological processes such as climate, soils and topography, but these are also intertwined with the local practices of humans as they have worked the land over generations. In an overcrowded land like the UK, many nature reserves also

© The Editorial Board of the Sociological Review 2003. Published by Blackwell Publishing Ltd, 9600 Garsington Road, Oxford OX4 2DQ, UK and 350 Main Street, Malden, MA 02148, USA

provide valuable local spaces for informal recreational practices like walking the dog. Through such material and social characteristics and uses, reserves can exemplify an approach to place as an emergent effect of relations between human subjects and agential nonhuman nature, often enacted through non-representational practices. The first section of this chapter elucidates such an approach.

There is a further layer to this, however, which gives the starting point for the second section of this chapter. Paradoxically, most nature reserves only continue to exist as distinctive local spaces because they exist also as standardized representations, such as species lists and habitat descriptions, in a much more universalized context. Through such representations, the local space of a reserve can be placed in frameworks of generic ecological knowledge and conservation evaluation, attributed value as a regional, national or international biodiversity resource, and consequently afforded some level of protection and management. The processes that, through protection and conservation, have maintained some local distinctiveness in a reserve also disembed it. The meanings of this particular, local space are distributed into institutional circuits of knowledge and meaning that spread across nations and continents. The practices and processes involved in turning a reserve into a scientific object are explored in the second section of the chapter. The abstracted, reductionist constitution of nature reserve sites that representations such as species lists and habitat descriptions offer appears to conflict, at a foundational level, with the fluid, relational performance of place that I outline in the first section.

However, what emerges from an analysis of the apparently divergent ways of performing nature reserves is an appreciation of the diversity of actors that share relational agency in the performance of place. Incorporating technological entities as well as natural nonhumans, universalistic knowledge as well as non-representational practices, into an account of one nature reserve results in a understanding of place as emergent not only from immediate practices of engagement between a human and the already present materiality of a site, but from a much more heterogeneous and distributed amalgam of relationships.

Reflecting the accommodation of nonhumans in my account of the performance of place, the chapter's two sections, outlined above, start from an exploration of two specific nonhuman entities, which exist a few hundred metres apart on a heath in Dorset. The first is a rock.

Godlingston's rock and the relationality of place

On Godlingston Heath, part of the Studland peninsula on the coast of Dorset, stands the Agglestone (Figure 1). This rock is a locus of meaning, as illustrated by the multiplicity of origin stories for it. One story has it that a giant threw it from the Isle of Wight in retaliation against the giant who threw what are now the pinnacles to the Isle of Wight. Another that the Devil, on the Isle of Wight, hurled the rock at Corfe Castle (a few miles to the west of Godlingston) but it

 © The Editorial Board of the Sociological Review 2003

Figure 1: *Agglestone Rock, from Swain (1893)*

fell short. A third that the Devil somehow mislaid it whilst on the way to drop it on Salisbury Cathedral. A fourth, that it was moved into place to top a barrow.[1] A fifth—that it is just a big rock that has been eroded in situ by the elements.

The Agglestone is striking in its physical context, roughly eight metres high and sitting on top of its own knoll, which elevates it strikingly above an immediate context of homogeneous, if wild, undulating heather dominated land. Its morphology has been more striking historically. Until it finally toppled in 1970, it was a logan-stone: all 500 tons of it could be rocked on the protuberance that it stood on.

What does it mean to suggest that the Agglestone is a 'locus of meaning'? The origin stories mentioned above as evidence of its meaning can easily be seen as cultural constructions laid over the materiality of the stone. Such an understanding of meaning in nonhuman nature would be coherent with the model under post-structuralist accounts of the meaning individuals or societies attach to material entities (see Barnes and Duncan, 1992).Within post-structuralist geography in the 1990s, the material reality that underlies 'landscape' is typically left as a passive backdrop upon which culture's meanings are inscribed (Thrift, 1996).

This position is part of the conceptual division between society and nature, and between human and nonhuman, that has been a near ubiquitous feature of social science at least since Emile Durkheim (Latour, 1993; Breslau, 2000).

Whether it is in terms of an autonomous Cartesian subject, or in terms of Durkheim's collective conscience of the social group, the nonhuman is left passive, constituting a mute world external to either the individual human subject or the collective subjectivity of society. For meaning to be found in relation to a radically separate nonhuman nature, it has to be something that human culture lays upon the semiotically silent materiality. The Agglestone, however, in its materiality and that of its surroundings, attests to the shallowness of such approaches, revealing the extent to which meanings are not laid upon materiality, but emerge from interaction with it.

The diversity of practices of engagement through which the meanings of the Agglestone emerge begin to present themselves simply in consideration of what it takes to experience the rock. No observer of the rock exists at some abstracted no-place. Most people who experience the Agglestone directly have to get themselves there by walking, running, cycling or horse riding. They have to engage with the place not only visually, but also corporeally. The knoll that the Agglestone sits upon means that from every direction anyone approaching it closely must ascend. Even approaching from the south, where the land is higher and the ascent therefore smaller, is enough of an ascent to register in one's 'muscular consciousness' (Bachelard, 1964; Ingold, 1993: 167).

These forms of bodily engagement are themselves transformative of the place. The paths leading to and from it on the north and south sides and the erosion control measures show how the rock draws people around it. The paths, along with the crater of bare sand surrounding the rock, are the product of the ground being eroded over decades and centuries as people pass by, walk around, climb on and off or sit beneath the rock. The rock itself bears testimony to how people engage with it. White marks on the rock are left by the chalked-up hands of rock climbers. Graffiti covers the easily carved multi-coloured sandstone.

With these interactions and relationships in mind we can talk about the rock as 'drawing the place around it'. It is clear that the place that the Agglestone draws around it is not fully accounted for by the physical reality of the place, its rocks, soils, paths and landforms. But neither is it a purely social product, a construct being laid upon the place by disembodied culture. The Agglestone, in the materiality of the rock and its surroundings, demonstrates clearly how place is constituted through an active relationship between people and things. The traces people leave—the chalk, the graffiti, the erosion—demonstrate how place is constituted through embodied engagement with materiality. The place that the rock gathers around itself exists neither in the materiality, nor as pure cultural construct; it exists in the relationships between the human and the nonhuman in local context. The nonhuman shares in the relational agency with which the place is made.

Understanding place as constituted through embodied practices engaged in the locality resonates with Martin Heidegger's concept of dwelling, which has become a frequent referent in sociological reflection on place, environment, landscape and nature over recent years (Harvey, 1996; Bender, 1998; Macnaghten and Urry, 1998, 2001; Malpas, 1998; Thrift, 1999; Cloke and Jones,

2001). To a large extent, the revival of the concept in this field has been via the work of Tim Ingold, particularly in his paper *The Temporality of the Landscape* (1993). As authors who have applied it argue, dwelling offers paths through key debates and dichotomies of current and recent social theory (Ingold, 1993, 1995, 2000; Thrift, 1996; Macnaghten and Urry, 1998, 2001). Ingold sees the 'dwelling perspective' as offering a means to:

> ... move beyond the sterile opposition between the naturalistic view of the landscape as a neutral, external backdrop to human activities, and the culturalistic view that every landscape is a particular cognitive or symbolic ordering of space (1993: 152).

Phil Macnaghten and John Urry (1998) present dwelling as offering a perspective that contests conventional divides between nature and culture and prioritizes the role of practices in understanding people's relationships with nonhuman nature. It is this focus on practice, and with it a relational understanding of human existence in which the material has an agential role, which means that a dwelling perspective can allow us to move beyond idealist/realist dichotomies. Meaning exists neither 'out there' in independent material reality, nor 'in here' as the representations of autonomous human mind. Indeed, it is this very division of outside and inside in relation to the human subject, a divide so near absolute in Cartesian formulations of the subject, which Heideggerian phenomenology undermines. Rather, meaning emerges from and exists in the practices of engagement between the human and the nonhuman.

Heidegger's theories have had considerable influence on a range of contemporary social science approaches that focus on practices and embodiment. Nigel Thrift traces this wide influence of Heidegger amongst theorists to:

> ... the fact that Heidegger 'does not ground his thinking in everyday concepts, but in average everyday practice; in what people do, not what they say they do' (Dreyfus and Hall, 1992: 2). Such a view of an 'engaged agency' (Taylor, 1993) leads Heidegger to jettison the Cartesian way of thinking of human beings, as isolated and disengaged subjects who represent objects to themselves, and to settle instead for the world-disclosing function of practices which always assumes a background of implicit familiarity, competence and concern or involvement. (1996: 10)

Consequently, a focus on embodied practices through which people engage with the materiality of a site gives a means of transcending the dichotomy of nature and culture as it can be applied, in different formulations, to our understanding of place. A focus on practices undermines the tacit understanding of place that exists under representationalist perspectives. From a representationalist perspective, place is an effect of the projection of social relations and cultural constructions on to material reality. The focus on embodied and embedded practices that a dwelling approach entails, on the other hand, reveals place as an emergent effect of the engagement between a human subject and the materiality of a site (Bender, 1998; Hetherington, 1997; Thrift, 1999).

However, whilst a focus on practices undermines the representationalist view of place, looking at the locally embedded practices of direct engagement does

© The Editorial Board of the Sociological Review 2003

little to confront the more general problem with concepts of place in the face of social scientific perspectives increasingly concerned with mobility, flows and hybridity. In particular, the dwelling perspective has a problematic focus on spatially and temporally immediate engagement. Dwelling as presented by Heidegger is not a universal characteristic of human being—it is rather a condition associated with a problematic valorization of locally 'authentic' cultural practices.

A number of authors have critically engaged with the dwelling perspective in relation to the limitations that arise from its reliance upon authentic and spatially proximal practices through which humans have a seemingly pure relation with nonhuman nature. For example, Paul Cloke and Owain Jones (2001) have explored the contemporary relevance of the dwelling perspective for considering place through the analysis of West Bradley, a traditional orchard in Somerset. The orchard is apparently a site of the continuation of authentic practices of productive and direct relations between humans and nonhuman nature, practices thoroughly embedded in local cultural heritage. However, on closer analysis, Cloke and Jones reveal the wide reaching flows of ideas, people and materials that converge in the orchard.

Mike Michael (2000a, 2000b) also critically engages with the dwelling perspective, as it is interpreted by Ingold in his concept of the taskscape. He compares the concept of taskscape, (with its implicit purity of co-constitutive relation between human and nonhuman) with the purity of relation (based upon the radical separation of human and nonhuman) seen to be the foundation of the romantic sublime experience of nonhuman nature. Although these two perspectives sit at opposite ends of the spectrum of ideas about the relationality between humans and environment, Michael argues that both 'posit a "pure" relation between humans and the natural environment' (Michael, 2000: 107). As a radical disruption of this purity, Michael highlights the role of mundane technologies in heterogeneously mediating all local exchanges between humans and environment.

Closer examination of the practices through which people engage with the Agglestone reveals a similar heterogeneity of both material and semiotic intermediaries in the interaction between human and nonhuman nature. In addition to their boots, there must be the tools with which some carve their names; the chalk that helps climbers' sweaty hands maintain their grip; the bottles of beer and cans of lager that tend to mediate people's interaction with the site (as evidenced by the empties they leave behind). As Michael highlights in his own analysis, each mundane object is itself constituted through and brings into the moment of interaction a range of relations stretching far beyond the locale.

This brings us to the crucial point in considering whether a relational understanding can help to revive place as an analytical concept of social science. Can a relational account of place hold up in the face of the distributedness and hybridity of the relations that crowd in to each moment in which place is performed? Following the distributed relations of another material entity close to

© The Editorial Board of the Sociological Review 2003

the Agglestone can lead us to confront just how distributed and hybrid the performance of place can be.

Godlingston's fence and the relationality of expert knowledge

A few hundred metres up the hill from the Agglestone, there is a fence. It is a typical stock fence, a nearly ubiquitous feature of the British countryside. However, it was not a feature of this bit of countryside a few years ago. The fence is there now because Godlingston is a habitat of international biodiversity importance. Godlingston is a lowland heath, a habitat recognized in international legislation such as the European Unions' Habitats and Species Directive, the Berne Convention and the Birds Directive. It was an early priority in the UK's Biodiversity Action Plan (BAP), part of the UK government's fulfilment of commitments to biodiversity made at the Rio Earth Summit in 1992 (Michael, 1996).

For lowland heath to come to have a place in international legislation or national priority frameworks, it has to exist as something that can be brought together with other entities, other habitats or species, in the limited spatial and cultural locales in which these decisions are made. Different habitats have to be brought together in a single building, perhaps even, at some stage on a single desk, so that they can be weighed against each other, priorities set, and conservation targets established. For this to happen, lowland heath has to exist as something mobile, something that as it moves between different spaces in the processes of description and prioritization has stable and transparent meaning, at least within the particular cultural contexts where these decisions are made. Latour uses the term 'immutable mobiles' to capture such characteristics (Latour, 1987).

To possess these characteristics, lowland heath has to exist as text: as habitat descriptions, floristic tables, species lists, as statistics of coverage and quality. Being a small number of sheets of paper, or a few fields in a database, lowland heath can be easily handled, it can be compared against other habitat descriptions, and it can be attributed relative value within frameworks of evaluation that reach across continents. As a result of these processes, lowland heath has been recognized as of international conservation and biodiversity importance, primarily based on the rarity of the species it supports and the history of decline in total area of the habitat, now standing in the UK at just one sixth of the coverage that existed in 1800 (Biodiversity Steering Group, 1995). As a result of such statistics in relation to the foundational bases for concern in nature conservation (rarity and relative loss) lowland heath became one of the first habitats to have a Habitat Action Plan as part of the UK BAP process. As part of the Habitat Action Plan, lowland heath has had national targets set for its conservation.[2] These targets have been established with the involvement of a range of governmental, voluntary and commercial bodies, and with the commitment of millions of pounds, mostly from public funds and from the UK's Heritage Lottery Fund.

However, these classifications, descriptions and evaluations would be meaningless if the entities that exist as text or data—as immutable mobiles—did not exist somewhere as a messy materiality of plants, animals, soil and rock. Conservation targets have to be realized on particular sites. Godlingston is one of those particular sites. It is in the process of contributing to the realization of targets for lowland heath maintenance and restoration that Godlingston, like many other heaths around the country, has a new fence. But why a fence?

Like most habitats of nature conservation importance in the UK, lowland heath is anthropogenic—a result of the interaction of people with the land in pursuit of livelihood. Typically, the origin of a lowland heath is traced back to the Bronze Age, when the clearance of woodland and attempts to cultivate the poor soils resulted in the further impoverishment of the soil to the point that the vegetation characteristic of lowland heath could become established. Lowland heath is characterized by low growing heathers and patches of gorse—vegetation that, without human management of the land, would in most places be replaced by woodland through processes of ecological succession. The habitat has only persisted over the millennia as a result of continuing human exploitation of the land. The history of the heath entails a picture of many different people scraping a subsistence livelihood through a diversity of small-scale practices including: the gathering of fodder; animal bedding and fuel; turf cutting; digging out of things like clay or gravel; and grazing stock—for which burning was used as a means of maintaining the most suitable vegetation. Although heath has been lost to agricultural improvement and building development, the greatest proportion of loss has been due to the lack of traditional management resulting in the encroachment of scrub and then woodland onto the heath. Such changes in vegetation represent a loss of biodiversity value on a site, when viewed within a national or international frame of reference.

Conservationists employ a range of practices to attempt to recreate the effects of past subsistence activities that maintained the heath. Over the 1990s, grazing came to be accepted as the most desirable and effective management practice. The main cost in setting up a grazing scheme is the erection of a perimeter fence to enclose the grazing stock, and one factor encouraging the dominance of grazing as a management practice has been the availability of funds for fencing, which exists not least due to the desire to realize BAP targets.

In the mid-1990s, a grazing scheme was designed for Godlingston heath, as part of the realization of the site's contribution to BAP targets. To keep the stock off the neighbouring golf course and the busy road, a fence had to be constructed. And so, Godlingston has its new fence.

The fence is a material transformation of a specific locale as a result of generic frameworks of description and evaluation. It is an effect of processes through which the generic uneasily becomes specific, where 'global' flows of texts, knowledge and meaning become material and static in a particular 'local'. The fence is a materialization of processes that constitute Godlingston as a scientific object, reduced to standardized mobile representations based on systematic and universalistic classifications. It represents what seems an understanding

© The Editorial Board of the Sociological Review 2003

Figure 2: *Captain Diver and colleagues survey Studland Peninsula*[3]

of place radically opposed to the immediate, relational and performative under-standing of place outlined above.

However, closer inspection of the processes through which Godlingston came to have its fence reveals how these processes are themselves composed of local, relational and heterogeneous practices. More significantly for understanding the relational performance of place, this exploration shows how even generic knowl-edge and international frameworks of understanding and evaluation come to share in the relational performance of place.

At least since subsistence practices on the heaths of the Studland peninsula ceased, few people have engaged with the nonhuman nature of them through practices so direct and embodied as those pictured in Figure 2. This is an action photo of the first stage of 'mobilizing' Studland Heath, the most dramatic trans-formation in the chains of translation that led to the international prioritization of lowland heath as a habitat of international biodiversity importance. In front of each surveyor is a simple wooden frame. Placed on the ground the frame defines the quadrat, a standardized sample of ground with its vegetation and fauna. This represents the first translation of the specific piece of ground in the process through which it must go to become something mobile, providing a man-ageable sample from the large area covered by the survey. In the hand of the middle figure, we can make out a pen or pencil with which he probes the vege-tation framed by his quadrat. We can imagine how the pencil will move occa-sionally, from probing the vegetation to inscribing, turning what the surveyor sees into text on the notebook by his side.

What we witness through the photograph is the convergence of specific natural nonhuman entities with universalistic taxonomy. Such a convergence

only occurs through an interaction of diverse actors, involving mundane technologies like pencils, quadrat frames and notebooks, as well as the surveyor, the
taxonomies, reference texts, and the organisms themselves. The taxonomies are
present, whether as internal knowledge of the surveyor or in material form as
a field guide. It is through this convergence that the mess of soil, plants and
animals that the surveyors are lying on undergoes its initial, most radical, translation—into the ordered text of mobile representation.

Dramatic though this translation is, an individual quadrat record is not
enough to make Studland travel far. The transient moment of sampling made
durable in the photograph above was part of what Sir Julian Huxley, in 1971,
described as 'the most exhaustive ecological survey ever undertaken of a large
area' (The Nature Conservancy, 1971: 2). This survey was one of the many
achievements of the man in the middle of the picture—Captain Cyril Diver
(1892–1969). By the early 1930s, having already established something of a
reputation from extensive work on the breeding of snails, Diver's interest turned
to the Studland peninsula. He was fascinated first by the dynamic coastal geo-
morphology of the peninsula, now the stuff of dozens of school field trips each
year. It was reportedly, however, the discovery of a pink grasshopper on match-
ing pink heather flowers that resolved Diver to study the flora and fauna of the
diverse habitats of the area (The Nature Conservancy, 1971: 2).

So began a major ecological survey of Studland. Through the 1930s to the
breakout of World War II, Diver spent his summer vacations surveying Studland with his wife and assistants, and with occasional help from a range of spe-
cialists. It is as an element within this vast undertaking that the turning of a
square foot of ground into inscriptions in a field notebook takes significance.
The point of this inscription is that the square foot of ground becomes mobile,
so that, along with thousands of other samples, it can go through another stage
of translation, combined into a single mobile that represents hundreds, perhaps
thousands, of samples. Each sample, whilst its individuality is lost in the new
inscription, reaches a new degree of mobility through its combination. At each
stage of translation Diver would not simply bring together the lower level
inscriptions but bring them together with his knowledge of ecology, as a means
to translate what was before him into representations that were ever more
mobile. It was through such processes that Diver authored and co-authored
around a dozen published papers drawn from his work on Studland, giving the
site national mobility through the circulation of journals such as the *Journal of
Animal Ecology* or the *Proceedings of the Royal Society*.[4]

By virtue of the interest revealed by an impressive survey, and embedded into
current debates through the articles, Studland became an ecological scientific
object. However, through the intensity of study afforded to Studland through
Diver's survey, the chains of translation can be traced further. As a result of
his reputation, built through the mobiles he constructed from his direct and embodied interaction with Studland Heath, Diver became a significant figure in
the institutionalization of nature conservation in Britain during the 1940s and
1950s. He was appointed to key committees in the processes that led to the cre-

 © The Editorial Board of the Sociological Review 2003

ation of the Nature Conservancy, Britain's first statutory nature conservation organization, as part of the 1949 *National Parks and Access to the Countryside Act*. Diver was appointed as the first Director-General of the Conservancy, until his retirement in 1952 (Merrett, 1971; Sheail, 1998).

As director-general, Diver had a significant role not only in shaping management priorities and the realization of statutory designations, but also in shaping the research carried out in the new institution, which in turn significantly shaped the professionalization of scientific ecology. As the locale that shaped and gave credibility to Diver's ecological expertise, and as what was then the most thoroughly researched, recorded and reported large area of ecosystem, it is reasonable to conjecture that Studland played a significant role in shaping generic understandings of heathland at this important time. Indeed, for Max Nicholson, Diver's successor as Director-General of the Nature Conservancy: 'Studland heath and its surroundings are, in a sense, sacred ground to ecologists, on account of what Cyril Diver achieved there' (Nicholson, 1975: 1).

More specifically, Studland clearly figured in Diver's decision on the siting of one of only two Nature Conservancy field research stations at Furzebrook, 10 km west of Studland. Studland, through its translation into immutable mobiles not only helped develop generic ecological knowledge of lowland heath. Through its role in establishing Diver as a significant figure in the institutionalization of nature conservation and thereby the siting of a key research station, the translations of Studland can be traced into the very heart of the development of nature conservation in post-war Britain.

Going a step further, we can see how these processes led on to the generation of concern not only about heathland but about habitat loss more generally. One of the first staff to arrive at Furzebrook, Dr. N. W. Moore, quantified for the first time the enormous loss of area of lowland heath in Dorset. Using old maps, he compared the coverage of heath in 1811, 1896, 1934 and 1960. Starkly displayed in a series of maps was the radical reduction in total area, and the fragmentation, of Dorset's heathland (Moore, 1962). Only one third of the heath present in 1811 remained in 1960, and the rate of loss seemed only to be increasing: 45 per cent of the area present in 1934 was lost by 1960. Moore's work was not only new in what it revealed about lowland heath. His work was unprecedented in relation to any habitat. The revelation of the extent to which an important habitat was disappearing galvanized conservation to the reality of habitat loss and fragmentation despite a decade and a half of statutory conservation.

Studland therefore played a small but significant role in the networks of things, places, people and processes (most notably also involving Diver, Furzebrook and Moore) that contributed to the shaping of conservation concerns and debates in the later 20th century. Along with thousands of other sites, mobilized through similar processes within the specific institutional and cultural contexts of ecology and conservation, Studland has contributed to the co-ordination of knowledge about the extent, fragmentation and loss of habitats across Britain and Europe. This knowledge has then formed the basis for setting conservation priorities on national and international levels, contributing to

© The Editorial Board of the Sociological Review 2003

frameworks of knowledge and concern, and legislation existing at international and global levels including the Convention on Biological Diversity.

This story has moved a long way from the fence. The point of tracing this tenuous history, from Studland in the 1940s to contemporary global biodiversity concern, is not to try to claim that Studland has been a uniquely powerful agent in creating European and global conservation concern. Its point is rather to show that even the most globalized generic understandings are produced from and through local, embodied and heterogeneous practices involving interaction with an agential nonhuman nature. Part of making an argument for the relationality of place is to recognize that a place can itself be agential, even in the construction of globalized and objectivist knowledge.

The insight that expert and universalistic knowledge is produced through local interactions between humans and nonhumans was established through the ethnographies of laboratories in the 1970s and 80s, and work that arose from them that directly challenged the distinction between micro and macro (Latour and Woolgar, 1979; Callon and Latour, 1981; Latour, 1983). Less often examined, however, is the way in which the processes of translation that lead to the construction of expert knowledge are 'reversed', passing through different pathways of translation, being transformed as it is negotiated into successive contexts of practice and decision making, on their paths back to the specific (for examples of such work see Disco and van der Meulen, 1998; and for a detailed account of specific translations in the same empirical field as this chapter, Waterton, 2002). By following the reversal of the processes of abstraction that turned Studland into a globalized actor, it becomes clear that expert knowledge passes through as many stages of translation on its way back to Studland as it did on its journey away from it. Once the narrative returns to the specificity of the Studland peninsula, the expert knowledge of this particular place is revealed not as something unproblematically identifiable with specific human individuals, whether professional scientists or conservation practitioners whose actions have some basis in and legitimisation from science. Rather, such expert knowledge exists locally as a collection of entities that, like so many others, have potential agency in the relational constitution of place.

As a Convention agreed at an international level, with 168 signatory nations, it was a considerable step of translation to make the Rio Biodiversity Convention something meaningful in the relative 'locality' of Britain, with its distinctive character in biodiversity terms as well as long-established structures of conservation. The UK government was amongst the first of the Convention's signatories to take definite and active steps towards fulfilling the commitments it had made. As a result of long processes of co-ordination, involving the always local processes of consultation between government departments, statutory conservation bodies and non-governmental organizations, the UK's Biodiversity Action Plan was launched in 1994. The Action Plan took the form of description of species and habitats identified as priorities for UK biodiversity conservation, and of action plans for that conservation (Biodiversity Steering Group, 1995).

© The Editorial Board of the Sociological Review 2003

As part of the UK's localization of the global convention, the 1994 BAP gave specific targets, proposed actions, responsible institutions and costings for the realization of the lowland heath action plan, all at a level of specificity unimaginable in a global convention. The two pages outlining the specifics of the UK's action plan still remain at too generic a level, however, to guide the specific material transformations needed to realize a target such as the reestablishment of 6,000 ha of heathland by 2005. The Lowland Heath Biodiversity Action Plan Steering Group (LHBAPSG) was set up in part to establish which areas of UK heathland were to be given priority in the realization of the BAP targets. Godlingston Heath was declared to be one such area. Consequently, a series of translations can be recognized stretching from the Rio Convention to Godlingston. At each successive stage of translation, the process has been made material only in mobiles, such as texts representing obligations, targets, project proposals and costings. In the final step the process reaches a stage that is deliberately immobile. The area to be fenced has to be identified, and the exact line of the fence decided, in negotiation between English Nature, the National Trust, the fencing contractors and the land itself. Deciding on the line is not simply a matter of finding the most practical route for the physical process of erecting a fence that will form an enclosure around the given area. The 'public' are also present in the negotiation, albeit through the proxy of the conservation staff's understanding of what they will require in terms of access, and what will be relatively acceptable in terms of siting.

Through these local co-ordinations of materials, people and land, the fence on Godlingston was finally erected, one part of the institution of a grazing regime to maintain and enhance the conservation value of the Studland NNR. In the fence, processes that had one small beginning—with Captain Diver crawling on his belly in the 1930s—followed complex paths of translation to the highest degree of abstraction, and subsequent reversal, to return finally to Studland in the form of a small material transformation. Following some of these paths demonstrates the extent to which place can be seen both as an emergent effect of globally distributed relationships, and as an actor in those relationships. The fence itself embodies these flows and relationships in the local space of Godlingston, sharing in the relational agency through which place is constituted. Indeed, its erection to enclose previously open heathland so challenged existing constitutions of the place that, like many other conservation fences on open ground in the UK, it caused significant conflict between local people and the conservation agencies.

Place is not only local, specific and static. A perspective that recognizes the relational agency of nonhumans in the performance of place denies understandings of place either as a locus of intrinsic meaning to be perceived by appropriately sensitive human observers, or as a passive context for the projection of cultural meaning. Rather, place is an emergent effect of practices that bring a diversity of relationships into the moment of interaction between a person and the materiality of a site. This understanding of place has of course been prefigured, not least by authors drawing on the dwelling perspective. For

Ingold (1993), the taskscape is emergent, something that exists only in the inter-actions between humans and the affordances, both material and semiotic, of the land around them. Thrift incorporates Heidegger to his re-conceptualization of places as something that 'must be seen as dynamic, as taking shape only in their passing' (1999: 310). Drawing on perspectives from STS, particularly from Latour and Law, he articulates his account of place as being:

> ... based in a *relational materialism* which depends upon conceiving of the world as associational, as an imbroglio of heterogeneous and more or less expansive hybrids performing 'not one but many worlds' (Law, 1997) and weaving all manner of spaces and times as they do so (Thrift, 1999: 317).

Also seeking to articulate a relational understanding of place, Hetherington argues that we should:

> ... bring materiality back in and ... see places as generated by the placing, arrang-ing and naming the spatial ordering of materials and the system of difference that they perform ... This does not mean that there is no space for the subject and sub-jective experiences and memories of a space; rather they become folded into the mate-rial world and each becomes imbricated in the agency of the other' (1997: 184).

A focus on nature reserves gives particular resources with which to confront a central limitation of approaches to place. As articulated earlier, a dwelling approach has often been used in ways which valorize immediate interaction between people and environment, closely contained within space and time, tending to a localism and valorization of seemingly 'authentic' practices and relations. There is no such explicit valorization of specific practices in the rela-tional approaches of theorists like Thrift or Hetherington. There remains in their work, however, and in Thrift's non-representational theory more broadly, a sense in which an approach that sees the world in terms of pre-linguistic prac-tices may tend towards a problematic localism, prioritizing practices of direct engagement between humans and the nonhuman world.

Nature reserves have particular characteristics that enable the analysis of the distributed and heterogeneous character of the performance of place. At the same time as affording informal and often non-representational practices of engagement, the materiality of a heathland reserve also affords practices that constitute it as scientific object. The ways in which field ecologists, reserve wardens and amateur naturalists bring together generic knowledge, such as taxonomies, mundane technologies such as quadrats or binoculars, and the materiality of a site, through their own embodied practices, is one way of exem-plifying how distributed and heterogeneous is the relational performance of place.

Nature reserves can support an unusually broad range of constitutions of place, from ones dominated by generic expert knowledge to ones constituted through informal non-representational practices, like walking the dog. Conse-quently, an analysis of how place is performed in nature reserves brings to light how heterogeneous and distributed place can be. In making such an analysis, I have indicated how the concept of place can be revivified as something mean-ingful for a social science wary of sedentary and localizing concepts and con-cerned to be aware of the flows, processes and hybridity of subjects, identities and spaces.

Notes

1 A barrow is a prehistoric burial mound.
2 Those targets for lowland heath are to maintain and improve all existing lowland heath and to encourage the re-establishment, by 2005, of a further 6000 ha of heathland (Biodiversity Steering Group, 1995).
3 Reproduced from Captain Cyril Diver (The Nature Conservancy, 1971: Figure 2) with the kind permission of the Natural Environment Research Council/Centre for Ecology and Hydrology.
4 eg. Diver (1934; 1936) For a review of Diver's published papers, see Merrett (1971).

Bibliography

Adams, W. (1996), *Future Nature: A Vision for Conservation*, London: Earthscan.
Bachelard, G. (1964), *The Poetics of Space*, Boston: Beacon Press.
Barnes, T. J. and J. S. Duncan (eds) (1992), *Writing Worlds: Discourse, Text and Metaphor in the Representation of the Landscape*, London: Routledge.
Bender, B. (1998), *Stonehenge: Making Space*, Oxford: Berg.
Biodiversity Steering Group (1995), *Biodiversity: the UK Action Plan. Volume 2: Action Plans*, London: HMSO.
Breslau, D. (2000), 'Sociology after Humanism: A Lesson from Contemporary Science Studies', *Sociological Theory*, 18(2): 289–307.
Callon, M. and B. Latour (1981), 'Unscrewing the Big Leviathan', in K. D. Knorr-Cetina and M. Mulkay (eds), *Advances in Social Theory and Methodology*, London: Routledge and Kegan Paul: 277–303.
Cloke, P. and O. Jones (2001), 'Dwelling, Place and Landscape: An Orchard in Somerset', *Environment and Planning A* 33(4): 649–666.
Disco, C. and B. van der Meulen (1998), *Getting New Technologies Together. Studies in Making New Sociotechnical Order*, Berlin: Walter der Gruyter.
Diver, C. (1936), 'The Problem of Closely Related Species and the Distribution of Their Popula-tions. In a Discussion on the Recent State of the Theory of Natural Selection', *Proceedings of the Royal Society (B)* 121: 43–73.
Diver, C. and R. Good (1934), 'The South Haven Peninsula Survey (Studland Heath, Dorset): General Scheme of the Survey', *Journal of Animal Ecology* 3: 129–132.
Doel, M. (1999), *Poststructuralist Geographies. The Diabolical Art of Spatial Science*, Edinburgh: Edinburgh University Press.
Dreyfus, H. and H. Hall (eds), (1992), *Heidegger. A Critical Reader*, Oxford: Blackwell.
Harvey, D. (1996), *Justice, Nature and the Geography of Difference*, Oxford: Blackwell.
Hetherington, K. (1997), 'In Place of Geometry: The Materiality of Place', in K. Hetherington and R. Munro (eds), *Ideas of Difference: Social Spaces and the Labour of Division*, Oxford: Blackwell, 183–199.
Ingold, T. (1993), 'The Temporality of the Landscape', *World Archaeolog, y* 25(2): 152–74.
Ingold, T. (1995), 'Building, Dwelling, Living. How Animals and People Make Themselves at Home in the World', in M. Strathern (ed.), *Shifting Contexts. Transformations in Anthropological Knowl-edge*, London: Routledge: 57–80.

Ingold, T. (2000), *The Perception of the Environment. Essays in Livelihood, Dwelling, Skill*, London: Routledge.

Latour, B. (1983), 'Give Me a Laboratory and I Will Raise the World', in K. Knorr-Cetina and M. Mulkay (eds), *Science Observed*, London: Sage: 141–170.

Latour, B. (1987), *Science in Action: How to Follow Scientists and Engineers through Society*, Cambridge Mass.: Harvard University Press.

Latour, B. (1993), *We Have Never Been Modern*, Hemel Hempsted: Harvester Wheatsheaf.

Latour, B. and S. Woolgar (1979), *Laboratory Life: The Social Construction of Scientific Facts*, London: Sage.

Law, J. (1997), *Traduction/trahision: Notes on ANT*, Department of Sociology, Lancaster University http://www.comp.lancs.ac.uk/sociology/stslaw2.html.

Macnaghten, P. and J. Urry (1998), *Contested Natures*, London: Sage.

Macnaghten, P. and J. Urry (eds), (2001), *Bodies of Nature*, London: Sage.

Malpas, J. (1998), 'Finding Place: Spatiality, Locality and Subjectivity', in A. Light and J. M. Smith (eds), *Philosophies of Place, Philosophy and Geography III*, Lanham: Rowman and Littlefield: 21–44.

Massey, D. (1991), 'A Global Sense of Place', *Marxism Today* (June): 24–9.

Massey, D. (1993), 'Power-geometry and a Progressive Sense of Place', in J. Bird, B. Curtis, T. Putnam, G. Robertson and L. Tickner (eds), *Mapping the Futures: Local Cultures, Global Change*, London: Routledge: 58–68.

Merrett, P. (1971), 'The Published Papers of Cyril Diver', in P. Merrett (ed.), *Captain Cyril Diver (1892–1969) A Memoir*, Wareham, Dorset: Furzebrook Research Station.

Michael, M. (2000a), *Reconnecting Culture, Technology and Nature: From Society to Heterogeneity*, London: Routledge.

Michael, M. (2000b), 'These Boots are Made for Walking . . .: Mundane Technology, the Body and Human-Environment Relations', *Body and Society*, 6(3–4): 107–126.

Michael, N. (1996), *Lowland Heathland: Wildlife Value and Conservation Status*, Peterborough: English Nature.

Moore, N. W. (1962), 'The Heaths of Dorset and their Conservation', *Journal of Ecology*, 50(2): 369–391.

National Trust (2000), *Wildlife Information Guide 2000*, Cirencester: National Trust.

Nicholson, E. M. (1975), 'Foreword', in *Furzebrook Research Station. 21 Years*, Dorset: Institute for Terrestrial Ecology.

Sheail, J. (1998), *Nature Conservation in Britain. The Formative Years*, London: The Stationery Office.

Swain, H. (1893), *An Artist's Rambles About Swanage*, South Kensington: Hume Swain.

Taylor, C. (1993), 'Engaged Agency and Background in Heidegger', in C. Guigon (ed.), *The Cambridge Companion to Heidegger*, Cambridge: Cambridge University Press, 317–336.

The Nature Conservancy (1971), *Captain Cyril Diver (1892–1969) A Memoir*, Wareham, Dorset: The Nature Conservancy.

Thrift, N. (1996), *Spatial Formations*, London: Sage.

Thrift, N. (1999), 'Steps to an Ecology of Place', in D. Massey, J. Allen and P. Sarre (eds), *Human Geography Today*, Cambridge: Polity Press: 295–323.

Waterton, C. (2002), 'From Field to Fantasy: Classifying Nature, Constructing Europe', *Social Studies of Science*, 32(2): 177–204.

© The Editorial Board of the Sociological Review 2003

Part IV
Unsettling life

Feral ecologies: performing life on the colonial periphery

Nigel Clark

'Performance is, if you like, a feral operator . . .' (Thrift and Dewsbury, 2000: 429)

Transplanting Europe

Recent years have seen an escalating concern over the human capacity to transform the natural world—focused especially, in the most developed societies, on new biotechnological modes of reproducing and manipulating living beings. Yet, long before anyone sought to clone individual organisms, vast energies were invested in the replication of entire regions. As historian Alfred Crosby has suggested, the European colonial project was in part an attempt to propagate 'new Europes' elsewhere on the planet (1986: 2–7). Having failed to remake the tropics in its own image, European attention was turned to those temperate regions girdling the Southern Hemisphere that had once seemed too remote to be of serious interest. This included the South African Cape, the grasslands of South America, and the regions I will be concentrating on, the south-west and east of Australia and almost all of New Zealand.

Along with its other permutations, the idea of recreating 'European life' on the colonial periphery was taken quite literally. Amongst those commentators who have grappled with the ground-level impacts of the European invasion of the temperate periphery there is a common refrain: colonization was as much a biological process as it was an economic, cultural or political one. Amidst all the forms of disorder and 'deterritorialization' accompanying colonization, biological forces stand out as the most irruptive and unpredictable—and the least amenable to re-containment. Either introduced intentionally, or smuggling themselves amidst licit cargo, hundreds of species from the temperate north traversed the oceans to the 'new worlds' of the south. What was so remarkable about this initially one-sided redistribution, as Charles Darwin and others noted, was that so many species seemed to fare better on the far side of the planet than they did on their home turf (Darwin, 1996: 164, 272).

In a similar way that pathogens from the Eurasian continent, when carried across oceans, cut a swathe through previously unexposed indigenous popula-

© The Editorial Board of the Sociological Review 2003. Published by Blackwell Publishing Ltd, 9600 Garsington Road, Oxford OX4 2DQ, UK and 350 Main Street, Malden, MA 02148, USA

tions, so too, did many plants and animals of the northern temperate zones turn out to be wildly opportunistic in their host environments. Cattle, let loose on the Argentine pampas to forage, proliferated into free-ranging herds so vast that they could not be counted, let alone corralled; a handful of rabbits released in Australia soon numbered hundred of millions; dozens of varieties of European plants, imported to New Zealand as fodder, garden or hedgerow plants jumped the fence and ran rampant over the countryside (Crosby, 1986: ch 8; Rolls, 1969). At first a boon for struggling settlers, feral biota could soon become a plague, threatening the livelihood of farming communities, displacing indigenous flora and fauna, and agitating the very soil of the newly-appropriated lands. Crosby is not overstating the case when he describes the biological introductions to Europe's temperate colonies as 'a grunting, lowing, neighing, crowing, chirping, snarling, buzzing, self-replicating and world-altering avalanche' (1986: 194).

The prodigious performance of so much of the transplanted life on the colonial periphery offers an early warning—largely unheeded—for the contemporary problem of species invasion. Today, intensive trade between distant parts of the globe has turned the trans-location of living organisms into a still greater threat to ecosystem integrity and biological diversity. Once predominantly a problem of the temperate settlement zones and oceanic islands, bioinvasion is now a fully global phenomenon, with no particular preference for destination (Bright, 1999: 173). Each trade route or mode of transport seems to offer its own opportunities: earth-working machinery carries caked-on, life-rich soil from country to country, containerized shipping and air freight disseminates seeds and small animals trans-nationally, while the ballast water in ocean-vessels redistributes marine creatures amongst the seas of the world (Bright, 1999: ch 7; Low, 1999: ch 14).

There is a further sense in which the biological misadventures of the settler societies might be premonitory. Current developments in biotechnology are raising concern over the ecological repercussions of releasing genetically-modified organisms into the 'field', with critics pointing to the possibility of unanticipatable proliferation and interbreeding with free-ranging relatives. 'Not only can these living things not be recalled', Barbara Adam writes, 'but they cannot even be traced as they migrate and mutate through the networked earth system of ecological relations' (1998: 19). Any mishap with genetically-modified life would constitute an 'undelimitable accident', Ulrich Beck has argued, bringing biotechnology into the realm of new and unprecedented 'manufactured' risks (Beck, 1995: 77–8).

But perhaps the runaway genetic event is not quite as novel as theorists of risk society would have it. The domesticated plant or animal which is transposed into an unfamiliar terrain—only to leap the fence and strike out for a new life in the wild—similarly defies limitation and re-containment. Every invasive organism is a potentially self-replicating package of genes—a bundle of code as well as a body on the move. Like a segment of genetic code snipped from one living thing and spliced into another, a population of organisms uplifted from one environment and dropped into a different one, ten thousand miles away, *is*

© The Editorial Board of the Sociological Review 2003

a genetic experiment: a field trial that takes entire countries or continents as its testing ground.

Performing live at the periphery

Environmentalists—and the social scientists who have heeded their message—have often presented the impact of human activity on the natural world in terms of an overwhelming and unilateral degradation. Such is the enthralment with the idea of a pervasive social undermining of biophysical forces and processes that environmentalists and social scientists alike are speaking of the 'end of nature' (McKibben, 1990; Strathern, 1992: 191–5; Giddens, 1994: 77). This end of nature thesis has been linked with the idea of undelimitable accidents, which are seen to extend the corruption of natural flows and cycles to a hitherto unthinkable depth (Beck, 1992: 81). In this context, bioinvasion might be taken as an epitome of fallen nature, a final and irrevocable effacement of biogeographic integrity played out on a global stage.

But if the capacity of transplanted organisms to work their way deep into unfamiliar ecosystems constitutes an exceptionally challenging environmental problem, at the same time it seems also to problematize the very idea of effacing or undoing nature. For what makes an invasive species troublesome is as much an affirmation of natural force and potentiality as it is a negation. Without the exuberance and adaptability that are defining qualities of life in general, there would be no problem. What the achievements of the invasive organism highlight is the extraordinary—or perhaps merely ordinary—ability of living things to improvise in new settings, to compose themselves into new rhythms and patterns and to recompose the milieus in which they dwell. And in this sense, we might look to the idea of the 'performativity of life' as more fruitful way of coming to terms with 'life out of bounds' than any sense of the total socialization or demise of the natural.

The growing interest in the performative dimensions of human existence amongst certain sectors of the social sciences and humanities has served to accentuate the 'doing' side of social life as opposed to the 'being' or givenness of particular social identities or categories. Attention is drawn to the multitude of repeated actions that make up everyday life: to the many small gestures and postures that configure the social world, and in so doing reconfigure the very bodies that perform them. A creative force, it is suggested, inheres in this microphysics of the most ordinary, as small differences or variations emerge out repetition, to resonate through the wider social body (Butler, 1993, 1997: ch 4).

While the performative focus has helped foreground the corporeal dimension of human social life, there seems to be further potential to address the continuities between human beings and the fuller range of embodied 'actors' that share our spaces or territories. The very idea of variation emerging out of repetition with small differences resonates profoundly with our understandings of the evolutionary dynamics of life in the broadest sense. As against the 'end of nature' argument, a performative approach invites a reading of human inter-actions with the non-human world that allows for opportunities as well as constraints, for mutual implications that might have generative as well as degenerative consequences. And it makes sense to look for such entanglements in those places where 'field trials' of introduced life have been iterated most often and most extensively.

It seems that a peculiar sensitivity to the performative dimensions of life 'in the general sense' has been percolating through the former colonial periphery for some time, and not always in conversation with discourses on the performative elsewhere. What is notable, particularly at Europe's 'antipodes', is the almost pre-emptive conjoining of interest in human and non-human performances. Indeed, as Australian/ New Zealand artist John Lyall proposes, the introduced organism running loose in an alien environment might be taken as the paradigmatic experience of the Australasian settler society. Over several decades of performance and installation, Lyall has been exploring the permutations of the 'feral': the transplanted entity that begins its tenure of a new land as a familiar, domesticated being before passing over the frontier in the direction of the wild and unknown. His many rehearsals of the feral refrain deal with the inherent uncertainty that comes with crossing an ocean and arriving somewhere that is never quite like the place of departure, however much its forms and features might appear to echo those on the other side of the world.

The host environment may be altered irrevocably by the presence of a new organism but so too, inevitably, is the one who runs wild transformed by the terrain in which it insinuates itself. If on the one hand, Lyall's feral art refers lit-erally to the biophysical implications of species introduction, on the other, he is making a much broader claim about any element or refrain that is subjected to radical displacement. The feral animal or plant, in this sense, figures for the entirety of objects, practices, and techniques that were uplifted from metropol-itan centres of the northern hemisphere and 'unleashed' at the colonial periph-ery. In Lyall's version of the performative, each and every introduction to some degree runs free and adapts in the unfamiliar terrain in which it finds itself. Human and non-human, cultural and biological elements, are all subject to the transformative force of repetition with distance-induced difference.

This interest in the variance spurred by passage into a new land following a sea-crossing is also central to the work of Australian ethno-historian Greg Dening. Dening has depicted the arrivals and the encounters constitutive of the history of Oceania as a kind of theatre—'the *theatrum mundi* of the Pacific': a version of the performative that pivots on the transition between land and sea (1992: 374). 'Crossing beaches', he notes, 'is always dramatic' (1980: 33). Dening foregrounds the many ingrained and embodied acts that make up everyday life, and what becomes of them in the extra-ordinary moment of encountering a new land. In the process of negotiating the marginal space between worlds, the integrity of iterated behaviour is quickly compromised. '[T]hings come across the beach partially, without their fuller meaning', Dening observes. 'The gestures,

© The Editorial Board of the Sociological Review 2003

the signals, the codes which make the voyager's own world no longer work' (1980: 34, 32).

Though his focus is on the smaller islands of the Pacific, rather than the land-masses on its south-western fringe, Dening's narratives seem redolent with the antipodean experience of living as strangers in a strange land. In particular, it is the ease with which he incorporates both human and non-human actors into his account that ties in with my theme of a peripheral 'performativity of life'. There is a striking—if incidental—resonance with Lyall's 'feral' theme, not only in this concern with life in its broadest sense but also in Dening's interest in the processes of improvisation that inevitably occur when new arrivals interact with unfamiliar terrain. Once again, this iteration with difference is seen as part of a mutual transformation implicating the newcomer and its milieu. As Dening puts it:

> Every living thing on an island has been a traveller. Every species of tree, plant and animal on an island has crossed the beach. In crossing the beach each voyager has brought something old and made something new. The old is written in the forms and habits and needs each newcomer brings. The new is the changed world, the adjusted balance every coming makes. On islands each new intruder finds a freedom it never had in its old environment. On arrival it develops, fills unfilled niches, plays a thousand variations on the theme of its own form (Dening, 1980: 31–2).

Embodying performance

Along with the individual contributions by Lyall and Dening, there is a third, and more communal, strand in the antipodean performativity of life refrain. This approach tends not to deal directly with the landscapes of the colonial periphery, but it *does* engage explicitly with those discourses on the performative that are more familiar to a northern metropolitan audience—and in this sense it provides us with a sort of a hinge between hemispheres. Over at least the last decade and half, Australian feminist philosophers have been engaging rigorously with the issue of embodiment and its relationship to language or discourse, shaping debates in this field far beyond their own shores. For all its multiple voices, the Australian feminist concern with the body has been identified as an 'emergent tradition', one that is recognizably distinct from its Anglo-American counterparts (Battersby, 2000: 4; see also Colebrook, 2000). One of the junctures at which this distinctiveness has become apparent is in the various engagements of Australian theorists with the work of the American feminist philosopher Judith Butler, whose discussion of the performative dimension of embodiment and sexuality has been widely influential.

What Butler sets out to do, through an appropriation of the notion of performativity from linguistic theory, is to show just how pervasive social coding or norms can be, and how their constant rehearsal inscribes them in the very contours of the human body. At the same time, she brings to light moments that occur within the heart of these strictures, episodes when acting out becomes acting up, and the operations of the codes themselves are exposed, questioned or resisted (1993: 1–4). Butler's most notable example of this is the subversion of the norms of heterosexuality through their inversion, parody and exaggeration by gays and lesbians (1990: ch 3). But it is the general idea of a resistance to prescribed behaviour that comes about through the 'constrained contingency' of their repetition that has proved inspirational in regard to numerous aspects of social life (1997: 156).

For Butler, the social norms in question are discursive. It is language which produces the 'identities'—the sexed, racialized, or otherwise marked bodies—that it then purports to describe (1993: 30). The enactments which both comply with and resist such investment might be thoroughly embodied, but these are bodies infused, shaped and activated by cultural forces. And it is in regard to this prioritizing of the discursive that Butler's notion of 'bodies that matter', as a number of Australian theorists have claimed, does not make enough of the materiality of bodies (Grosz, 1995: 211–214; Kirby, 1997: ch 4; Wilson, 1998: 59–62; Kerin, 1999). While Butler's 'embodying' of the performative may at first appear to overcome the duality of discourse and body, or language and matter, Jacinta Kerin argues, what it rests on is an understanding of the materiality of the body as something which is both unknowing and ultimately unknowable— unknowing, because bodily matter is seen to be inarticulate and unreflexive; unknowable in the final instance because it is only culture's representations of matter which offer us any purchase on it (Kerin, 1999: 93).

For Elizabeth Grosz—drawing on the philosophy of Giles Deleuze, Butler's performative unsettling of the category of gender could be pushed much further by a recognition that there is play or contingency not only in the cultural coding of sexed bodies, 'but within the very instabilities of the category of sex itself, of bodies themselves' (Grosz, 1995: 213–214). Other Australian theorists draw on a particular reading of Jacques Derrida's philosophy to make a related point about the biological body's own capacity to generate difference. Where Butler makes use of Derrida's writings to argue for the impossibility of accessing the body 'outside' of text or language, Kirby and Wilson offer alternative readings of the same Derridean injunction: suggesting that bodies themselves might be viewed as participating in the play of language or textuality. Looking at the capabilities of the biological body, its ability to register stimuli, to transform itself, to communicate between its various levels and parts, these theorists ask why we should not consider the very stuff of the body as intelligent and articulate.

Language, in this sense, would cease to be seen simply as a force which contours and inscribes bodies from the outside, and come to be viewed as a capacity inhering in the flesh, implicit in the working of cells, tissues, organs, and all their interconnections. As Kirby puts it: 'we could embrace even biology, with all its entailments, within the scene of writing . . . as an integral expression of the performativity of language in the general sense' (1997: 98; see also Wilson, 1999). This is not simply an antipodean intuition, however. Chiming with the thoughts of Kirby, Wilson and other Australian 'deconstructive' feminist philosophers, the American microbiologist Lynn Margulis has argued unequiv-

 © The Editorial Board of the Sociological Review 2003

ocally that all life is mindful, perceptive and self reflexive. 'Life' she claims, 'has been recognizing itself long before any biology textbooks were written' (Margulis and Sagan, 1995: 32).

The work of Australian feminist theorists fleshes out the possibility of a performative force that animates not only the depths of the human body, but the bodies of all living things. This is not to undo Butler's notion of the performative, which has proved so productive, but it *is* to extend it radically, beyond the scope of the social, the cultural, or the linguistic that conventionally delineates the social sciences and humanities. Once we acknowledge a differentiating force, a 'literacy' or a communicative competence implicit in living matter, then nature and culture cease to appear as self-enclosed spheres, and at least the hint of a mutual intelligibility opens up. In this way, just as it is possible to identify a whole range of social constructions and conditionings of the natural world, so too, is it conceivable that biophysical forces never cease to animate and articulate the socio-cultural domain.

This is not to say that biophysicality 'determines' culture—or itself for that matter, for as soon as we admit of a performativity intrinsic to life, the unwavering course of 'determination' cedes to the unsettling effect of rehearsal and improvisation. Viewed performatively, life is neither free to pursue any or every option, nor destined to reproduce itself in a constant and self-identical fashion (see Grosz, 1999: 42). Refusing either of these polarities is a notion of biological becoming in which bodies and their environment are construed as mutually conditioning and mutually transformative. 'Constrained contingency', by this logic, inheres deep in the workings of the living world.

Biopolitics of centre and periphery

The interest of Australian feminists in reclaiming biophysical agency has its own particular, and often clearly explicated, philosophical lineages. While some of these writers draw connections between their interrogation of material life and their own positioning at Europe's antipodes (see for example, Lloyd, 2000), direct links with the settler histories implicated in this location are more occasional than consistent. But the insistence on culture's openness to biophysical forces that many Australian feminist theorists share with neighbouring writers and artists who engage with colonial 'life' invites further consideration; not merely because of a common geographical locus, but because the very idea of culture being open to its 'outside' is an exhortation to take geographical difference seriously.

To question culture's enclosure, in this way, is to challenge the idea that nature and society constitute ontologically distinct domains. The nature/culture duality is a notion with a long and complex heritage but, in the form in which it has been disseminated around the planet, it bears the signs of its gestation in northwest Europe. While this duality may be coming under question in numerous intellectual contexts and locations around the world, there are good reasons why its inadequacies and tensions are being, and have been, experienced with particular acuteness at Europe's southern peripheral colonies. For these were the places, as we have seen, which were intended to inherit more of Europe's thought and practice than any other region, whilst also being located at the greatest geographical remove from the model they were to aspire to. This spacing of Europe and its 'antipodes', however, is not the only significant factor we need to take into account: there is also the matter of the timing of the attempted transplantation of Europe to the southern periphery.

As Michel Foucault (1991) suggested, what goes by the name of European 'modernity' can be seen as a set of transformations in which aspects of 'life' once left to their own local and particular devices were subjected to increasingly rigorous social control. Gaining pace around the end of the 17th century, the changes in question had largely been achieved in north-western Europe by the turn of the 19th century. Foucault's focus, famously, was the raft of institutionalized practices which came to regulate the 'performances' of human bodies—both individually and collectively. But Foucault also gives numerous indications that he viewed this unprecedented concern with the deportment of human bodies as part of much more encompassing project which sought to comprehend and to reorganize 'life' in the broadest sense (see 1989: 263–279).

This new concern with life as a force or set of powers was evident in the rise of the discipline of biology. But as Foucault notes, it also had a more practical dimension. New capacities to understand and harness the force of biological life played an important part in the receding of famine and the other great 'ravages' of human existence that had cast their shadow over pre-modern and early modern Europe. While Foucault (1990: 142) makes passing reference to the transformations that contributed to this relaxation of biological risk, including the improvement of agricultural techniques, other writers have taken these insights further. The changes in the practice and organization of farming that occurred in 17th century Europe, usually referred to as the 'agrarian revolution', Manuel De Landa suggests, can be viewed as a far-reaching 'disciplining' of organic life (1997: 162–164).

As De Landa observes: 'animals and plants . . . fell under a net of writing and observation', with systematic breeding, documented by centralized recording of pedigrees, contributing to an unprecedented genetic homogenization of livestock (1997: 162). New fodder crops were introduced, along with innovations in soil management; free-burning fire and fallow periods declined, while heavier use of manure and other tightened forms of the cycling of nutrients advanced (De Landa, 1997: 164–166; Pyne, 1997: 4). These transformations sought to iron out the vagaries of biological and geographical difference, constituting a kind of 'biopolitics' directed towards the performances of bodies of all kinds—a rural 'field trial', we might say—for the later urban regulatory measures that Foucault brings to our attention.

The waning of famine and the burgeoning of urban populations in north-western Europe, however, was premised not only on the 'rationalization' of agricultural production on the home front. It was also conditioned by the massive

© The Editorial Board of the Sociological Review 2003

appropriation of labour, energy and biomass from annexed or enslaved regions. The establishment of tropical colonies by northern Europeans, from the 17th century onwards, was premised on very different disciplinary regimes to those emerging on the home front: more brutal on human bodies and usually far more disruptive in ecological terms. But the later extension of the 'colonial outfield' to the southern temperate periphery was intended to be a more civilized and civilizing process. Not only were the lands in question visibly and climatically reminiscent of north-western Europe in certain ways, but their 'opening up' came at a time when the disciplining of the European landscape and its populace was nearing its accomplishment.[1] On these grounds, there was every reason to believe that the southern colonies would replicate the degree of regulation and the intensities of production that had so thoroughly transformed the bio-political contours of north-west Europe.

It has been said of the New Zealand context, and it is equally applicable to Australia, that the aim of colonists was to 'carry with them everything of England but the soil and the climate' (Lamb, 1999: 81). Both colonies were to experience lengthy periods of prosperity based on agricultural production: the sheer extent of exploitable land and broadening markets saw to this. But along the way, 'the furious, meticulous work' of remaking Europe at 'the earth's extremes' was to encounter some sudden and shocking setbacks (see Park, 1995: 21). In Australia, pastoral farmers—lulled into overstocking the land during good years—were struck by successive waves of drought, leading to soil erosion on a vast scale (Flannery, 1994: 351–353). Across the Tasman, deforestation resulted in chronic gulleying and subsidence over great swathes of the New Zealand countryside. The boundary-pegs and fence-lines, so pivotal for regimenting unruly landscapes, were themselves frequently swept away by floods, landslides or erosion. Or in the case of the gorse hedgerows introduced from Europe 'to delimit wildlands into fields and paddocks', they absented themselves, proliferating wildly and choking the very pastures they were intended to delineate (Pyne, 1997: 435). Moreover, the livestock evolved and selected for northern conditions were far from appropriate for southern lands. In both Australia and New Zealand, the complete lack of co-adaptation between local vegetation and the hoofed livestock introduced from the north played such havoc with the topsoil that some observers feared a complete collapse of the biophysical infrastructure (Crosby, 1986: 288–291).

In short, so many of the techniques that served to train or discipline the agrarian landscape of Europe, when applied in an unreconstructed way on the far side of the world, had radically counter-productive effects. As the New Zealand natural historian Herbert Guthrie-Smith summed it up, 'the pioneers of every colony set in motion machinery beyond their ultimate control' (1999: 294). And as he knew full well from a lifetime of observation, it was the biological component of this 'machinery' that defied control most emphatically and irrevocably. As Crosby would later write of the animals introduced by Europeans to the temperate periphery: 'Because these animals are self-replicators, the efficiency and speed with which they can alter environments, even continental environments, are superior to those for any machine we have thus far devised' (1986: 173).

Performing the feral

Whereas the agricultural techniques introduced from Europe could be adapted, transformed or reinvented for local conditions—and thus 'brought into line'— free-ranging biological life would do its own adapting, transforming, and reinventing. And this meant quite the reverse of coming back into line. Biological life, in other words, refused and continues to refuse to be the raw material that simply precedes culture, or falls outside of its range. At Europe's antipodes there would always be reminders that whatever started out as familiar, domestic or 'encultured' could become progressively unfamiliar, wild, and 'naturalized'. This is why, as John Lyall's feral thematic suggests, the southern settler societies also *unsettle*: why they demonstrate with particular clarity and prescience the ambivalence of a modernity which defines itself by its ordering impulses. And it is why the notion of the performative, with its repertoire of permutations wrought by the particular, seems peculiarly relevant—too pertinent to be restricted to the play of culture or discourse.

Lyall's performance works have a complex structure: they explore the transmutations of the biophysical environment that issue from the European advance into the southern colonies at the same time as they inquire into the transfor-

Figure 1: *Requiem for Electronic Moa,* directed by John Lyall, Soundculture (1999)

© The Editorial Board of the Sociological Review 2003

mation of European modes of representing 'nature' that are effected by their radical relocation across the planet. At the core of these works is a set of tasks that a cast of performers must struggle to complete in the allotted time and space, using a combination of resources they bring with them or find on location. Many of these operations demand an improvisation of techniques of display and artistic expression which are ill-adapted to the context at hand, a reference to the pressures placed on European aesthetic canons and practices by the encounter with a distant and different world. But always at the heart of Lyall's work is the feral motif: the insistence that the aesthetic or cultural performance, and all its makeshift strivings, is continuous with the ongoing inventiveness of biological life when it is faced with the challenge of a novel or changing environment (see Clark, 1996).

In the *Requiem for Electronic Moa* performances (Lyall, 1999, 2000), amongst a host of other iterations of the transformative events of the antipodean periphery, the audience can catch a glimpse of 'feral' life-forms, proliferating and dispersing in real time (Figure 1). Utilizing an early generation (and rather obsolete) computer game, one of the performers 'breeds' a set of simple, organic forms. These digital creations include representatives of the species that have been introduced and the organisms that are indigenous to the Australasian lands (Figure 2). Over the course of the performance these life-forms interact, competing for the resources and space of the computer program. Some evolve into new forms

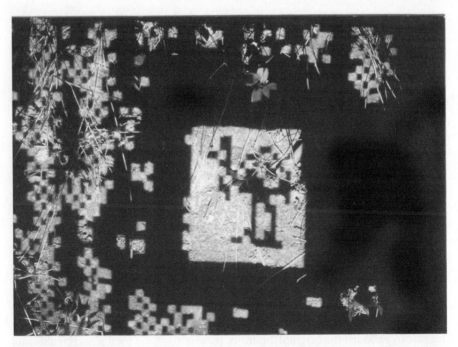

Figure 2: Pixellated Moa, John Lyall, from *Requiem for Electronic Moa* (1999)

173

Figure 3: Towards a Hyper-Feral Art, Aotearoa: A Universal Appliqué – Tiger, John Lyall (1995)

while others may die out; but the outcome is never predictable, as the program is open-ended enough to allow for a great range of possible permutations.

What Lyall is doing here is using the idea of basic computer 'evolutionary' programs—structured around their own hidden core of coded instructions—as a medium to explore the scrambling and re-coding process that occurs under the selective pressures of a novel environment. The significance of this strand of the performance becomes clearer if we look at Lyall's photographic work, which has been exhibited separately, but which also features as slide projections in the *Electronic Moa* performances. In *Towards a Hyper-Feral Art, Aotearoa: A Universal Appliqué*, Lyall again uses simple computer programs to construct generic organisms—which take the form the form of minimum recognizable signifiers of surface patterning or body shape (Lyall, 1995, see also 1997). Photographed from the computer screen onto slide film, these images are projected onto a bank of exposed earth and re-photographed (Figure 3). This earth surface is nothing more than the trans-section of soil and clay which is to be found wherever excavations occur: its grainy textures, irregular surfaces and sprinkling of plant-life serving to subtly distort the images projected on it (see Clark, 1996: 56). In this way, Lyall suggests that the particularities of the local context work their transformative effects on every incoming entity to which it plays host. However 'disciplined' or rigorously encoded the original 'figure' is, there is always at least a partial undoing and remaking when it touches down on fresh soil.

174

Lyall's enactments of biological improvisation have a reference point in the observed evolutionary consequences of translocation for colonising species. Colonizing biota tends to find itself in a situation where it is free from familiar predators and pathogens, and often lacks its usual competitors. A novel set of selection pressures, the availability of vacant niches in host ecosystems, and genetic drift[2] all increase the likelihood of physiological divergence in an invasive species (Low, 1999: 242–3). Studies of free-ranging, introduced biota in New Zealand and Australia not only offer evidence of the return of previously suppressed genetic expressions, but suggest that actual divergence of species from their parent populations is taking place (see Wodzicki, 1965). It has been argued, for example, that there are now rabbits 'unique to Australia'. As ecologist Laurie Corbett claims, '[t]he physiological and genetic differences between rabbits in Australia and the original Spanish rabbits are due to their interaction with the peculiarities of the Australian environment' (cited in Morton and Smith, 1999: 163–164).

So, too, are there signs that local or indigenous biota can adjust to the presence of new arrivals. In New Zealand, there is evidence that native plants are becoming more resistant to the damage done by the possum, an Australian import. There are, moreover, examples of endangered Australasian native species becoming dependent on weedy, runaway exotic plants as food sources (Low, 1999: 241). At the same time, the exotic coniferous forests of New Zealand have become an important habitat for native birds, to the extent that they may support higher densities of bird-life than some native forests (Wodzicki, 1965: 440). An earlier 'irony' of invasive biology was the unexpected but vital role played by exotic weeds in stabilizing the soil of the new colonies. When the hooves of introduced livestock had churned and loosened the topsoil, it was often the uninvited and accidentally disseminated weeds of Europe—the botanical 'lowlife' that had snuck into the colonies amongst the seeds of 'respectable' fodder crops—which took root on the bare earth and mitigated further erosion (Crosby, 1986: 288–91; Guthrie-Smith, 1999: 276).

The territorial refrain

The impact of introduced biota—for better or worse—on vegetative cover, and on the stability and composition of the soil of the temperate periphery, offers a cogent reminder of the deep interconnection of life-form and landform. Just as Lyall's projections of 'life' onto soil warp and reshape the figure of the living being, so too, does the transmutation work in the other direction. Indeed, so implicated are living organisms with the ground they inhabit that antipodean earth and life scientists have been wont to describe life as 'the uppermost geological layer' (Gray, 1989: 797; Grehan, 1988: 480). What a sense of 'rocks and flesh' as co-creations suggests is that the performative force of the living is not simply played out on a static and pre-given stage. No longer a mere a substrate, the 'ground' or the 'space' of life's intricate dramas begins to well up into the realm of generative iteration.

© The Editorial Board of the Sociological Review 2003

It is time, then, to add some literal grit to Butler's metaphor of 'sedimenta-tion' (1993: 11; 1997: 159). We have seen that Kirby and other Australian fem-inists are less than satisfied with Butler's unwillingness to consider the capacities of matter in any sense other than as a 'materializing effect' of language or dis-course. Once, however, that the privileged enclosure of human language as the site of differentiation and articulation is opened to an 'outside', a 'beyond', or a 'beneath', this deconstructive movement can be pushed still further. 'Flesh'—the realm of the biophysical—can in turn be opened to its outside: a world of inorganic matter imbued with the generativity and self-organizing capabilities that are the very condition or possibility of life (see Wilson, 1999: 16). Indeed, as each successive 'substrate' turns out itself to be a mutable arrangement of other elements, the very idea of an ultimately stable ground gives way to endless deferral—or what Derrida has described as 'the indefinitely articulated regress of the beginning' (1981: 333–334).

In this way, just as we have been viewing social and biological identities as the provisional outcome of many iterated acts, so too, can 'landform', 'space', 'territory' or 'environment' be construed as a kind of enactment: the outcome of shifting, sifting, sorting and literal sedimentations rather than a pre-given state. 'Space then is not an anterior actant to be filled or spanned or con-structed', as Gillian Rose has put it, '. . . . space is practised, a matrix of play, dynamic and iterative' (1999: 248). Philosophers Gilles Deleuze and Felix Guattari make a similar claim about the particular space or territory we call 'home'. As they would have it, 'home does not pre-exist', it is a form of orga-nization, a demarcation that is enacted through gestures and markings, selec-tions and exclusions (1987: 311). Derrida, too, has made the point that the whole idea of a primordial 'homeland' as a pure and unadulterated place of origin serves to conceal an inevitably messy genesis. A homeland, he argues, is always a retrospective tidying up, an imagining that excludes the many coming and goings, meetings and mixtures that have made all places what they are (Derrida, 1981: 21, 304).

In the context of accelerating globalization, questions of belonging and ter-ritorial identification have risen to prominence in political discourse over recent decades. Today, few critical thinkers are willing to admit that peoples spring forth from a native soil or that they belong, by any natural or absolute right, to a fixed parcel of land. In this light, politically sensitive commentators on bio-invasion have taken pains not to allow their cautionary words about the inva-sive species problem to slip into a condemnation of migrants, refugees or other mobile human groups. 'We want a world in which people are as free as possible to travel and to exchange goods and ideas', Chris Bright declares, 'but at the same time, we *need* a world in which most other living things stay put' (1999: 200). The implication of such intentions however, is that human beings are exceptional, and thereby discontinuous with the rest of the nature. Territorial-ity might be practised or enacted on the part of our own species, but with regards to other life-forms, it appears to be pre-existent and inviolable. This is precisely the kind of dualism that each of our 'antipodean iterations' of the per-

176

formativity of life refrain have been attempting to disavow. And if we look more closely at what Derrida, or Deleuze and Guattari are saying about homelands and territories, it is also clear that no such scission between humankind and the rest of the world is implied.

Whereas most social scientists have shied away from possible connections between human territoriality and that of other forms of life, Deleuze and Guattari (1987) have no such hesitation. For them, the territorial inclination found amongst certain human social groups is continuous with similar impulses discernible not only throughout the biological realms, but also in the inorganic world. A central concern in Deleuze and Guattari's collaborative work is the spontaneous, self-organizing processes through which new forms or structures emerge, not only in the social realm but at all levels and domains of existence. For them, the emergence of patterns or discernible 'refrains' out of more inchoate or diffuse states is constitutive of the physical world, as well as the bio-logical or social realms (1987: ch 11).

Such generative events are always improvisations, variations on a theme that reflect the specific context or milieu in which they emerge. Every 'refrain', in this sense, expresses a relationship with the particular place from which it emerged: 'it always carries earth with it, it has a land . . . as its concomitant', (Deleuze and Guattari, 1987: 312). As Deleuze and Guattari suggest, emergent patterns or refrains tend to settle down over time into expressions which constitute more stable spatial forms—as in the territories marked out by birds with distinctive songs, or in the space of nationhood articulated by human collectivities through border-posts or anthems (see 1987: 314). 'Territory', viewed in this way, is a certain kind of entrenched patterning or refrain, a spatial organization that emerges as the outcome of many itera-tions. For Deleuze and Guattari, such enactment of territory is first and foremost an act of differentiation from within: it is a way that an expression of distinctness of identity emerges out of sameness or disorganization (1987: 319–320).

In this light, Derrida's perspective on the acting out of territoriality has an alternative focus, in that for him it is primarily the encounter with something or someone strange that institutes a border. He proposes the border or demarca-tion of territory cannot pre-exist the arrival of 'strangers' or 'others' or 'aliens', for it is only through successive encounters with the strange and unfamiliar that the distinction between belonging and not-belonging can sediment itself (Derrida, 1993: 33–5). Deleuze and Guattari's differentiating force from within, and Derrida's differentiating force from without may not be in full agreement, but they are equally intimating of an iterated or enacted take on territoriality. And they are perhaps ultimately complementary—for as Lyall's concept of the 'feral' reminds us—the border between insiders and outsiders, between the strange and the familiar, can be crossed in more than one direction. That which we encounter as recognizable and known may once have been strange to us, but those that confront us from 'beyond the pale' may once have belonged within our fold.

© The Editorial Board of the Sociological Review 2003

Lessons for/from colonial life

Whichever aspect of the constitutive traffic of 'territorialization' we chose to foreground, a generalized 'performative' perspective prompts us to think about spatial relations as patternings that emerge out of movements, encounters and improvisations. In this light, the introduction of a species—or a cultural trait—from a distant territory is less an absolute rupture with an essential nature than an intensification of a potential for making and remaking territories that inheres deep in the working of the world. But a vision of earth and life as the congealing of so many performances does not mean such mobilizations should be taken lightly. Derrida cautions that any opening up of a new path is a creative act, yet 'presupposes a certain violence' (1978: 200). In a related sense, Deleuze and Guattari emphasize that once territories have taken shape, any rupture or movement between them is at once potentially generative and devastating: 'a too-sudden deterritorialization may be suicidal, or turn cancerous' (1987: 503).

Analogously, Lyall's *Requiem for Electronic Moa* interleaves its recognition of generative transmissions with acknowledgements of loss, not least being the titular genus of great flightless birds of Aotearoa New Zealand. Moa were already extinct when Europeans arrived, a reminder that earlier Polynesian migrations had also come at a price (Figure 4). Likewise, Dening's paean to insular breachings and improvisations is counterposed with the narrating of

Figure 4: The Naming of the Parts: Moa Reflecting, John Lyall (1998)

 © The Editorial Board of the Sociological Review 2003

cultural and biotic devastation on the islands in question (1980). Yet, for all the danger of novel transmissions that has attended the various phases of human venture into 'blue water', trans-oceanic mobility is far from the prerogative of our own species. The populating of islands by rich—if often eccentric— biotic communities, as evolutionary theorists from Darwin's era onwards have recognized, is indicative of the momentous role played by occasional ocean crossings. Moreover, such migrations intimate that the oceans themselves are more than simply 'absences' or empty intervals. For the sea, as Dening reminds us, plays a constitutive role in the sifting and sorting of the elements that pass through or over it (1992: 307). And even the oceans are not unchanging in their breadth, depth or composition.

But there is no escaping the charge that intensifying human mobility across oceans and continents is unravelling and reweaving long-established territorial refrains at a rate which is without precedent. In the majority of cases, the long-distance translocation of life—in all its forms—has induced damage and loss both for the transported population and for the worlds it encounters. This is especially so in the opening phases when territorial settlings are most rapidly rent. There is plentiful evidence of such devastation and no shortage of reasons to give consideration to those who urge greater caution—in any realm of transmission. In this regard, the point of acknowledging the continuity between human and non-human, organic and inorganic 'performances' is not to imply that 'anything goes', or to abjure accountability or judgement on our part.

It is, rather, to underscore our degree of implication in the materiality of the world, and in this way to extend the sphere of human responsibility rather than to delimit it. Even the rarefied realms of aesthetic thought and practice, as John Lyall's performance works intimate, have biotic and earthy entanglements. Or as Herbert Guthrie-Smith once observed of the imbroglio of Antipodean cultural and biotic life, even a provincial musical recital would have its own particular part to play in the dissemination of weedy, invasive plants. 'Top-hats, violins, ground resin, old catgut, long hair, and broken piano-wire would doubt-less . . . produce their specialised flora', he notes—a playful reminder that where conditions are particularly conducive even the most unlikely cultural practices may have significant biological repercussions (Guthrie-Smith, 1999: 295).

But a sense of the performative that breaks with culture's self-enclosure must also concede that the responsibility for deterritorializing life and landform does not rest entirely with our own species. Just as the very process of evolution is an accretion of immense numbers of individual decisions on the part of living things themselves, so too, should we keep in mind that invasive organisms play an active role in their dispersions and ongoing improvisations—and are often more than willing instigators of their own relocation (see Margulis and Sagan, 1995: 185; Waddington, 1965: 1). In this sense, the feral escapees and trans-oceanic stowaways that have populated the southern temperate zones are at least partially consensual participants in a vast 'series of experiments in evolution' (Waddington, 1965: 1).

© The Editorial Board of the Sociological Review 2003

The lessons we can learn from these unfinished and interminable experiments have relevance far beyond the former colonial 'periphery' where they have been concentrated. Biological introductions, geneticist C. H. Waddington has observed, offer a huge amount of evidence about the ways in which organisms cope with evolutionary challenges. Presciently, he further noted that our knowledge about how colonizing biota adjust to new environments can also cast light on the experience of populations which stay at home—but find themselves forced to respond to changes in their own environment (1965: 5). And quite often it is these changes—such as habit fragmentation, shrinkage and disturbance—that increase the likelihood of invading organisms becoming established, and thereby turn bio-invasion into a fully global and multi-directional phenomena (see Bright, 1999: 173).

While many of the earlier 'runaway' events of Europe's antipodes have been at least partially 'reterritorialized', Europeans are now being reawakened to the unruliness of biological life—as they contemplate rising domestic bio-invasion problems as well as the possibility of new biotechnologically-induced disseminations. With increasing frequency, life-forms from the southern colonial periphery and elsewhere are establishing themselves in the northern temperate zones. And as we contemplate this counter-flow, so too might we ask what will become of the 'feral' theme in antipodean thought and practice, should it gain a foothold in territories half a world away from the site of its inception. In an era of intensifying global exchanges, it seems ever more likely that 'peripheral' refrains will take their turn to unsettle the metropolitan landscape (see Deleuze and Guattari, 1987: 50). This is the possibility intimated by Lyall's *Dis-located Moa* performance (2000)—the re-enactment of an antipodean event under very different conditions 12,000 miles to north. What might happen, we are left to ponder, when metropolitan cultural and biological forms which have run loose and adapted in the Southern Hemisphere, are encouraged to make the return trip 'home' a century and a half later?

Notes on photographs

All photographs are copyright of John Lyall.
Figure 1. cibachrome print documenting performance (photo: John Lyall)
Figure 2. cibachrome print documenting installation of a computer drawing
Figure 3. cibachrome print documenting installation of a computer drawing
Figure 4. cibachrome print

Notes

1 The role of Australia as a British penal colony, in this sense, offers a bridging point between domestic discipline and the geographical extension of the European model.
2 Genetic drift refers to the random changes in gene frequency that are especially pronounced when there is a small 'founder population'.

© The Editorial Board of the Sociological Review 2003

References

Adam, B. (1998), *Timescapes of Modernity: The Environment and Invisible Hazards*, London and New York: Routledge.

Battersby, C. (2000), 'Learning to Think Intercontinentally: Finding Australian Roots', *Hypatia*, 15(2): 1–17.

Beck, U. (1992), *Risk Society: Towards a New Modernity*, London: Sage.

Beck, U. (1995), *Ecological Politics in an Age of Risk*, Cambridge: Polity Press.

Bright, C. (1999), *Life out of Bounds*, London: Earthscan.

Butler, J. (1990), *Gender Trouble*, London: Routledge.

Butler, J. (1993), *Bodies that Matter: On the Discursive Limits of 'Sex'*, New York and London: Routledge.

Butler, J. (1997), *Excitable Speech: A Politics of the Performative*, New York and London: Routledge.

Clark, N. (1996), 'Towards the Feral: John Lyall at Karekare', *Art New Zealand* 78: 54–57.

Colebrook, C. (2000), 'From Radical Representations to Corporeal Becomings: The Feminist Philosophy of Lloyd, Grosz, and Gatens', *Hypatia*, 15(2): 76–93.

Crosby, A. (1986), *Ecological Imperialism*, Cambridge: Cambridge University Press.

Darwin, C. (1996 [1859]), *The Origin of Species*, Oxford: Oxford University Press.

De Landa, M. (1997), *A Thousand Years of Nonlinear History*, New York: Swerve.

Deleuze, G. and F. Guattari (1987 [1980]), *A Thousand Plateaus: Capitalism and Schizophrenia*, Minneapolis: University of Minnesota Press.

Dening, G. (1980), *Islands and Beaches: Discourse on a Silent Land: Marquesas 1774–1880*, Honolulu: University Press of Hawaii.

Dening, G. (1992), *Mr Bligh's Bad Language: Passion, Power and Theatre on the Bounty*, New York: Cambridge University Press.

Derrida, J. (1978 [1968]*)*, *Writing and Difference*, London: Routledge.

Derrida, J. (1981 [1972]), *Dissemination*, Chicago: University of Chicago Press.

Derrida, J. (1993), *Aporias*, Stanford, CA: Stanford University Press.

Flannery, T. (1994), *The Future Eaters: An Ecological History of the Australasian Lands and People*, Kew, Vic.: Reed Books.

Foucault, M. (1989 [1966]), *The Order of Things: An Archaeology of the Human Sciences*, London: Routledge.

Foucault, M. (1990 [1976]), *The History of Sexuality, Volume 1: An Introduction*, London: Penguin Books.

Foucault, M. (1991 [1975]), *Discipline and Punish: The Birth of the Prison*, London: Penguin.

Giddens, A. (1994), 'Living in a Post-Traditional Society' in U. Beck, A. Giddens and S. Lash (eds), *Reflexive Modernization: Politics, Tradition and Aesthetics in the Modern Social Order*, Cambridge: Polity Press, pp. 56–109.

Gray, R. (1989), 'Oppositions in Panbiogeography: Can the Conflicts between Selection, Constraint, Ecology, and History Be Resolved?', *New Zealand Journal of Zoology* 16(4): 787–806.

Grehan, J. R. (1988), 'Panbiogeography and Evolution', *Rivista di Biologia Biology Forum*, 81(4): 469–498.

Grosz, E. (1995), *Space, Time and Perversion*, New York and London: Routledge.

Grosz, E. (1999), 'Darwin and Feminism: Preliminary Investigations for a Possible Alliance', *Australian Feminist Studies*, 14(29): 31–45.

Guthrie-Smith, H. (1999[1921]), *Tutira: The Story of a New Zealand Sheep Station*, Auckland: Godwit.

Kerin, J. (1999), 'The Matter at Hand: Butler, Ontology and the Natural Sciences', *Australian Feminist Studies* 14(29): 91–104.

Kirby, V. (1997), *Telling Flesh: The Substance of the Corporeal*, London: Routledge.

© The Editorial Board of the Sociological Review 2003

Lamb, J. (1999), 'The Idea of Utopia in the European Settlement of New Zealand' in K. Neumann, N. Thomas and H. Ericksen (eds), *Quicksands: Foundational Histories in Australia and Aotearoa New Zealand*, Sydney: University of New South Wales Press, pp. 79–97.

Lloyd, G. (2000), 'No One's Land: Australia and the Philosophical Imagination', *Hypatia* 15(2): 26–58.

Low, T. (1999), *Feral Future*, Ringwood, Vic.: Viking.

Lyall, J. (1995), 'Toward an Hyper-Feral Art, Aotearoa', in *The Nervous System: Twelve Artists Explore Images and Identities in Crisis*, Te Whare Toi, Wellington: City Art Gallery.

Lyall, J. (1997), 'Toward an Hyper-Feral Art, Aotearoa: A Projected Journey: given both a Pixellated Bestiary and an Uncertain arCADian Plane', in *alt.nature*, Auckland: Artspace.

Lyall, J. (1999), *Requiem for Electronic Moa*, dir. J. Lyall, performed at *Soundculture*, Auckland, NZ, March 1999.

Lyall, J. (2000), *Requiem for Dis-located Moa*, dir. J. Lyall, performed at Between Nature, Explorations in ecology and performance, Lancaster University, Lancaster UK, July 2000.

McKibben, B. (1990), *The End of Nature*, London: Penguin.

Margulis, L. and D. Sagan (1995), *What is Life?*, New York: Simon and Schuster.

Morton, J. and N. Smith (1999), 'Planting Indigenous Species', in K. Neumann, N. Thomas and H. Ericksen (eds) *Quicksands: Foundational Histories in Australia and Aotearoa New Zealand*, Sydney: University of New South Wales Press, pp.153–175.

Park, G. (1995), *Nga Uruora: The Groves of Life: Ecology and History in a New Zealand Landscape*, Wellington: Victoria University Press.

Pyne, S. J. (1997), *Vestal Fire*, Seattle and London: University of Washington Press.

Rolls, E. (1969), *They All Ran Wild: The Story of Pests on the Land in Australia*, Sydney: Angus and Robertson.

Rose, G. (1999), 'Performing Space' in D. Massey, J. Allen and P. Sarre (eds), *Human Geography Today*, Malden, MA: Polity Press, pp. 247–259.

Strathern, M. (1992), *After Nature: English Kinship in the Late Twentieth Century*, Cambridge: Cambridge University Press.

Thrift, N. and J.-D. Dewsbury (2000), 'Dead Geographies and How to Make Them Live', *Environment and Planning D: Society and Space*, (18): 411–432.

Waddington, C. H. (1965), 'Introduction to the Symposium' in G. H. Baker and G. L. Stebbins (eds), *The Genetics of Colonizing Species*, New York and London: Academic Press, pp. 1–6.

Wilson, E. A. (1998), *Neural Geographies: Feminism and the Microstructure of Cognition*, New York and London: Routledge.

Wilson, E. A. (1999), 'Somatic Compliance- Feminism, Biology and Science' *Australian Feminist Studies*, 14(29): 7–18.

Wodzicki, K. (1965), 'The Status of Some Exotic Vertebrates in the Ecology of New Zealand' in G. H. Baker and G. L. Stebbins (eds), *The Genetics of Colonizing Species*, New York and London: Academic Press, pp. 425–460.

© The Editorial Board of the Sociological Review 2003

Slow activism: homelands, love and the lightbulb

Wallace Heim

To come into conversation can be a disturbing thing, exposing, altering and aesthetic. How the conversation is made can conduct the speakers in an unknown direction, towards friendship, argument, silence, the emergence of something new. The intentions and allure of the speakers colour the exchange. The timing, location and milieu can enfold the speakers in a world at once marked out from and embedded within the everyday. For example, to talk with a stranger about love, home and ecological interdependency—while sitting in the back of a large truck parked on a fast-trafficked street—rests those conversations within the social conventions and ethical demands of speaking together in public, while inviting an event into existence, one in which the aesthetic, imaginative, and transformative may be realized.

During the last thirty years, artists-performers-activists have been creating events and actions in which a conversation with a public is the performative core, and in some, conceptions of nature-human relations are imagined and spoken into being. As created events, they allow for experimentation of how a public space can be created, however transiently, through the speaking together about those relations. They initiate rehearsals of a culture in which those public conversations are possible, within situations imbued with the aesthetic, and which have purposes, however indirectly drawn, to bring about a change. And, as created works, they allow for a critical viewing of those processes.

My questions in this chapter are methodological. 'Method' is not taken in terms of replicable procedures, but as the processes through which an event is created and has bearing and potency. 'How do these works "work"?' and 'How do they form a mode of understanding nature-human relations?' are questions addressed first through the particular. This chapter interprets the methods of one work of social practice art: HOMELAND, a nomadic public dialogue action by PLATFORM. HOMELAND is not paradigmatic of that diverse family of art, but it does show the potential and fragility of these works which are hybrids of activism, performance, and conversation. It exposed the delicacy of that balance between creating the space for an equitable public exchange and using conversation as an indirectly persuasive medium. HOMELAND may not have evoked the responses it intended, but its methods allowed for an experience of public dialogue, which, in turn, allowed for the

© The Editorial Board of the Sociological Review 2003. Published by Blackwell Publishing Ltd, 9600 Garsington Road, Oxford OX4 2DQ, UK and 350 Main Street, Malden, MA 02148, USA

unexpected to emerge, not in contradiction to the work's purposes, but in an enrichment of them.

My emphasis is on that potential for change, the performative methods for disclosing and altering an habitual action, thought, or perception, and for transporting the participants to a new recognition or understanding. One, more private and reflective method, is through the operation of imagination as it mediates between the metaphoric elements of the *mise en scène*. Other, more social methods are through conversation and the spoken exchanges of narratives. These, too, have imaginative and heuristic force, the capacity to open up new dimensions of reality, to allow for new values and subjectivities to be tried out. The 'doing' of conversation, the give and take of questioning and listening influenced by the directed content, can be an experience approximating the democratizing, moral conversation described by communicative and dialogic ethics.[1] As a form of rhetorical argument, conversation can be a practice of collective reasoning, contingent and fallible, in situations of uncertainty. For the conversations to persuade, they need also to be occasions of character, in which the phenomena of an ethics of character or virtue can be experienced. Following Hans-Georg Gadamer (1989), the process of conversation is analogous to that of coming to an understanding, or of interpreting a work of art; in these events, conversation is the 'work' of art, an understanding mutually created.

Attributes of performance apply to these works: ephemeral, ambiguous, improvisatory, risky. They are also a form of social reason, occasions for talking together, in public, about nature-human relations. They are also a form of activism, politicized interventions advancing an idea, but proceeding in the time it takes to engage in conversation. Some works continue to have effect beyond the event, reverberating in the stories about it, passed along like a slow contagion.

HOMELAND in the family of social practice art

PLATFORM is a social practice collective working in London, England. It started in 1983, and at present is comprised of core members Dan Gretton, James Marriott and Jane Trowell. PLATFORM's members work as artists, educators, historians, performers, activists, writers. Trowell describes their work as 'intimate acts of exchange and trust, proposal and re-imagining' (2000: 100). Conversation is a method of PLATFORM, a medium and skill developed through practice within the collective and 'listening' actions.[2] Each project develops its own form and timescale, and brings together its own interdisciplinary team; for HOMELAND that was Gretton, Marriott, and John Jordan, a core member at that time. HOMELAND was commissioned by the 1993 London International Festival of Theatre, following PLATFORM's work *Still Waters*, begun in 1992, which consisted of four events and projects each marking a buried or canalized tributary of the River Thames.[3]

© The Editorial Board of the Sociological Review 2003

HOMELAND continued with that idea of making visible something unseen: light itself—the actuality of how the city is lit, and metaphorically, how it illuminates feelings and conceptions of home, territory and environmental interconnectedness. A large furniture truck, a pantechnicon, housed the event, parking each day of the 10-day Festival on a London street. Inside, an installation formed the *mise en scène* for conversations between a member of PLATFORM and a public participant.

PLATFORM's intentions, as I interpret them, were to enable connections to be made, firstly between one's sense of 'home', and the imagined sense of 'home' by someone in a distant country. That possible projection of feelings outward, from the near-by and familiar to an unknown person in a distant country, could be extended to a feeling for the land on which London rests, to the lands on which the city depends, and for the possible damage to other homes and lands which that dependency could incur. The urban home's inseparability from other landscapes was shown through an explication of the manufacture of a lightbulb, tracking the city's dependency for its functioning and liveliness on the extraction of minerals from other landscapes, on the processes of energy production, manufacturing and transport which cross political boundaries. The unseen provision of electricity, the ubiquity of artificial light, the everyday habits of turning on the light-switch were to be made apparent and the effects of those actions made intimate and visceral through their connection with feelings of home, belonging, land and responsibility. Those feelings were to be extended through connecting one's narrative within a pattern of other, imagined, emotional territories.

In the wider context, in 1993, the Balkans were at war. Europeans were killing each other over nationalist and economic claims, and to achieve 'ethnic cleansing'. Against this background, PLATFORM were asking the public to disperse their concepts of home, to de-territorialize the spatial identifications of home, to blur the emotional marks which limit their extension of belonging.

'Nature' in this work was not the lost river symbolizing the flow of civic dreams, but spoken into being in the narrated landscapes. As the conceptions of 'homeland' were to be dispersed, so too, was 'nature', represented as unseen lands and the mined elements of those lands lost into the hard surfaces of the everyday, industrialized in the provision of energy.

The family of social practice art

The methods for declaring and realizing PLATFORM's intentions were to offer to the public face-to-face questioning, open-ended conversation, symbolic objects and contemplative actions. These methods place HOMELAND within the loosely associated, international family of art works and actions known as social practice art, social sculpture, littoral art, dialogic art, new genre public art.[4] These terms refer to heuristic approaches more than formal categories. These works can be hybrids of differing forms of performance, image-making,

© The Editorial Board of the Sociological Review 2003

activism, and social research. They can be marked out as aesthetic works and be indiscernible from everyday activities; they can exist as transient events, or be settled in a location over an extended timescale. But there are shared patterns of formal methods, predominantly the incorporation of dialogue between the artist(s) and participant(s).

Because these works are resolutely *between* conventional forms, criticism from one disciplinary perspective can find the works lacking. From the visual arts, the absence of an object, the durational aspect, and the inclusion of dialogue have required the development of new critical frameworks (see Kester, forthcoming). Likewise, the expectations of theatre, in which extremes of emotions can be conveyed and fictional identities entertained, will not be met by works which are embedded in the everyday, which are constrained by the ethical imperatives and social conventions of speaking face-to-face with another person. The apparent lack of control and blending of 'art' and 'life' can identify the works as Actions or Happenings; but many are not 'events' and beneath the improvisation can be a strong activist, politicized directive to transport participants towards a given or mutually decided change in thought or perception. As instances of activism, though, they can be without displays of provocation or demonstration. They are without the collective, festive suspension of quotidian norms which are evident in some protests. They seldom present a narrowed issue against which a clear sense of resistance can be achieved.

The polyvalence and indeterminacy of 'performance'—as ephemeral event, as process and practice—can describe aspects of these works. HOMELAND was a performative event, 'the creation of an occasion of experience', in the terms of the philosopher of aesthetics Arnold Berleant, a circumstance which happens in which perceptual activity is immediate and intrinsic (1991: 154). The performative event, as defined by theatre theoretician Bert O. States, is '[t]he manipulation of empirical reality toward what is . . . an artistic statement being made about reality' (1996: 16). According to States, the phenomenon of performance is transformation. Something is always transformed, something is brought into existence and in some way made recognizable, and this way of seeing involves collaborative and contextual relations between the work and the spectator or participant. Performance offers the fundamental pleasure of transformation, and it involves memory as a creative ability (States, 1996: 20–22). But 'performance' does not entirely capture the phenomenon, the feelings of alteration and potential which can attend to these works.

That desire for transformation is directed by variations in the liberal social and environmental ethos which infuses most works in this 'family'. The transformation intended can be perceptual and conceptual; works also can instigate consensually determined decisions and actions, negotiate issues of environmental justice, bring the aesthetic into processes of collaboration. Some incorporate public dialogue in projects which are physical interventions in a natural environment, transforming landscapes. Ideals of the procedures of dialogue, of the democratic value of communicative processes in effecting social change, are critical markers. The political perspectives and moral accountability of the artists

© The Editorial Board of the Sociological Review 2003

have become part of the critical remit, as has the artists' skill in creating equitable, dialogic situations, in creating public spaces for conversation imbued with the aesthetic. The intentions of the artists, as articulated and as perceived by a participant, have returned as elements for criticism, and can be considered as thematic ground to be compared with their expressive, performative methods.

'Conversational drift' to slow activism

The artists Newton and Helen Mayer Harrison use the term 'conversational drift' to describe their method of initiating conversations and storytelling between publics, policy makers and environmental scientists in projects which re-map a region or watershed (Adcock, 1992: 39, 45). The 'drift' is in the non-argumentative fluidity of the conversations. The diverse perspectives brought forward by the 'drift' can evolve towards creative responses to complex patterns of social and environmental problems.

There is another dimension to 'drift' I would add, which is that the artist creates the conditions for conversation to continue beyond the reach of the event. Consistent with Hannah Arendt's understanding of 'action', the conversation produces stories which extend beyond the speaking, moving unpredictably through the social realm as they are told and re-told (see Arendt, 1958). These stories may be made visible through art works, objects and documentation (Arendt, 1958: 184). But in conversational works, the speaking is the 'art', and with some, there is the intention and possibility that the conversation set loose will carry its contents and manners adapting and drifting into the future. The artist initiates an exchange which 'works' not only in the immediacy of the event, but could 'work' in unforeseen situations. That initial exchange, and its setting and narrative, can be recounted and storied. Those stories can continue to reverberate as uncontrollable extensions of the work, with new meanings emerging in unexpected, untraceable places; they become feral. An experience of conversation which is transformative is also a practice, a rehearsal for another. That initial public meeting cannot be reproduced, but the methods and the ethos bringing the situation into being can be adapted, experimented with in other contexts, not only by the artists but also by the public participants, who have already mutually created the event. It is an experience which makes further experience possible (see Gadamer, 1989: 346–362).

This is slow activism. The slowness refers not only to the duration of the event and the drift which can be momentary or extend over years, but to its temper. There is a resistance in slowness which responds to the reductive aspects of haste and frenzy. The locus of change is one person at a time, in a process of communication which is dependent on finding enough common meaning between the artist and participant to sustain a dialogue. This mutual adjustment is method. It is not only a prerequisite, but inherent; it is a process which forms the work. The activist potential for change develops in the time it takes to speak about something, and for it to be 'listened' into existence. This involves not only the matter conversed, but the subjectivities engaged, which are, in the action, opened to change.

This does not imply a necessary connection between emotional and perceptual responses and a change in moral values or a disturbance of conceptual orientations. An event can insulate, confirm, and irritate; conversational methods could be used repressively. Not all conversation is transformative, or art. But in those works that do propose the democratic and ethical effects outlined, the artists are attempting to question and respond to social and environmental conditions, in ways which go with the fabric of the everyday but attempt not to replicate the languages and spaces of those conditions. As Alasdair MacIntyre writes, '[t]he ability to respond adequately to this kind of cultural need depends of course on whether those summoned possess intellectual and moral resources that transcend the immediate crisis, which enable them to say to the culture what the culture cannot say to itself' (MacIntyre, 1981: 3–4, quoted in M. Smith, 2001: 14). There are works in this 'family' which have asked challenging questions, in protected spaces, suffusing those public encounters with imaginative, aesthetic and sensuous knowledge. What they may elicit is the previously unspeakable, spoken not only by the artist, but by someone else.

HOMELAND—what was offered

PLATFORM's research in preparation for HOMELAND identified three junctions in the provision of electric light: 1) the quarrying of silica sand and the

© The Editorial Board of the Sociological Review 2003

manufacture of lightbulbs at General Electric's factory in Hungary; 2) the mining of copper ore for electric cable by Rio Tinto Zinc in Portugal; and 3) the mining of coal by the then British Coal in Wales. The pantechnicon was parked each day in front of the corporate offices of RTZ, GE, or British Coal, or by a building representative of one of the countries involved: two Portuguese cafés, two British-Hungarian societies' meeting rooms, and the London Welsh Centre.

On the exterior of the pantechnicon was an image which was composed of two photographs, one of a bombed rural dwelling and one of a burned forest landscape with the words:

WHAT DO YOU LOVE MOST
YOUR HOME OR YOUR LAND?

Once the pantechnicon was parked, the back shutters were opened and white steps set out onto the street. The area nearest the opening was laid with artificial grass and set with garden tables and chairs. The public were welcomed to step up onto this garden terrace and invited to sit down. They were given a brochure, with questions printed in English, Hungarian, Welsh and Portuguese:

Across Europe people are killing each other over different meanings of *home*—What is Home for you?
Is there a place you love above any other?
Is this your *home*?
When you think of *home* what do you see or hear?
How much is your *home* built of memories?
Where are you most at *home*? In your street? Your town? Your region? Your country? Your continent?
Where do you feel you stop belonging?
How often do you think about the future of the place you call *home*?

PLATFORM would initiate conversations using these questions. If the person agreed, the dialogue would be recorded but kept anonymous. The length of each recording was limited to ten minutes, but the conversations found their own lengths, from a few minutes to several hours. The conversations had two stages: the first, directed by the printed questions, elicited a narrative. In the second, PLATFORM introduced questions and information about environmental interdependence, responding to that narrative. There was no fee charged, and of the people who entered, about half were passers-by, a quarter from the designated buildings, a quarter from the Festival audience.

The public were given a map of Greater London photocopied onto tracing paper and asked to mark the boundaries of their home territory, or a place that was special to them. They were invited to draw or write representations of home on small squares of paper using coloured pencils and pens. People were offered a lightbulb in a carton and told its narrative, tracing its production and entry into London.

© The Editorial Board of the Sociological Review 2003

Further inside the pantechnicon, backing the terrace and bathed in light, was a mock house with pitched roof, painted white. On the door were the words:

HOMELAND
MINHA TERRA
SZÜLŐFÖLD
FY NGWLAD I

The house was divided into a two room installation. Inside, the public were invited to photograph one of their hands, resting on a tray of earth, palm upwards. The side walls of the first, the 'Home' Room, were honeycombed with rows of hundreds of small squares. The transparencies of hands and the drawings of home were hung over these and back-lit. Each drawing and hand was anonymous, but numbered, identifying it with a numbered conversation tape, which was available at a desk, along with the marked maps and documentation from PLATFORM's preparatory research.

The dividing wall between the two rooms was a lapped wooden fascia with a door simulating the exterior of a house. On the door were the words:

THE FOOTPRINTS
OF YOUR HOME
STRETCH ACROSS
A CONTINENT

This 'Land' Room was darkened; as the public stepped over the threshold, they activated the room light. Three walls each had a mock door, with two back-lit panels of glass, one at eye level behind which ran a video of an opened hand, and a lower panel onto which a poem was etched, recounting the journeys of copper, coal and the lightbulb, and eulogizing the hands that mined and made them.

Not everyone spoke. Some people passed through, read, drew, mapped, photographed, or just listened. Had sufficient funding been available, HOMELAND would have travelled to Hungary, Portugal and Wales, then returned to London.

Coming to a recognition

Interpreting HOMELAND can only be a provisional exercise. In addition to those who watched from the street and those who did not speak, the work consisted of more than 300 conversations, or 300 events, mostly without witness. There are material traces but there is no one coherent performance to recall. My interpretation is derived from speculations on the potential of the elements offered to achieve the work's persuasive purposes—more specifically, the interplay of differing modes of metaphor and communication. It is based on experience of the event, subsequent conversations with PLATFORM, and a review of the documentation.[5]

The persuasive movement of the work was towards bringing the participants to a recognition, to an understanding of their position within a newly defined

© The Editorial Board of the Sociological Review 2003

world, to a knowledge about themselves within the context of patterns of nature-human relations which they may not have previously known. This would be a recognition of how others determine one's possible actions, one's identity. From the *Poetics*, Aristotelian recognition, *anagnôrisis*, is 'a change from ignorance to knowledge', disclosing a relationship (1996: 18–19 (52b) and 26–27 (55a)). It generally involves a perceptual act, seeing a sign or object, or observing human action. It can come about through memory, or from inference, or through the course of events. It is provoked through a social interaction, a questioning within a community, and can involve false, surprising or unanticipated consequences. Adaptations of those dramaturgies were apparent in HOMELAND, but with a difference. What is to be known, in classical tragedy, is fixed. In HOMELAND, recognition came about in a dynamic event, and what was to be recognized could not be predicted. Part of the work of PLATFORM was to create the capacity to recognize; through questioning and listening to make the preparations for a participant—and themselves—to see a disclosure of something not already known, which was collectively created, and not already fixed. In Gadamerian terms,

> The joy of recognition is rather the joy of knowing *more* than is already familiar. In recognition what we know emerges, as if illuminated, from all the contingent and variable circumstances that condition it; it is grasped in its essence. It is known as something (Gadamer, 1989: 114).

Although the overarching metaphors in the work were of sight and enlightenment, a trope through which HOMELAND can be interpreted is 'hearing'. A
performed event can be the co-mingling and extension of horizons of perception
and understanding. What is created in the experience, the new, is just beyond one's
existing horizons, and like sound, may reach the subject before it is disclosed to
sight. Recognition was 'heard' before it was seen through the operation of imagination in two regards: the experience of the symbolic and aesthetic aspects of
the material context of HOMELAND, its *mise en scène*; and in the heuristic force
of narrative. Both are described in Paul Ricoeur's theory of imagination in discourse and in action (1991: 168–187). A second 'hearing' refers to the out-loud
conversations within that framework of imagination. More than their informa-
tional content, the conversations were, in P. Christopher Smith's terms, 'original
argument', a form of rhetorical culture, to which I return below (1998: 1–12,
35–56). The conversations and the *mise en scène* animated and housed each other.
In HOMELAND, the sensual and ethical experience of conversation set the
ground by which one 'hears' oneself, and one's relations with nature, differently.

Hearing the new before it is seen: imagination as method

The nomadic truck inscribed an urban spatial story, in Michel de Certeau's
terms, conducting those protected and contained narratives over the frontiers
and bridges of homeland, the exiled, and the corporate (de Certeau, 1984:
115–130). Parked, the truck was a hesitation in the transport of carbon, a temporary siding in that traffic where the city exchanges goods and energy. In
Michel Foucault's terms, it was like a heterotopic site, a counter-site, reflecting
the surrounding commercial landscapes while creating a space which exposed
the illusions of those surrounding sites (Foucault, 1986: 22–27). It arrived
on the street, and drew the performance to it. It allowed for slow passage, silence,
touch and darkness, for enough of a suspension of the everyday for imagination to come into play.

The *mise en scène* of HOMELAND was a collocation of elements each of
which could be read for their symbolic value in communicating something
of nature, enlightenment and relationality. HOMELAND also afforded an embodied experience of the metaphoric which can be described by adapting
Ricoeur's theory of imagination (1991: 168–174). Ricoeur theorizes imagination
as method rather than as a visual scene in a mental theatre. He relates the operation of imagination to language, exemplified by the metaphorical process. It is
through the metaphoric that one has access to the phenomenon of imagination.
As method, imagination mediates the shock and dissonances produced by
metaphor. New meaning emerges out of the disturbance of semantic innovation
in metaphor as it is made in written discourse. Imagination is the operation of
grasping the similarity in dissimilars, of 'seeing as . . .'. Following Kant, Ricoeur
suggests that imagination is the process of coming to new concepts, of giving
an image to the emerging meaning brought about by the innovation of

© The Editorial Board of the Sociological Review 2003

metaphor. We hear the new before it is seen: 'we see images only insofar as we first hear them' (Ricoeur, 1991: 168–174).

The poet engenders and shapes a metaphor; the poetic image allows for a suspension of signification in which imagination comes to the new. Ricoeur refers to Gaston Bachelard, in finding that the poetic image unfolds for the reader in a procedure of reverberation (Ricoeur, 1991: 172–174; see Bachelard, 1964: xi–xiv). As the imagination of the reader schematizes the metaphorical, the process is one in which 'imagination is diffused in all directions, reviving former experiences, awakening dormant memories, irrigating adjacent sensorial fields' (Ricoeur, 1991: 173).

Ricoeur is, I think, using 'hearing' itself metaphorically, to distance the operation of imagination from the bias towards perceiving it as a visual mental scene or projection. 'Hearing' is in the quasi-sensorial experience of written fiction, poetry and narrative. This view of 'hearing' can be adapted to the experience of activities, material objects and settings. A performative view of imagination as method would take 'hearing' again metaphorically, but the experience would be explicitly sensorial and temporal. The poetic and metaphoric qualities of the experience of elements, spaces and objects have been shown by Bachelard (1964). Mikel Dufrenne has explained how the world created by a work of art or performance establishes the conditions which allow the material elements to 'speak' to each other. In the ensemble, they become significant beyond their literal meanings, changed by the presence of the viewer or audience (Dufrenne, 1987: 128–133).

These operations are familiar to the experience of any installation or performed work. In HOMELAND, the public moved through and activated new combinations of elements and activities—the predicates of metaphor. The elements were ordinary; the activities were creative: drawing and mapping your territory on paper, reading poems, opening doors, touching glass, photographing your hand on earth to be added to the shrine of transparencies. Mingling with the tangible were the overheard snatches of other conversations, the recollection of your own, and the ambient traffic. This layering of light, hands, earth, homes, landscapes and voices could be read as an undefined connection between strangers, a temporary proximity, an enlightening. PLATFORM set the atmosphere, the texture and range of combinations, but the connections and symbolic resonances were left radically open, undirected.

The spoken narratives can be considered through another dimension of imagination brought out in Ricoeur's theory. The heuristic force of fiction and narrative is their capacity to open up new dimensions of reality, not only to re-describe a reality which is already there. Again following Kant, for Ricoeur imagination is 'the free play of possibilities in a state of non-involvement with respect to the world of perception or of action' (1991: 174). Imagination provides the 'luminous clearing' in which motives, desires and obligations in the world can be compared. New values, subjectivities and ideas can be tried out. For Ricoeur, the Kantian 'free play' of imagination is imagination's function of coming to the possibilities for practical action (1991: 174–181).

The stories of HOMELAND were made in the 'between' of a liminal situation of passage but one embedded in social conventions—the social imaginary and the demands on conscious awareness of speaking with another person. The descriptive narratives were ephemeral and unpredictable; the possibility was open to not tell the truth. But whether fictive or not, the stories were self-defining by the tellers, and were already relational, belonging to the occasion and to both speakers. The exchanges in response to PLATFORM's further questioning on interconnectedness were, ideally, those in which new subjectivities could be created, tried out, not only as the private reflection on an authored story, but through a process of shared creation. Action was not to be taken then, but another subjectivity was spoken into possible existence, a tentative narrative created that could be returned to through memory and imagination.

The sound carries

The second aspect of the 'hearing' trope concerns the physical experience and flow of conversation. The voice compels an attentiveness to the other person in the midst of other sounds. In HOMELAND, a world was created through the conversational give-and-take. It is on conversation as method that I want to focus; the way in which the conduct of a conversation creates an occasion of experience with persuasive and ethical force. There are three aspects I want to develop: conversation as a mode of rhetorical argument; conversation as an experience of practical and moral reasoning in an uncertain world; and the event as an occasion of character, one which has transformative potential.

HOMELAND's conversations were not directed towards a collaborative project, nor were they intended to approximate an exchange of reasoned argument or the deliberative reaching of a consensus.[6] Rather, the initial demand of the work was in setting the conditions of conversation, which I found to be more like the moral and methodological ideals described by Seyla Benhabib:

> In conversation, I must know how to listen, I must know how to understand your point of view, I must learn to represent to myself the world and the other as you see them. If I cannot listen, if I cannot understand, and if I cannot represent, the conversation stops, develops into an argument, or maybe never gets started . . . Discourse ethics projects such moral conversation, in which reciprocal recognition is exercised, onto a utopian community of humankind (Benhabib, 1992: 52).

PLATFORM's practice, which can be seen as a making of 'moral conversation', brought into being an experience of that kind of public talking-together. The exchanges depended on the talents of the participants and PLATFORM to respond to the insights, fallibilities and allure of each other, and on their abilities to improvise with the stutterings and inconsistencies of conversation. But the conversations were piloted, however tactfully, within an activist and aesthetic context. PLATFORM's processes of questioning and listening were an indirect persuasion; a movement with the participant's narrative towards a recognition of interdependency.

 © The Editorial Board of the Sociological Review 2003

To start in Aristotelian terms, persuasion is the art of rhetoric, and is directed to a particular audience about practical matters, to bring them to a decision and so to action (Aristotle, 1991: 74–79 (1356a–1358a)). There are three modes of rhetoric through the spoken word: those that reside in the character of the speaker; those that induce an emotional state in the audience; and those that demonstrate persuasive arguments. Judgement of those arguments depends on judgement about the credibility of the speaker—whether they have good sense and are reliable, and whether they have moral character and can be trusted (Aristotle, 1991: 74 (1356a)).

In HOMELAND, the flow of the conversations approximated rhetorical argument, or what P. C. Smith calls 'original argument,' the spoken exchange of reasoning together with another person, which was historically prior to demonstrational logic and formal dialectic (Smith, 1998: 1–49). Following Martin Heidegger's reinterpretation of Aristotle's *Rhetoric*, Smith sets out original argument as the structure and nature of argument as it occurs in everyday speech, in how we are with one another. It takes place through telling a narrative which reasons sequentially, by how one thing follows another, not by logical demonstration or from first principles. The argument is open-ended, possibly stopping and starting, but continuing, and continually open to question. Through rhetorical argument, it is not only how one sees things which is to be changed, but how one feels about them, and how one might reach a decision on what to do as a result of hearing what the other person has said. The speaking is not addressed to onlookers, but to the listeners (Smith, 1998: 1–9).

The HOMELAND tapes, by my hearing, show the range and fluctuations of narrative modes: confessional, argumentative, reminiscent, curious, confused, obdurate, intimate. As the conversations progressed through questioning, the give-and-take became more like a form of reasoning than an exchange of stories or information. Gerald Bruns, in 'The Hermeneutical Anarchist', expands on Smith's rhetorical mode, seeing it as a 'ground level' rationality. The practical reasoning in this mode is *phronesis*, which Bruns, following Aristotle and Gadamer, interprets as:

> . . . a condition of moral knowledge at the level of particular situations . . . knowing what a situation calls for in the way of right action, even when the situation is so complex and unprecedented that one experiences the shortfall of one's principles, beliefs, or patterns of conduct, or even one's sense of how things should go if they are to go right . . . *Phronesis* is . . . reason that shows itself in timeliness, improvisation, and a gift for nuance rather than in the rigorous duplication of results (Bruns, 2002: 47–48).

Continuing with Bruns, rhetoric is a way of improvising moments of order; it presupposes a world of complexity, randomness and contingency. Rhetoric is a mode of responsibility, not only a mode of knowledge. '[Rhetoric] responds to the need for action by producing a consensus in the absence of sufficient (that is self-evident) reasons' (Bruns, 2000: 51). HOMELAND did not so much rely on a commonly shared rhetorical culture as create the conditions for it, within which there was the potential to reason together about human actions within unpredictable worlds.

The conversations of HOMELAND were like conversations with someone familiar, a friend. To return to Smith, again following Heidegger, he finds that original argument begins somatically in the body, inseparable from the tone of voice, the tenor and bearing of the speakers and the temporality of bodily experience. It is a speaking together in a face-to-face relation where *ethos* and *pathos*, character and feeling, provide the conditions that make *logos*, reasoned argument, possible. The logical content is not a wholly separable entity, but infused with and understood through the somatic, ethical and emotive qualities of the experience. Mood and attunement, which are fundamental conditions of everyday existence, are the deep structures of feeling and cognition by which we 'hear' an argument. How things sound and how they look is not the manipulation of appearances but has to do with argument's deepest, pre-logical and rhetorical structure, a structure of feeling as well as cognition. To be persuaded, the listener must be brought to feel a certain way about something, to be moved. For Smith, the contingencies, contradictions and open-endedness of original argument are kept from becoming fallacious by the 'ethical matrix' in which the conversation is held. The character of the speakers who are engaged in it, their reasonableness, virtue and goodwill, their talents, are the ethical pre-dispositions which form social reason. The validity of the argument is tested by the measure of the character of the speakers, their tone and whether they can be trusted (Smith, 1998: 4–12, 38–54).

In rhetorical works like HOMELAND, it is not so much the performative identity of the artist, or their iterative ability to instantiate and modify that identity that matters—as in some performance art and liveart. Nor is it so much the enactment of chosen virtues projected onto a situation, or articulations of an ethical theory, as in some theatre. Rather, it is the ability to create the experience of that ethical matrix, an occasion of character. That experience will be particular, somatic, and transient—and one which is mutually 'performed' between the artist and participant.

I do not want to define 'character' beyond a most general view which is as a constituent of an ethics which begins with the human subject in everyday experience, which expresses a sense of human flourishing and virtue, and which is influenced by principles, habits and social pre-dispositions (see Statman, 1997). Those qualities, principles and virtues which constitute 'character' will be informed by pre-figured views, but each performed occasion will specifically create those relations through which character is understood.

The occasion does begin with the artist. Her or his comportment will carry the presence of 'character'. The occasion and the perceptions of character are, however, created within the productive ambivalence of performance. They are inseparable from the everyday, with a suspicion of the 'rhetorical' as manipulative and deceptive. As a counter to this, in many of these works, information and tactics are presented as verifiable and transparent, claiming an authority based on factual correctness. This extends to the artists presenting themselves

© The Editorial Board of the Sociological Review 2003

as open and honest; as themselves, in ordinary dress, with their variable skills in public dialogue, 'performing' a task but not a role. The authenticity of the artist's character and the work's conceptual validity are always questionable and immediately exposable by their partners in conversation.

At the same time the occasion is a suspension of the ordinary, more at ease with the playful and emotive and the possibility of change. The artist is a threshold through which transformation may happen, and that change is undergone without shock, Brechtian *verfremdungseffekt*,[7] or spectacle. The allure and the provisional trustworthiness of the artist can draw one into the pleasure of an ethos of listening, and into feelings associated with care and friendship. To become attracted to, even imitative of, their comportment and tone can be a transformative experience.

To bring about that experience requires more than an empathy on the part of the artist towards the participant, or the artist's negotiation of disparities in social and dialogic skills and differences in cultural power. It requires making the occasion, the event, in which each person can begin with the knowledge they have, including that of how to act and of what constitutes character, and then move to a questioning of that knowledge. The ethical matrix is more than simply a check on fallaciousness; creating the experience of that matrix is method.

To return to Ricoeur and imagination, within the social imaginary, the function of an utopian 'no-where' is as a mode of social subversion, the place from which the imagination wanders and constitutes a possible different social sphere (Ricoeur, 1991: 181–187). Much of PLATFORM's work—and other artists' work—has an utopian force, which like the metaphoric, is not explicitly drawn. The feeling is evoked that another reality can be figured, in the marked-out event, while the experience is rehearsed of how humans might be with one another. From my experience, the tacitly communicated ethos, and the gestures, voices, and presence of PLATFORM, create the feelings that whatever is spoken will be welcomed and questioned, and that in this process, one is carried into surprising thoughts and ideas.

'It no longer exists, but I always long for it'[8]

HOMELAND proposed to be both an activist action in communicating an idea, and an experiment in its methods which were to allow something new to emerge. The riskiness of the experiment prevailed; what emerged was not the anticipated public response. Most people talked about home and their sense of place; most conversations were nostalgic. The careful piloting by PLATFORM evoked recollections of protection, abandonment, childhood, identity, happiness, isolation, homelessness. Their tact may not have had enough force to critically interrogate the public about their concepts of belonging and territory, or to introduce novel ideas. Conversational works can reinforce pre-figured views. In HOMELAND, confined to a theatre-like timeframe in which the 'audience' arrived once, the conversations could not evolve over time and generate a growing familiarity between the partners, allowing both to refine their sensibilities and PLAT-FORM to adapt their methods.

Nature 'performed', but not as expected. It appeared in almost all the drawings and many spoken descriptions as a landscape, a park, a garden, the lands left after exile or lost to urbanization, trees, rivers, mountains, sea, flowers, animals. The shrine of drawings and hands was one to a nature lost, remembered, spoken into being again, of the future, inseparable from 'home'.

HOMELAND disclosed the fragility of conversational works against the persuasiveness of memory, if what was expected was efficacy in delivering a message. But HOMELAND allowed the unanticipated to emerge, and so did something different and richer, when slowness is taken into account.

It asked a question of necessity—how does the maintenance of your way of life depend on other lands, labours and lives, in ways which you might prefer not to recognize—in terms of a familiar object, an element and emotion. From the tapes, it seems that environmental interdependency and tracing an artefact's manufacture were unfamiliar to most participants;[9] answers to those questions were not already rehearsed, the information about them not easily exchangeable, the re-figuring of one's habits was not already justified. Starting with 'home' weighted the conversations towards an intimate sphere of strong personal emotions. This may have limited any projection to other 'homes'. But that framing also meant that the questions, when considered, required bringing the emotional force of unidentified prejudices into the domestic and familiar. It also meant that the 'footprint' outwards was recognized not only as the tangible effects of manufacture and capital, but as the differences in the patterns and qualities of love and care as they extended beyond one's immediate spheres.

During the event, the metaphor of light seemingly was not strong enough against the feelings of home to carry the intentions of the work. Electricity and the lightbulb were too distant from the body, too cold, too invisible to come into

© The Editorial Board of the Sociological Review 2003

play. Those 'natural' constituent elements in everyday artefacts did not have the immediate agency, liveliness, or comfort of a buried river, of food, of a pair of trainers—objects used in other art works and media documentaries.[10] But with time, in recollection and re-cognition, the imagery of light as an element which flows over boundaries and which transforms perception, and of the lightbulb, in its brittleness, have remained potent, entering one's home and habitual actions—at least for me. The discomfort of the mismatch between 'nature', home and electricity has kept the themes of HOMELAND unsettled and alive as it progresses in the re-telling drift.

HOMELAND was not exemplary. There were decisions, such as the gender imbalance of the three artists, which could have been made differently. But HOMELAND 'worked.' To 'not work' would have been to lack character; to have lacked character would have been to neglect the other person's voice, to force the conversations towards a prescribed end. Returning to Gadamer:

> We say we 'conduct' a conversation, but the more genuine a conversation is, the less its conduct lies within the will of either partner. Thus a genuine conversation is never the one that we wanted to conduct . . . a conversation has a spirit of its own, and . . . the language in which it is conducted bears its own truth within it—ie., that it allows something to 'emerge,' which henceforth exists (1989: 383).

HOMELAND entered the flux of everyday life, listened and spoke with the city. The longing was, as well, for the public space in which to speak; to not only view a work of art, but to be heard through one.

Acknowledgements

I would like to thank James Marriott, Dan Gretton and Jane Trowell of PLAT-FORM for all our conversations. PLATFORM's current work, *90% Crude*, is a series of projects investigating the end of fossil fuel dependency and the dismantling of trans-national corporate culture, including: *Killing Us Softly; Unravelling the Carbon Web; Loot! Reckoning with the East India Company*.

I would like to thank Hester Reeve for her helpful comments on a draft. And especially thank Claire Waterton and Bronislaw Szerszynski for our altering conversations and for their support as editorial buddies, and more. Responsibility for this chapter is mine.

All photographs are provided by, and copyright of, PLATFORM.

Notes

1 The relations between a performative event as experienced, its content and the ethical are uneasy and complex. Fitting with views of performance as relational and improvisatory are those theories which address the ethical as experienced—embodied, contingent and practiced—rather than as predominantly rule-based. This includes some relational ethics (eg. Baier, 1989; Putnam, 1991; see also Varela, 1992); ethics of care (for overviews from ecofeminist perspectives, see

Cuomo, 1998; Plumwood, 2002); and virtue-based ethics (for an overview, see Statman, 1997). A critique of 'performed' conversation can be informed by theories of the procedures and democratic ideals from communicative and dialogic ethics (see Benhabib, 1992; Habermas, 1990). Although these events contain ethical dimensions, they are not circumscribed by, nor instrumentally representational of a theory; the co-evolving of the ethical and the event is an element for interpretation, directed to the particular event. As a further note, equitable conversation between humans can be seen as a model for relations between humans and nature, humans and other living beings (see Dryzek, 2000; Plumwood, 2002; Smith, 2001). This chapter takes the view that the performing of conversation between humans about their relations with nature, the doing of it and its articulated content, can also be an environmentally ethical act.

2 PLATFORM's project *Tree of Life, City of Life* in 1989 involved James Marriott and John Jordan walking from the English Channel to the River Thames in London, where they lived in a tent for ten weeks, at five places on the south bank—pulse points of the city. The tent was a 'listening' place, drawing in random people to converse about the city, the 'nature' within it, its traffic, ingestion and waste.

3 The four projects were: *Listening to the Fleet*, a ceremonial walk from Hampstead to the Thames along the course of the River Fleet; *Walking on the Walbrook*, a daily ritual on the streets of London's financial district; *Unearthing the Effra: Effra Redevelopment Agency*, in which Jordan and Andrea Phillips, posing as venture capitalist developers, opened a shop-front in South London presenting plans for uncovering the River Effra; and *Delta*, which began as a project building a micro-hydro over the River Wandle lighting part of a local school. PLATFORM's ongoing dialogues with the communities in the Wandle watershed have continued, and the project has evolved into RENUE, a major renewable energy project in South London.

4 There are significant differences in antecedents, methods, and directives within these groupings, and artists are continually innovating and re-defining the fields. Broad generalizations can be made as follows. 'Social sculpture' is the term coined by the artist Joseph Beuys, and can refer to both an ethos, and to methodological elements. The artist is the transformer, the provocateur; to 'sculpt' or create within the social realm is both the vocation of an artist and an inherent capacity of every human. See Tisdall (1979) and The Social Sculpture Research Unit: www.brookes.ac.uk/schools/apm/social_sculpture/index.html. Littoral is the shifting region of the shoreline between high and low tide, and refers to works which are communicative actions between differing communities. See www.littoral.org.uk for the work of Littoral, formerly Projects Environment; and http://novelsquat.com for the work of Bruce Barber. Grant Kester uses the term 'dialogic art' to describe a wide range of art practices using dialogue, from the visual arts perspective (see Kester, forthcoming). New Genre Public Art is a term used by Suzanne Lacy to distinguish works involving collaborations between artists and communities and communicative actions, from 'public art' as a display of sculpture outside the gallery (Lacy, 1995). Additionally, ecoart is an emerging field of artists working within natural environments, some of which incorporate performative elements and dialogue (see Spaid, 2002).

5 I have chosen not to include transcribed conversations for several reasons. Conversations extended beyond the recordings. Although the tapes are anonymous, and were available in the pantechnicon for the public to hear, I do not think the conversations were entered into for public display in the way the drawings and photographs were. Listening to the tapes was necessary to understand the work, but I am interpreting the methods of HOMELAND, rather than providing an analysis of the 'results' or 'data'.

6 For those works which are directed towards reaching a consensus or instituting an ongoing public space for dialogue, the theories of Jürgen Habermas (1990) can inform an interpretation of those procedures. My emphasis in this chapter is on method as experienced.

7 *Verfremdungseffekt* is a complex of dramaturgy and theory. Theatrically, it is a 'making strange', a de-familiarization of the habits of the everyday, one in which those habits are exposed, and one in which an empathy with a character is diminished.

8 Statement on a drawing of a house within a forested landscape, with gardens, rivers, animals, sun; printed with permission of PLATFORM.

© The Editorial Board of the Sociological Review 2003

9 In some conversations, there was an understanding of environmental interdependency, but it was not articulated in terms similar to the 'ecological footprint'. Wackernagel and Rees did not publish *Our Ecological Footprint* until 1996.
10 See also Shelley Sacks' *Exchange Values: Images of Invisible Lives*, an exhibition on banana production, which includes the recorded voices of farmers: http://apm.brookes.ac.uk/exchange

References

Adcock, C. (1992), 'Conversational Drift: Helen Mayer Harrison and Newton Harrison', *Art Journal*, 51(2): 35–45.
Arendt, H. (1958), *The Human Condition*, Chicago and London: University of Chicago Press.
Aristotle (1991), *The Art of Rhetoric*, tr. H. C. Lawson-Tancred, London: Penguin Books.
Aristotle (1996), *Poetics*, tr. M. Heath, London: Penguin Books.
Bachelard, G. (1964), *The Poetics of Space*, Boston: Beacon Press.
Baier, A. (1989), 'Doing Without Moral Theory?', in S. Clark and E. Simpson (eds), *Anti-Theory in Ethics and Moral Conservatism*, Albany, NY: State University of New York Press, pp. 29–48.
Benhabib, S. (1992), *Situating the Self. Gender, Community and Postmodernism in Contemporary Ethics*, Cambridge: Polity Press.
Berleant, A. (1991), *Art and Engagement*, Philadelphia: Temple University Press.
Bruns, G. (2002), 'The Hermeneutical Anarchist: *Phronesis*, Rhetoric, and the Experience of Art', in J. Malpas, U. Arnswald and J. Kertscher (eds), *Gadamer's Century. Essays in Honor of Hans-Georg Gadamer*, Cambridge, Mass. and London: MIT Press, pp. 45–76.
Cuomo, C. J. (1998), *Feminism and Ecological Communities. An Ethic of Flourishing*, London and New York: Routledge.
de Certeau, M. (1984), *The Practice of Everyday Life*, tr. S. Randall, Berkley and London: University of California Press.
Dryzek, J. S. (2000), *Deliberative Democracy and Beyond. Liberals, Critics, Contestations*, Oxford: Oxford University Press.
Dufrenne, M. (1987), *In the Presence of the Sensuous: Essays in Aesthetics*, tr. M. S. Roberts and D. Gallagher, Atlantic Highlands, NJ: Humanities Press International.
Foucault, M. (1986 [1984]), 'Of Other Spaces', tr. J. Miskowiec, *Diacritics—a Review of Contemporary Criticism*, 16 (Spring), 22–27.
Gadamer, H-G. (1989), *Truth and Method*, tr. J. Weinsheimer and D. G. Marshall, London: Sheed and Ward.
Habermas, J. (1990), *Moral Consciousness and Communicative Action*, Cambridge: Polity Press.
Kester, G. (2004, forthcoming), *Conversation Pieces: Community and Communication in Modern Art*, Berkeley: University of California Press.
Lacy, S. (1995), *Mapping the Terrain: New Genre Public Art*. Seattle: Bay Press.
MacIntyre, A. (1981), 'A Crisis in Moral Philosophy', in D. Callahan and H. T. Engelhardt Jr. (eds), *The Roots of Ethics: Science, Religion and Values*, New York: Plenum Press.
PLATFORM (1993), HOMELAND, London: London International Festival of Theatre, 23 June–11 July, 1993.
Plumwood, V. (2002), *Environmental Culture. The Ecological Crisis of Reason*, London and New York: Routledge.
Putnam, D. (1991), 'Relational Ethics and Virtue Theory', *Metaphilosophy*, 22(3): 231–238.
Ricoeur, P. (1991), 'Imagination in Discourse and in Action', tr. K. Blamey, in *From Text to Action. Essays in Hermeneutics, II*, London: Athlone Press, pp. 168–187.
Smith, M. (2001), *An Ethics of Place. Radical Ecology, Postmodernity, and Social Theory*, Albany: State University of New York Press.
Smith, P. C. (1998), *The Hermeneutics of Original Argument. Demonstration, Dialectic, Rhetoric*, Evanston, Ill.: Northwestern University Press.

Spaid, S. (2002), *Ecovention. Current Art to Transform Ecologies*, Cincinnati: greenmuseum.org, The Contemporary Arts Centre, and ecoartspace.

States, B. O. (1996), 'Performance as Metaphor', *Theatre Journal*, 48(1): 1–26.

Statman, D. (ed.) (1997), *Virtue Ethics*, Edinburgh: Edinburgh University Press.

Tisdall, C. (1979), *Joseph Beuys*, London: Thames and Hudson.

Trowell, J. (2000), 'The Snowflake in Hell and The Baked Alaska: Improbability, Intimacy and Change in the Public Realm', in S. Bennett and J. Butler (eds), *Locality, Regeneration & Diver[c]ities. Advances in Art & Urban Futures Volume 1*, Bristol and Portland Ore: Intellect Books. pp. 99–109.

Varela, F. J. (1999), *Ethical Know-How. Action, Wisdom and Cognition*, Stanford, Stanford University Press.

Wackernagel, M. and W. E. Rees (1996), *Our Ecological Footprint. Reducing Human Impact on the Earth*, Gabriola Island, BC and Philadelphia: New Society Publishers.

© The Editorial Board of the Sociological Review 2003

Technology, performance and life itself: Hannah Arendt and the fate of nature[1]

Bronislaw Szerszynski

Introduction

In this chapter I want to explore issues concerning performance, nature and technology using ideas developed by Hannah Arendt in *The Human Condition* (1958). Arendt does not herself use the term 'performance', but her ideas can nevertheless help us to make important distinctions between different kinds of human performance, and to recognize the different ways in which these performances relate us to the natural world and to life's self-reproduction. Furthermore, I will try to show how Arendt's analysis can help illuminate the nature of contemporary problems. In particular, I want to suggest that her analysis of human activity in terms of labour, work and action can furnish us with a powerfully critical account of the way that contemporary capitalism and technoscience alter our performative relationship with the natural world.

At first glance Arendt's work may seem an unlikely place to look for a framework for a critical politics of environment and technology. After all, Arendt is in many ways profoundly anthropocentric, concerned above all with human beings and what makes them different to the rest of nature. A recurrent emphasis in her work is the resistance to any naturalization of the human, to any attempt to describe the human person as a biological entity like any other—a position that would seem to put her at odds with most ecological thought. Furthermore, Arendt's analysis of human activity is in terms of a hierarchical schema, in which the move from labour, to work, and then to action represents a kind of ascent from nature and necessity into humanity and autonomy. Yet, as I hope to show, these features of Arendt's thought strengthen rather than compromise her usefulness for ecological thought.

Arendt (1906–1975) was born in Germany to a secular Jewish family, and studied with Martin Heidegger and Karl Jaspers before writing her doctoral dissertation on the concept of love in Augustine. Her writings, published after she fled the Holocaust and settled in America, are chiefly inspired by the turmoil of twentieth-century European history, and the need to defend—in both thought and practice—the essential dignity of the human person. Her first major work was *The Origins of Totalitarianism* (Arendt, 1951), which explored Nazism and Stalinism as part of the same, novel phenomenon. *The Human Condition* (1958)

© The Editorial Board of the Sociological Review 2003. Published by Blackwell Publishing Ltd, 9600 Garsington Road, Oxford OX4 2DQ, UK and 350 Main Street, Malden, MA 02148, USA

appears to be very different in approach, being a systematic analysis of the *vita activa*, the active human life, but in fact addresses many of the same themes. Later works included *On Revolution* (1963b), which explored the French and American revolutions as temporarily opening up spaces for individuals to deliberate and act together, and *Eichmann in Jerusalem: The Banality of Evil* (1963a), which controversially represented Adolf Eichmann as enacting the Holocaust due to a lack of imagination rather than any monstrous evil or malevolence.

In *The Human Condition* Arendt traces the way that the *vita activa* has been continually denigrated from the Greeks onwards in favour of the *vita contemplativa* of theoretical reflection or prayer. But she also identifies three moments within the *vita activa*—labour, work and action—arguing that the distinctions between them have become increasingly blurred, to the detriment of our capacity to recognize and realize the fulfilled human life. *Labour*—the meeting of biological needs—and *work*—the fabrication of enduring objects—have their rightful, essential place as part of the human condition. But for Arendt it is in *action*, the exchange of speech and deed, that our humanity is most fully realized, since of all forms of human activity it is action that is most closely linked to the features that Arendt sees as most constitutive of the human: *natality*—human beings' capacity to initiate radically new things in the world—and *plurality*—their ineradicable uniqueness—that 'men, not Man,[2] live on the earth and inhabit the world' (p. 7).[3]

On the basis of this systematic exploration of the active powers of human beings—in the present context, one might say their capacity to engage in radically different kinds of performance—Arendt erects an incisively critical analysis of the modern age in terms of the corruption and distortion of these powers. Here the target of her critique is not just totalitarianism but also Western liberal society, which she presents as being pervaded by conformism, consumerism and subjectivism. But her concerns are not narrowly psychological, centred on the effects of modern society on human beings' inner nature. Her attention is always focused on the way that human beings inhabit the artificial and natural environment around them, an inhabitation that has been disrupted in the modern age, resulting in alienation from both a common, artefactual human world and our embedding in nature.

Labour, work, action

Let me start by exploring in a little more detail Arendt's typology of the *vita activa* in order to show how it helpfully distinguishes different kinds of 'performance'. Commentators discussing Arendt in terms of performance have generally focused on the performative nature of her concept of action, and of politics in particular,[4] but it is possible to see all of the forms of activity that Arendt identifies as different kinds of performance. Her first category of activity is that of labour. As labouring (and consuming) animals, humans engage with 'earth'

© The Editorial Board of the Sociological Review 2003

(by which Arendt means the natural world), in a constant, never-ending performance or activity which serves to meet their physical needs for sustenance, warmth and shelter. Labour is the activity we share with animals—we labour as *animal laborans*.[5] In so far as we labour, then, we are aligned with life, we foreground the fact that life is a kind of performance, one that serves only itself, and that we are part of that performance.[6] For Arendt, labour is a cyclical process, necessary for survival, but one that leaves no trace behind; its products are consumed as they are used. Subsistence forms of life in particular have this kind of character, with their cycles of use and replenishment, plenty and paucity. And even in developed economies this kind of temporality is arguably dominant in the domestic sphere—in activities such as cooking, cleaning, shopping for consumables or the maintaining of human health (see Szerszynski, 2002: 183–4). But Arendt argues that labour has also invaded the public sphere in modern societies, as mechanization and the division of labour break up even skilled tasks to the endless repetition characteristic of labour.

Although Arendt considers labour to be the lowliest, most basic form of human activity, she acknowledges that it is not without its pleasures. Labour allows us 'to experience the sheer bliss of being alive which we share with all living creatures . . . toiling and resting, labouring and consuming' (p. 106). But at the same time that labour is a 'blessing', it also represents a kind of imprisonment. As the requirements of necessity are never finally fulfilled, humans are compelled to labour unceasingly. The 'redemption' of this imprisonment can only come from *outside* labour, from another form of activity—work.

Oriented not to necessity but to utility, work is a very different kind of performance—a goal-directed, means-ends form of activity, guided by a model, goal or blueprint, which leaves behind itself an enduring artefact such as a tool, a table or a building. Whereas *animal laborans* is a servant of nature, *homo faber*—the human being as fabricator—conquers nature, removing material from its location and from the cycles of growth and decay (p. 139). Arendt distinguishes tools from the lasting artefacts they are used to make. Tools can ease the pain of labour, but they can also be used to create what Arendt calls the 'world', an ensemble of objects that assemble us into a shared reality, one that outlasts us and provides an enduring setting for human affairs. Through work humans carve this world out from the endless flux of nature. And *some* labour— that put to the service of the human world—has the function of policing the boundary between world and earth, of protecting the former from the processes of growth and decay that are characteristic of the latter.[7] However, although the world is made by *homo faber*, by craft, it must not be ruled by him. Left to *homo faber*, the world would be trapped in meaninglessness. There would be no way of discerning the value of anything except by reference to its usefulness to something else; this in turn could only be valued in relation to a third, and so on in endless chains of utility. Like labour, work has to be redeemed from outside itself, in terms not of utility but *meaning*. So the world becomes the setting for another mode of being, which Arendt calls action.

© The Editorial Board of the Sociological Review 2003

With action, her third (and highest) category of human activity, Arendt is closest to theatrical notions of performance. She uses this term to refer to meaningful interaction with other persons, through speech and deed. People reveal themselves through action, which paradigmatically takes place in the public sphere or *polis*. Like the world, the *polis* has to be crafted; the laws which set out a space for the *polis* are the products of making, of work (pp. 194–5); boundaries also need to be crafted between the private and the public, so that the freedom of the public sphere can be insulated from the necessity of the private sphere.[8] But the form of activity that actually constitutes the *polis* as ongoing performance is not fabrication but action. Action is not futile and transitory, like labour; but neither does it leave behind a physical product modelled on the blueprint that guided it, like work. Rather, because of the nature of human beings and relations, action sets into train unpredictable and uncontrollable effects, spiralling away from the actor's control.

Like work, action is productive: the products of our self-revelation through speech and action are stories, remembered and retold by others. However, these are stories that we are characters *within* rather than authors and controllers *of*. As Arendt puts it, 'nobody is the author of his own story' (p. 184). Besides, the very plurality of human perspectives make interpretations and responses to anything we say or do inherently unpredictable. This 'frailty' of action cannot be redeemed from outside action itself; we are now at the top of the internal hierarchy within the *vita activa*, so cannot look to another form of activity as a solution to action's frailty. The inherent irreversibility and unpredictability of human action can only be tamed through specific forms of action, forms that try to control this irreversibility and unpredictability through binding speech acts—such as forgiving (in which the past is reversed) and promising (in which the future is secured).

As components of the *vita activa*, labour, work and action are all kinds of 'performance', but differ in a number of ways. For example, action alone is performed for its own sake[9]—this sets it aside from work, with its goal of making an enduring end product, but also from labour, which is compelled by necessity, by the requirement to meet human needs. A further contrast lies in action's essentially public nature—it needs the presence of others to give it meaning. Labour, by contrast, is essentially solitary—it is the individual body that labours. People labour in gangs—but here they are simply labouring alongside each other, doing the same activity side by side. Work is even more solitary, performed alone—although craft workers have to meet in the market place in order to exchange their goods (pp. 159–67).

Stability in world and earth

But perhaps the crucial difference here is that, although labour, work and action are all kinds of performance, work alone produces something that continues to exist *without* performance. Indeed, it is the fact that work produces something

 © The Editorial Board of the Sociological Review 2003

that endures that makes it an activity that does not itself endure—it reaches a natural conclusion in the completion of its product, and thus is what Aristotle called a 'self-destroying' activity (Aristotle, 1976, 10: iv; Szerszynski, 2002: 183). Labour and action, by contrast, are both naturally ceaseless; there is no inherent reason within either form of activity for them to come to a close—labour is the continuing self-reproduction of life itself (p. 105), and action is part of the endless 'conversation of mankind' (Oakeshott, 1962: 197 ff.). With labour and action, then, it is their *performance* that endures; with work, it is that which is produced *by* the performance that endures.

For Arendt the various kinds of endurance inherent in these different forms of performance are crucially significant to questions of human survival and dignity. And it is central to Arendt's critical analysis of contemporary society that these different forms of durability are being dangerously threatened by technological and social change. I want to focus on two particular forms that this threat takes. Firstly, the permanent artefactual world of created objects that provides a setting for meaningful human action has come under threat from industrialization and capitalism, which displace work by labour and turn objects into products to be consumed. In the round of labouring and consuming, through which we participate in the life process, things have no enduring quality, but are absorbed into the performance that is life itself, threatening the worldliness of the world, and thus its capacity to sustain human meanings. Secondly, through new technologies such as biotechnology and nanotechnology humans are acquiring the capacity to 'act' into nature—to introduce into our relations with the natural world the characteristics of unpredictability and irreversibility that characterize interactions in the human social world. This both imperils the capacity of the performance of life to continue, and also, by making action rather than fabrication the organizing principle of technology, compromises further science's capacity to 'know' nature. I will expand on these claims in the next section; but in the rest of the current section I want to explore further the enduring characteristics of both labour/life[10] and the products of work.

The ceaselessness of nature is an inescapable part of the human condition, in that as humans we are also animals. When we labour we do so as animals; labour is life performing itself. But in nature, in 'earth', there are no enduring objects or subjects, only eternal movement. Nature—particularly as understood since the advent of modern biology in the nineteenth century—is not a collection of interacting, enduring things but a *process* (pp. 18–19, 137, 296). Unlike human beings, other animals, who dwell in earth alone and not world, are immortal—not because individual animals never die, but because they are part of this never-ending flow; as a species their immortality lies in the sheer repetition of procreation. It is only in the enduring context of the artefactual world that human beings can retain their own continuing identity—and only against this stable background that human beings can be seen as mortal, as having a recognizable life story (*bios*) from birth to death (p. 97). Deprived of this lasting background human beings would be reduced to the 'bare life' (*zoë*) of mere biological function, as happened in the Nazi death camps (see Agamben, 1998; Arendt, 1951).

Thus, although for Arendt the world in its durability and objectivity is not *sufficient* for a meaningful human life—for that humans also need to engage in action—it is nevertheless *necessary*. Although utility is the grounding principle of *homo faber*, the world and the objects 'he' creates are not to be valued for their mere usefulness alone, but also as a setting for the creation and exchange of meaning. The durability of the artefactual world thus has a much wider role in sustaining humanity than simply materially insulating people from the forces of nature. Firstly, the products of fabrication serve to stabilize relations between people and to provide a stable background for action—they provide addresses which locate people in the human world, and places and objects in or around which people can congregate and engage with each other. Secondly, work and its products give humans the experience of objects as enduring, bounded things. Fabricated products outlast their use and even their users, and can become the objects of agreement between spectators. It is in the fabricated artefact that we find the paradigmatic experience of a stable object, one which takes on an objectivity and worldly quality from being perceived from many points of view. Only once granted such an experience can humanity take that experience outside the human 'world' and apply it to the earth; only then can they approach nature as made up of objective, isolated things that can be objects of agreement or disagreement, rather than simply as the flow of life's self-performance (pp. 57, 137). Fourthly, these artefacts—and by extension natural things—also serve as objects not just of knowledge, but also of judgement and appraisal using criteria such as beauty and elegance, criteria which can only emerge through debate, through action, in the public realm. As Kerry Whiteside argues, the existence and preservation of a common artefactual world may thus be necessary for the possibility of approaching nature as a domain not just of life itself but of value. The valuing of nature may be grounded not outside but inside the city wall—in the experience not of wilderness but of civilization and culture (Whiteside, 1998: 31).

But, as I suggested above, labour/life too produces its own kind of permanence. However, rather than this permanence being something that stands outside the performance, signalling its terminus, this is a permanence *of* performance. I want here to isolate two aspects of the endurance of labour/life. Firstly, life's ongoingness is necessarily part of the human condition. Human finitude may only be intelligible against the backdrop of world, but it is only necessitated by our embeddedness in earth—by our organic nature. The meeting of earthly needs is just as much what makes us human—as opposed to angelic or divine—as our transcendence of them in work and action. This is something Arendt is insistent on. As well as the 'world-alienation' Arendt identifies in the modern world, the erosion of a strong sense of a common public world, she also discusses the danger of 'earth-alienation'—a sense of estrangement from humanity's embedding in the life process. She finds manifestations of such an alienation in modern science's promise to 'think in terms of the universe while

© The Editorial Board of the Sociological Review 2003

remaining on the earth', to describe the world from a point outside of the human world (p. 264), but also in the practical technological desire to escape the bonds of earth, the limits of our organic nature (pp. 1–2). Against such angelic pre-tensions—which if realized would end our human-ness—Arendt reminds us of our interest in the maintenance of the life process, and of our bonds with it.

Secondly, the ongoingness of labour/life is not just one of fleetingness, but also produces its own form of stability, and hence its own kind of worldliness. Arendt herself emphasizes the ephemeral nature of the products of labour/life: for her, whereas work is a transient activity that produces enduring products, labour/life is an enduring activity that produces transient products. The very performance of labour/life thus grants it its own distinctive form of permanence, one that resides in the performance itself. In order to illustrate this, let us see how Arendt's ideas might be extended to a topic not really considered in her own work—that of nature as 'landscape'.

A landscape confronts us as a more-or less stable 'thing' or assemblage of things. Viewed through Arendt's concepts, however, landscape is at most only partly 'made', partly object. As Tim Ingold has argued, a landscape is rightly understood as 'the congelation of past activity', as 'a pattern of activities "collapsed" into an array of features' (Ingold, 2000: 53–4, 197–8). Using the concept of 'taskscape' to describe this pattern of activities, Ingold is saying that a landscape is nothing more than a taskscape made visible. A path across a patch of grass is the activity of 'walking' collapsed into a feature; it is a place where walking happens, but it is also produced by walking—not in the same way that an object is deliberately produced by fabrication, but through the sheer repetition of the act. Similarly, a field is both a place of activity and a place produced and maintained in being by that activity. Arendt insists that cultivation is not work, even though it produces cultivated land, since its product 'needs to be reproduced again and again in order to remain in the human world at all' (pp. 148–9). Yet labour's own *conatus* to repetition can be seen as conferring a durability no less real than that conferred by fabrication. The same can be said more generally of life's own permanence; species, habitats, patterns of predation—all endure not as objects but as more-or-less stable patterns in the performance of life itself.

Thus, Ingold (though not himself using Arendtian terms) in effect shows us how labour is a mode of performance that can leave enduring traces—not in its direct products, which are consumed as fast as they are produced, but in its very iteration and the effects of its iteration. The landscape itself is given form by the repetition of tasks of labour. Paths, clearings, fields are all produced—and have to be continually reproduced—through labour.[11] But to say landscape is performed is not necessarily to say it is 'constructed'. The landscape is not fab-ricated; there is no enduring model which is held in the mind of anyone, on the basis of which nature has been 'made'. Rather, landscape takes its form through the repetition of labour/life; it endures as an epiphenomenon of repetition. In this landscape simply manifests a more general characteristic of nature—that it is life's iterations made visible.

What is striking—and here I am using the very power of Arendt's ideas in order to stage a partial disagreement with her[12]—is that the 'collapsing' of patterns of activity into enduring structures such as landscapes and ecosystems gives labour/life the capacity to produce its own enduring 'worldly' structures— albeit ones that are constantly maintained in and through labour/life's own performances.[13] For example, the 'desire path'—the path that is worn into a patch of grass, or through a hedge, by countless human movements—is no less part of the 'world' than the path that is designed and fabricated through work. The landscape produced by the repetitions of labour/life can itself be a 'world'—can serve as an enduring backdrop to human biographies, can provide places and objects for meaningful human interaction, can serve as objects of appraisal and judgement. It may be that without the activity of fabrication, and the artefacts which it produces, humans could never have had the experience of a common 'world' as a setting for action and judgement. But now that we can approach reality as 'world', as having worldly qualities, nature itself can be related to as a realm not just of necessity but also of ethics, aesthetics, politics and culture. From such an analysis environmentalism can be seen as the extension of culture to nature, the granting of worldliness to 'earth', the expansion of the *polis* beyond the city walls.

Stability under threat

Despite the need for these slight but significant revisions to Arendt's discussion of nature, her investigation into the historical fate of the *vita activa* can furnish us with a critical analysis of the modern age which is hugely relevant to contemporary debates about environment and technology. For, due to social, economic and technological change, both of the forms of permanence discussed in the previous section—of the products of fabrication, and of the very performance of labour/life—have come under threat in the modern world. Under capitalist conditions of production and consumption, the pattern of transience and durability that is characteristic of fabrication—whereby finite, purposeful activities produce enduring, knowable objects—has been compromised by the injection of labour/life's infinite performativity into the human world. Similarly, changes in the character of modern technology, and in the relationship between technology, science, and wider society, have resulted in the kind of performativity characteristic of human action—with its irreversibility and unpredictability—being introduced into our dealings with the natural world. I will take both of these developments in turn.

Arendt argues that, in the age of modern, industrial capitalism, the durable human 'world' has been invaded by the cyclic, endless forms of activity characteristic of 'earth'. No longer do most people experience the activity of fabrication as a bounded activity, guided by a blueprint or model, which produces durable products. Instead, production and consumption have become an endless round, where questions of utility—of what is being done for the sake of what—

© The Editorial Board of the Sociological Review 2003

become as impossible to answer and as irrelevant as they are in nature. Pre-figuring Foucault's notion of bio-power (Foucault, 1979), Arendt describes this as 'the public organisation of the life process', in which all communities were transformed into 'societies of labourers and jobholders . . . centred around the one activity necessary to sustain life' (p. 46). In a related process, the stability of 'property', which had provided individuals and families with a location in the world, was displaced by monetized 'wealth', with its capacity to flow and accumulate, its status as sheer earning and spending power betraying its character as an extension of life's own metabolic powers (p. 124). Through such developments, labour/life—the activity of the human meeting its animal needs—escaped from the private sphere, entered the public stage and realized its capacity to produce surplus. Growth thereby overcame the decay that had hitherto held labour/life in check, setting it free from its entrapment in eternal recurrence; the expansive logic of industrial, mercantile capitalism was set in motion. Correlatively, politics in Western societies was gradually turned from a realm of action and excellence into the mere administration of this self-propelling life process.

Yet this setting free of labour/life was not the redemption but the extension of its futility; the performance of life was unleashed into the human world, threatening the latter's permanence (pp. 46–7). Labour threatens the world in this way because, whereas work serves the world, labour serves only life itself (*zoë*). For Arendt the liberation of labour into the human world reached its theoretical acme in Marx, who merged work with labour, in service of life, and for whom 'all things would be understood, not in their worldly, objective quality, but as results of living labour power and functions of the life process' (p. 89). In Marx the unending character of labour appears as an extension of the fertile life process, but Marx did not recognize that labour's fruits cannot be piled up—they do not contribute to the *world* (pp. 101–9). Only in the permanence of the world and fabrication are means and ends separable; in the life process, by contrast, the labouring body and its implement merge, and technology comes to dominate the human being (pp. 145–7).

For Arendt, technological development took a decisive turn when steam power—the imitation of natural and manual processes, extended by arts and crafts—gave way to electricity and thence to automation. Technologies that were powered by human bodies or steam worked through 'killing natural processes or interrupting them or imitating them'; with such technologies earth and world still remained distinct. In the electric age, by contrast, we 'unchain natural processes of our own . . . and instead of carefully surrounding the human artifice with defences against nature's elemental forces, keeping them as far as possible outside the man-made world, we have channelled these forces . . . into the world itself' (pp. 148–9). Arendt suggests this 'channelling of natural forces into the human world' has compromised the purposefulness of the world, making it all-but impossible to ask questions about purpose or utility (p. 150). Just as the existence of natural entities is inseparable from the process that brings them into being, under conditions of automation means and ends are blurred. In the automated world, *homo faber*, with his means–ends thinking, thus has no place.

Homo faber invented tools to serve 'the world and its things'; contemporary technologies, by contrast, simply aid and fuel the life process which threatens the world's permanency (pp. 150–1).

Thus the mechanization of production, the reorganization of the human world around labour and consumption, and the transformation of politics from a realm of excellence and self-revelation into the 'administration of life', constituted an erosion of the boundaries between earth and world. This erosion has allowed the performativity of 'life' to pour into the human world, compromising its world-like character. A result of this is a growing 'world-alienation', whereby people abandon the togetherness of a shared public world, retreating instead into the subjectivism of consumption or therapy. Viewed from this perspective, the most fundamental problem of consumer capitalism is not simply that it threatens the 'earth' through resource use, pollution and habitat loss, but that it threatens the 'world', without which there can be no meaning or value. Similarly, it would be misleading to describe contemporary environmental problems in terms of nature being threatened by the artefactual world, life by non-life; the modern human world should be understood as a *hypertrophy* of life's potency, an 'unnatural rise of the *natural*' (p. 47), which compromises the integrity and purpose of the artefactual world and then turns on and threatens the rest of life. When nature was viewed from a human world that still retained its artefactual integrity, it achieved objectivity; when viewed from a human world that has been colonized by labour/life, by contrast, the natural world loses its objectivity—and hence its capacity to stand as a world for us, as a backdrop and context for meaning and value—and is absorbed instead into the runaway life process of capitalism. The very imbalance toward growth and productivity, unchecked by cyclical decay, that is exhibited by the capitalist life process, seems to be calling forth in the natural world an expansion of the powers of decay, the diminishing of earth's recuperative powers.

But I also want to consider a second, complementary disturbance in the patterns of performance and durability operating in our relations with nature. Just as the performativity of *life* has been allowed to flow into and dominate the *human* world, so too has the distinctive performativity characteristic of *action* been increasingly directed into the *natural* world—humans have in effect begun to 'act into nature' (p. 231). Developments in the both the character and the application of technology—manifest particularly today in the area of biotechnology—mark a shift from *fabrication* to *action* as the dominant way of interacting with and knowing nature. Rather than being organized around the activity of creating durable objects on the basis of a pre-existing model or idea, many contemporary technologies, relying on the human capacity to 'act', to create radically new elements, organisms or life processes, result in the initiation of unpredictable, irreversible processes that generate new kinds of uncertainty in the human relationship with the natural world (see pp. 231–2). Just as the injection of life into the human world both threatened the durability of the artefactual world and distorted the human relationship with nature, the directing of action into the natural world disrupts not only nature's own durability—its pat-

© The Editorial Board of the Sociological Review 2003

terns of self-reproduction—but also alters the human capacity to 'know' nature.

Arendt's thinking about the rise of technology-as-action is not as developed as that concerning the invasion of life's performativity into the human world; given the newness of this emergent phenomenon at the time she was writing it is perhaps extraordinary that she theorized it at all. But, drawing out the implications of her few comments on 'acting into nature', it is possible to identify a number of levels at which this new form of the *vita activa* manifests itself. Firstly, Arendt herself draws attention to the nature of the forces used in contemporary—or, as she styles it here 'future'—technologies. 'If present technology consists of channelling natural forces into the world of the human artifice', Arendt writes, 'future technology may yet consist of channelling the universal forces of the cosmos around us into the nature of the earth' (p. 150). What she seems to be indicating here is the way that many emergent forms of technology do not simply 'harness' forces that are immanent to the life process, as one harnesses a horse to channel its strength, but 'unharness' quite alien processes, directing them into life's performance, thereby creating novel, hybrid processes. Just as modern science seeks to *know* nature from an 'Archimedean point . . . a universal, astrophysical viewpoint, a cosmic standpoint outside nature itself' (pp. 264–5), so modern technologies *act on* nature from such a standpoint, from outside life's performance. Acting into nature is not done for the human world; it does not add to the durability of things. But neither is it done for the earth; only life maintains life.[14]

Secondly, in a development Arendt could hardly have anticipated, the shift towards acting into nature has also been strengthened by a transformed relationship between science, technology, politics and commerce. With scientific knowledge playing such a central role in the activities of wealth creation and governance, the boundaries between science and other domains have been eroded. The dominant mode of knowledge production is now what Michael Gibbons *et al.* call 'Mode 2', where knowledge is generated in the context of its application (Gibbons *et al.*, 1994; Nowotny *et al.*, 2001). As Bruno Latour puts it, the cold, detachment of 'science' has given way to the warm, risky, engagement of 'research' (Latour, 1998, cited by Nowotny *et al.*, 2001: 2). In such a context the boundary between science and technology, between experiment and application—always impossible firmly to maintain—has become even harder to draw; contemporary technologies are in effect tested in the field, resulting in what Wolfgang Krohn and Johannes Weyer call 'real-life experiments' (Krohn and Weyer, 1994).

It was Gunther Anders in *The Antiquatedness of Man* who first suggested that nuclear bomb tests were not experiments at all, since the classical experiment takes place in a carefully isolated space. The effects of the bombs, he wrote, are of such a scale that 'the laboratory becomes co-extensive with the globe'. Under such conditions 'the distinction between "trial" and "execution" has lost its meaning; every "experiment" has turned into a "real case"'.[15] 'What we call "experiments" are thus already parts of our reality, of our historical reality'

(Anders, 1956: 260–261).[16] Krohn and Weyer relate how in the seventeenth century, experimental scientific method was made possible by the way that the laboratory structure granted exemption from the social consequences of error. This exemption operated as long as (a) operations within the laboratory were without material effect outside, and (b) scientific discourse and everyday discourse were insulated from each other, so that scientific truth claims could easily be recalled, ending their circulation in society (Krohn and Weyer, 1994: 174). Under conditions of the risk society, however, where the potential effects of technological disasters are potentially unlimited, both geographically and socially, and risks are invisible to the senses and only rendered visible through technical and scientific instruments, procedures and discourses, these conditions no longer apply (Beck, 1992); real-life experiments produce un-recallable effects at the level of both materiality and discourses.

Thirdly, the shift from fabrication to action as the primary form of activity inherent in contemporary technology thus results in a radical transformation in the conditions of knowledge production. From the seventeenth century, the mode of knowledge of things promised by modern science was one based on the experience of not just made but *making* things. As Arendt writes, science taught people not to trust their senses, which could always be deceived; being and appearance thus parted company. Truth no longer was felt to appear spontaneously through contemplation or observation, so 'there arose a veritable necessity to hunt for truth behind deceptive appearances'. Knowing became conceived of as the result of an activity: in order to know one had to do—and specifically to *make* (p. 290). So, recalling Giambattista Vico's dictum '*verum ipsum factum*' (Vico, 1984), the scientist worked as *homo faber*, knowing through making, recreating nature within the experiment. The laboratory operated as a space of fabrication which provided the conditions for the creation of knowable phenomena (Hacking, 1983: 220ff). The classical, experimental scientist was thus *homo faber* elevated to his apotheosis—one who made from the standpoint of the creator, and made only in order to know. By making nature, *homo faber* sought to glimpse the 'model' by which it was made. And as he ceased to fabricate and simply contemplated this model, he would grasp the natural law underlying the process whereby nature had come into being (pp. 297, 295). Scientific knowing was thus a contemplative gesture within the performance of experimental science; a mode of thought immanent in the act of fabrication which was elevated to become the very *telos* of the experiment: the scientist did not contemplate the model in order to make, but made in order to apprehend the model.

But under the contemporary conditions described above, as the experiment is moved *outside* the laboratory, scientific knowing shifts from 'making' to 'acting' as its practical template. What might Arendt have said about the epistemological implications of this move, had she theorized it in any depth? To combine her own language with that of Latour quoted above, contemporary technoscience proceeds not so much in the 'cold', bounded activity of fabrication, creating enduring products and uncovering timeless laws, but in 'warm',

© The Editorial Board of the Sociological Review 2003

boundless action. And the boundlessness of action consists not only in its cease-lessness—the fact that, unlike fabrication, as an activity it has no natural end-point—but also in the self-multiplication of its consequences (Arendt, 1998: 233). In acting into nature, what would have been 'data' in the context of the classical, laboratory experiment, becomes instead real-world 'risk events', emer-gencies, in which nature responds to our actions and to which in turn we have to respond. Knowing nature thus becomes much more provisional: nature comes to be known not as a fabricated object is known but as we know a participant in a dialogue. Human acting can thus incited nature itself into action-hood, transforming our interactions with it into a 'conversation'.[17]

And it is in the logic of conversation that we do not 'know' an interlocutor as something we have made; instead, they are an actor with which we are bound in a conversation. In such a context scientists are no longer the creators of objec-tive facts; but neither are they the authors of their own stories, being merely players within them (p. 184). It is only those who follow us who may be able to apprehend our actions into nature and their consequences as a coherent story. As contemporary technologies permit the distinctive performativity of action to spill into nature, we are in danger of disrupting not only the ongoingness of life's own performance, but also humanity's status as a knower and master of nature.

Conclusion

In this chapter I have used Hannah Arendt's way of looking at human activity to explore issues about the human place in the natural world. Although, as I said in my introduction, Arendt's main concern in *The Human Condition* and elsewhere is to identify and defend what it is that makes human beings *more* than simply part of nature, I have tried to show how her thought nevertheless can be of great value in grasping aspects of the contemporary environmental problematic. Her analysis of the distinctively human in terms of the *vita activa* in fact continuously connects to questions concerning nature. Our animal nature, caught up in the endless reproduction of life itself, remains an essential part of the human condition; and in as far as we transcend life's ceaseless self-performance in fabrication and action, it is in these very forms of activity that the capacity to approach nature as an objective realm of value is nevertheless grounded. Furthermore, I would suggest, it is in the very midst of her defence of human distinctiveness—rather than in an ontology that emphasizes the con-tinuity of humans and the natural world—that an ecologically critical account of contemporary society can best be mounted.

But if the thought of Hannah Arendt has been invaluable for helping us arrive at a diagnosis of our situation, does it offer any clues as to possible solu-tions? Arendt's consistent commitment to a vision of a performative politics of free association and debate, rather than one involving societal plans and pro-jects, means that we will look in vain in her writings for specific descriptions of how society ought to be. Nevertheless, if Arendt reminds us of the importance of enduring objects (prompting the reflection that our problem may not be that Western societies value objects too highly but that they do not value them enough),[18] she also clearly reminds us of the need for action in the public sphere. For it is not in the isolated crafting of theoretical analysis but in interaction between free individuals—in speech and deed—that value and objectivity emerge. Arendtian action, with its intrinsic rather than extrinsic goals, relates people together in a way that can counter the relentless instrumentalization of modern life. It is surely out of a worldly politics, engaging with and reasserting the meaningfulness of the common world, that any remedy must come.[19]

Notes

1 I would like to thank Wallace Heim, Claire Waterton, Dave Littlewood, Brian Wynne, Garrath Williams and Nina Moeller, who have all helped by commenting on earlier drafts of this chapter, or have filled in gaps in my argument through answering my endless queries.

2 Here and elsewhere I reproduce intact Arendt's gendered language since resolving the issues it raises would need a lot more than simply replacing 'men' by 'human beings', or 'him' by 'him or her'.

3 All citations in this form refer to pages in the 1958 edition of *The Human Condition*.

4 For an overview, see the discussion in d'Entrèves (1994: 89–90, 152–5).

5 Arendt does not use terms like *animal laborans* and *homo faber* to refer to different empirical groups of human beings, but rather to different forms of human being-in-the-world.

6 This sets her against Karl Marx, for whom it is the capacity to labour that sets humans *apart* from other animals. Marx uses 'labour' in a slightly different way to Arendt—indeed, she argues that he fails to distinguish between labour and work, thus compromising his critical analysis of the modern age.

7 Although technically it is only in the context of the human 'world' that nature can be said to grow and decay—only against a backdrop of permanency (Arendt, 1958: 97–8).

8 Arendt sees the private, domestic sphere as dominated by labour—the meeting of animal needs—and hence by necessity. It is only through appearing in the public sphere that we can realize true human freedom.

9 Although action can be employed instrumentally, in order to bring about a particular state of affairs, for Arendt this is a distortion of action's orientation to meaning, self-revelation and human excellence and also to vainly try to stem its indeterminacy of outcome. To use action instrumentally is to turn it into a form of 'making', where a 'blueprint' of the desired outcome is used to guide action, rather than being open to action's indeterminacy.

10 I use this compound term to denote the life process including its extension in human labouring.

11 And from Ingold's 'dwelling' perspective, even buildings are not necessarily 'made', built things, but can emerge from the act of dwelling in a given place (see Heidegger, 1975).

12 To be fair, in *Between Past and Future* (1961) Arendt herself describes how Roman civilization combined its own ideas about the cultivation and care of land with Greek aesthetic attitudes to the artefactual world to develop non-instrumental values of nature (see Whiteside, 1998). Such an account is more than consistent with my analysis of how the temporalities of labour/life can create the conditions for nature to be approached as 'world'.

13 There are lessons here for sociological treatments of nature, which often use the language of 'construction' to describe the performance into being of nature by human society, with the implication—intended or otherwise—of intentional design and enduring products. Firstly, can be misleading to apply terms borrowed from the world of work and fabrication to nature, which is often better characterized in terms of life and labour. Secondly, talk of '*social* construction'

© The Editorial Board of the Sociological Review 2003

assumes a human/natural divide which is problematized by Arendt's concept of labour; many 'social constructions' of nature can best be understood not as humans performing nature (through fabrication) but as life performing itself (in labour).

14 This is not to say that no action can be performed for the earth. Environmental politics, as Whiteside and Torgerson emphasize, should at least partially be conceived as action—as speech and deed—between humans, in the human world, that is for and about the earth and our relations with it.

15 *Ernstfall*—which also means 'emergency'.

16 I am grateful to Nina Moeller for providing and translating this extract.

17 This is not to constitute nature as a whole as an actor in this sense; rather, actor-hood in nature would emerge within particular contexts of activity.

18 I am indebted to Russell Keat for this thought.

19 Douglas Torgerson in particular has used Arendt's writings to advance a model of green politics with performative political debate at its heart (Torgerson, 1999; see Healy, this volume). It is worth noting that Torgerson's development of Arendtian politics offers a defence of participatory politics which at the same time can act as a critique of the increasing instrumentalization of participation in citizens juries and other policy-making mechanisms.

References

Agamben, G. (1998), *Homo Sacer: Sovereign Power and Bare Life*, tr. Daniel Heller-Roazen, Stanford, CA: Stanford University Press.

Anders, G. (1956), *Die Antiquiertheit Des Menschen: Vol. I: Über Die Seele Im Zeitalter Der Zweiten Industriellen Revolution*, Munich: Beck'sche Reihe.

Arendt, H. (1951), *The Origins of Totalitarianism*, New York: Harcourt Brace & Co.

Arendt, H. (1958), *The Human Condition*, Chicago: University of Chicago Press.

Arendt, H. (1961), *Between Past and Future*, New York: Viking Press.

Arendt, H. (1963a), *Eichmann in Jerusalem: A Report on the Banality of Evil*, London: Faber & Faber.

Arendt, H. (1963b), *On Revolution*, London: Faber.

Arendt, H. (1998), *The Human Condition*, second edition, Chicago: University of Chicago Press.

Aristotle (1976), *The Ethics of Aristotle: The Nichomachean Ethics*, Harmondsworth: Penguin.

Beck, U. (1992), *Risk Society: Towards a New Modernity*, tr. Mark Ritter, London: Sage.

d'Entrèves, M. P. (1994), *The Political Philosophy of Hannah Arendt*, London: Routledge.

Foucault, M. (1979), *The History of Sexuality Vol. 1: An Introduction*, tr. Robert Hurley, London: Allen Lane.

Gibbons, M., C. Limoges, H. Nowotny, S. Schwartzman, P. Scott and M. Trow (1994), *The New Production of Knowledge: The Dynamics of Science and Research in Contemporary Societies*, London: Sage.

Hacking, I. (1983), *Representing and Intervening: Introductory Topics in the Philosophy of Natural Science*, Cambridge: Cambridge University Press.

Heidegger, M. (1975), 'Building Dwelling Thinking,' in *Poetry, Language, Thought*, New York: Harper and Row, pp. 145–61.

Ingold, T. (2000), *The Perception of the Environment: Essays in Livelihood, Dwelling and Skill*, London: Routledge.

Krohn, W. and J. Weyer (1994), 'Society as a Laboratory: The Social Risks of Experimental Research,' *Science and Public Policy*, 21(3): 173–83.

Latour, B. (1998), 'From the World of Science to the World of Research?,' *Science*, 280(5361): 208–9.

Nowotny, H., P. Scott and M. Gibbons (2001), *Re-Thinking Science: Knowledge and the Public in an Age of Uncertainty*, Cambridge: Polity.

Oakeshott, M. (1962), *Rationalism in Politics and Other Essays*, London: Methuen.

Szerszynski, B. (2002), 'Wild Times and Domesticated Times: The Temporalities of Environmental Lifestyles and Politics,' *Landscape and Urban Planning*, 61(2–4): 181–91.

Torgerson, D. (1999), *The Promise of Green Politics: Environmentalism and the Public Sphere*, Durham, NC: Duke University Press.

Vico, G. (1984), *The New Science of Giambattista Vico: Unabridged Translation of the Third Edition (1744) with the Addition of 'Practice of the New Science'*, tr. Thomas Goddard Bergin and Max Harold Fisch, Ithaca, N. Y.: Cornell University Press.

Whiteside, K. H. (1998), 'Worldliness and Respect for Nature,' *Environmental Values*, 7(1): 25–40.

© The Editorial Board of the Sociological Review 2003

Notes on contributors

Nigel Clark lectures in Geography at the Open University, Milton Keynes. His current research looks at the ethical dimensions of life on a geologically and biologically turbulent planet. He is also an occasional art essayist and has curated two shows: *Shrinking Worlds* (1999) and *alt.nature* (1997).

David Crouch is Professor of Cultural Geography, Tourism and Leisure and Director of the culture, Tourism Consumption and Environment Research Centre at the University of Derby, and Visiting Professor of Geography and Tourism at the Universities of Karlstad and Kalmar, Sweden. His research focuses on the space-encounter of human life in tourism and leisure. Recent publications include *Visual Culture and Tourism* (ed. with N. Lubbren, Berg, 2003) and *The Art of Allotments* (Five Leaves Publications, 2003).

Ronald L. Grimes is Professor of Religion and Culture at Wilfrid Laurier University, Ontario, Canada. One of the founding editors of the *Journal of Ritual Studies*, he has written many articles and books on ritual, including *Deeply into the Bone: Re-Inventing Rites of Passage* (University of California Press, 2000) and *Readings in Ritual Studies* (Prentice-Hall, 1996).

Stephen Healy lectures in the School of History and Philosophy of Science, University of New South Wales, Sydney, Australia. His teaching and research interests encompass energy policy and politics, issues of global environmental change and community involvement in technoscientific decision-making. He has worked for Greenpeace UK, and is a keen competitive cyclist.

Wallace Heim is completing a PhD in Philosophy at the Institute for Enviroment, philosophy and Public Policy at Lancaster University on the dramaturgies of nature and the ethics of created performance, on how the event is a mode of understanding nature-human relations. She has also exhibited sculpture internationally, initiated social practice actions, and designed for theatre, television and film.

Dave Horton is a Postdoctoral Research Fellow at the Institute for Environment, Philosophy and Public Policy at Lancaster University. His research is into cultures of sustainability. He is an environmental activist, and co-founder of Shift-

© The Editorial Board of the Sociological Review 2003. Published by Blackwell Publishing Ltd, 9600 Garsington Road, Oxford OX4 2DQ, UK and 350 Main Street, Malden, MA 02148, USA

ing Ground (www.shiftingground.org), a workers' co-operative dedicated to forging links between the worlds of academia and activism.

Hayden Lorimer teaches human geography in the Department of Geography and Geomatics, University of Glasgow. His research considers how ideas of landscape, nature, science, memory and movement have been variously brought to bear on the understanding of geography in Scotland.

Katrin Lund lectures in the School of Anthropological Studies, Queens University, Belfast. Her primary research field was on landscape, mobility, place and perception in Andalusia, Spain. Before her research at the University of Aberdeen on *Pedestrian Geographies*, she was visiting lecturer at the Victoria University of Wellington, New Zealand.

Garry Marvin is a social anthropologist at the University of Surrey Roehampton, London, with a particular interest in human/animal relations. He has written on performance in Spanish bullfighting, on cockfighting, and on zoos. At present he is writing an ethnography of English foxhunting and has embarked on a study of human/wolf relationships.

Peter Simmons is Lecturer in Environmental Risk in the School of Environmental Sciences, University of East Anglia. His current research interests include narrative approaches to risk and place; spatial representation and risk management; and public participation and deliberation in risk policy.

Bronislaw Szerszynski is Lecturer in Environment and Culture at the Institute for Environment, Philosophy and Public Policy, Lancaster University. His research interests include risk, environment and new technologies; citizenship and social movements; and religion and culture. His forthcoming publications include a monograph on nature and the sacred for Blackwell. He is also a singer, guitarist and songwriter.

Claire Waterton is Lecturer in Environment and Social Policy at the Institute for Environment, Philosophy and Public Policy, Lancaster University. Her research and teaching centres around science, knowledge and environmental policymaking and she is currently taking part in an ethnographic study of UK naturalists, scientists and policymakers involved in Biodiversity Action Planning.

Matt Watson is Research Associate at Durham University's Department of Geography. His research explores how practices are co-constitutive with knowledge, materiality, technologies, spatiality, embodiment, identities and power in professional, recreational and domestic contexts.

© The Editorial Board of the Sociological Review 2003

Index

abstraction 2, 7–8, 131–2, 142–3, 157;
    mountains as 133, 138
action 25, 193; Arendt and 187, 204,
    206, 207, 208, 212–15, 216
activism (*see also* environmental activism)
    184, 186; slow 10, 187–8
activity 2, 114; Arendt and 204–16
actor network theory 97, 105;
    performance and 97–101
Adam, B. 164
adaptation 9, 112, 114, 126, 165, 166,
    171, 172, 180
agency 3, 5, 6–7, 27, 114
Agglestone Rock 146–7; engagement
    with 148, 150–1; meanings of 147,
    148
agricultural improvements 170
alienation 208–9, 212
allotments 5, 18; holders of 21–3, 27, 28;
    as performance event 19–21
Anders, G. 213
Arendt, H. 10, 187; *The Human
    Condition* 203–16
argument 192, 195, 196
Aristotle 195, 207
artefacts 25, 28, 131, 198–9, 207, 208
art 19–21, 24, 25, 26, 27, 28, 166, 172–4,
    176, 179, 180, 183–202
audience, accidental/integral 52–3
Australia 101; agricultural production
    171, 175; colonization of 163–4,
    171

Bachelard, G. 193
Barnes, T. 142, 143
Barth, F. 126

Beck, U. 96, 164
Bell, C. 114
Bell, M. M. 50
Benhabib, S. 194
Berleant, A. 186
Berry, T. 31
Biodiversity Action Plan 151, 156–7
Biodiversity Convention 156
biogenetic structuralism 37–8
bioinvasion 9, 164, 165–6, 171, 175, 176,
    178–9, 180
biological colonization 163–5
biological life 170–1, 172
biophysicality 169
biopolitics 170
bio-power 211
biotechnology 163, 164, 212ff
bird watching 111
Bloom 98 18, 19–21, 25, 27, 28
body (*see also* embodiment) 138–9
body-encounter 25, 28
Booher, D. 99–100
Bourdieu, P. 6, 67, 68, 126
Bowker, G. 113, 125
Brandon, S. G. F. 35
Bright, C. 176
Bronte Catchment Project (Sydney)
    101–6
Bruns, G. 195
Buddhism, and environmental ritual 32
Burns, T. 81
Burton, M. 19
Butler, J. 3, 17, 26, 122, 167–8, 176

capacity building 104–5
capitalism 207, 210–11, 212

car ownership 76n; among environmental activists 71–4
categorization 116–17, 122, 125, 127n
character 196–7; ethics of 184
Chemical Industries Association, Responsible Care 83
chemical production 82–3; emergency handling 86–9; performance of safety 81–6
choreography 17, 122, 125, 127n
citizen's jury, for environmental deliberation 101, 103–4, 105
Clark, N. 3, 9, 11, 12
class, environmentalism and 66–7
classifications 8, 111, 112–14, 153–4; as disciplinary-based practice 115–16, 125; of mountains 133–6; of movement 116–17, 122–4; National Vegetation Classification 116, 117–20; as performance 112, 116, 120–2, 133–6
Cloke, P. 150
codes 3, 7, 33, 47, 59n, 60n, 68–9, 73, 75, 124, 136, 137–8, 141, 167, 174
colonization 163–5, 171–2, 180
communicative action 96
communities: capacity-building 104–5; in faulty environments 81–2, 83, 84, 90; participation *see* public participation; performance of safety 81–4
communities of practice 114, 125
compasses 139, 140
construction of nature 18, 147, 149, 169, 217n
conversational drift 187–8
conversation 10, 11, 183, 184, 189, 192, 215; as method 194–7
cooperative discourse 97
Corner, J. 142
cosmologies 44
Council of All Beings 31
counter-activity 80, 90
counter-readings 7, 84–6, 89–90
countryside, as space for foxhunting 49–51, 151
creative nature of performance 5–6, 9, 99, 165, 173, 184, 186
Crosby, A. 163, 164, 171

Crossley, N. 24, 25
Crouch, D. 5, 140
cultural codes, green 68–9, 70; and car ownership 72–3; and food 71
cultural performance 47–8, 116
culture: body and 168–9; classifications and 113; nature and 35–6, 149, 169–70

d'Aquili, E. 6, 37
dance 122
Darwin, C. 3, 163
de Certeau, M. 135, 192
decision-making, environmental 95–7, 101–2, 103–4
definition of situation 79–80, 80–1, 87, 89, 90–1
Deleuze, G. 24, 168, 176, 177, 178
deliberation 98–9, 99–100, 106
Dening, G. 166–7, 178–9
Derrida, J. 168, 176, 177, 178
deterritorialization 163, 178, 185
disciplining of nature 170–2
distinction 215; green 64, 66–7, 74
Diver, C. 154–5
Dufrenne, M. 193
durability 98, 207–10
dwelling 18, 26–7, 148–9, 150, 158

earth 207, 208, 210, 211, 212
Earth Charter 33
Earth First! 65
ecological anthropology 39–43
ecosystems 43, 165, 208
electricity 185, 188–9, 198–9
embodiment 167–9; in performance 17, 22, 23–4, 138–40
emotion 33, 36, 41, 96, 48, 50, 59, 185–6, 188, 195–8
end of nature 165
endurance 207–10
environmental activism, and identity 63–76, 210; different styles 65, 69
environmental ethics 11–12, 33, 179
environmental hazards 81–2
environmental management 105–6; community understandings 95, 101–2, 104
environmental ritual 31–4, 36, 43–4

ethics 6, 11–12, 33, 184, 199–200n
Europe, southern colonies 163, 166,
    170–2
event, performance as 3, 9, 12, 35, 52,
    116, 183, 186, 188, 192
everyday 3–7, 15, 17–30, 46, 49, 51, 53,
    58, 63–4, 70, 72–4, 78
evolution 3, 31, 175, 179
experiments 213–14, 111–2, 117, 125–6
expressivity 24, 34, 36, 47, 58, 187

fabrication 207, 208, 210–15
facts 133, 135, 142; collection of 135
faulty environments 81–2
feminist philosophers 167–9
feral biota 164, 166, 172; performativity
    of 172–5
festivals 52
food 7, 22, 67, 70–1
force 116–17; spatialization of 122, 123
Foucault, M. 170, 192, 121
foxes 50–1, 55–6
foxhounds 56–7
foxhunting 6, 46–7, 48–9, 59;
    participants in 52–5, 58; as
    performance 47–8, 50, 55–9;
    spaces for 49–51
framing 7, 79, 80
Franklin, A. 18
Friends of the Earth 65

Gadamer, H.-G. 191, 199
Game, A. 28
gardening 5, 18
Geertz, C. 115
Gibbons, M. 213
Giddens, A. 90
Global Positioning Satellite (GPS) devices
    140–2
Godlingston Heath 146, 151, 157; fence
    for 152–3, 157
Goffman, E. 7, 78–81, 89, 90
grassland, classifications of 116–24, 125
green lifestyles 65–6, 67, 74–5; identity
    performance and 67–74; material
    culture of 63–4
Green Party 65
green values 6–7, 25, 66–7, 70–1
Gregson, N. 79

Gretton, D. 184
Grimes, R. 5–6
Grosz, E. 17, 26, 168
Guattari, F. 176, 177, 178
Guthrie-Smith, H. 171, 179

Habermas, J. 96, 200n
Habitat Action Plan 151
habitats 151, 209
habitus 67, 68
Hannah, M. 142, 143
Harre, R. 23
Healy, S. 7
'hearing' 192–4
Heidegger, M. 148, 149, 203
Heim, W. 9–10, 11
Hetherington, K. 145, 158
hill-walking 132; identity and 134–5;
    navigation 136–8, 140–2; as
    performance 138–40
holiness 41
homeland 176, 177, 185
HOMELAND 183, 184–5, 186–7,
    189–92
Hoppe, R. 97
Horton, D. 6–7, 11
Hunts 49, 50, 53; members of 50, 53
Huntsman 48–9, 53–4, 57–8
Huxley, J. 36–7, 154
hybridity 94

identity 22; green 64, 65–6, 67–70, 70–5;
    hill-walking and 134–5
imagination 184, 192–4
impression management 79, 80, 82, 83,
    84–5, 87
improvisation 4, 7, 89, 132, 167, 175,
    177, 186, 194, 195; classification and
    8, 112, 114, 122, 126
industrialization 207, 211
Ingold, T. 18, 26–7, 131, 140, 149, 158,
    209
Innes, J. 99–100
instrumental-technical reasoning 96

Jacob, C. 137
Jaspers, K. 203
Jones, O. 150
Jordan, W. 31

Kerin, J. 168
Kester, G. 186, 200n
Kirby, V. 168
knowledge 4, 94–5, 106, 121, 122; expert
    156; as practice 141, 143; production
    of 213–14
Kristeva, J. 25
Krohn, W. 213, 214
Kroll-Smith, S. 83

labour 204–5, 207, 209, 211
Lancaster, green networks 64–5, 70–1
Landa, M. de 170
landscape 25, 49–51, 209–10; and identity
    formation 134; visualization 137
language 2, 42, 168, 176
Latour, B. 94, 151, 213
Laughlin, C. 37
Law, J. 98, 111, 120
lay understandings 95, 97, 98
Levidow, L. 96
life, biological 9, 170–1, 172, 175, 180,
    207–8; performativity of 165–6,
    167–9, 212–13
lifestyle *see* green lifestyles
lightbulbs 188–9, 198–9
Linnaeus, K. 113, 123
liturgy 35, 37, 41
Lorimer, H. 8
loss of species 178–9
lowland heath 151–2, 153, 155, 157
Lund, K. 8
Lyall, J. 166, 172–5, 178, 179, 180
Lynch, M. 111, 120

MacIntytre, A. 188
Macnaghten, P. 1, 18, 25, 149
Maffesoli, M. 25
map reading 136–8
Margulis, L. 168–9
Marriott, J. 184
Marris, C. 96
Marvin, G. 6
Marx, K. 211
Massey, D. 145
material culture: and green lifestyles 63–4;
    and performance of identity 70–4
materiality: nature as 2, 3, 25, 27, 148,
    179; relational 98, 105, 158

Matless, D. 137
McFague, S. 34
meaning(s) 21, 47, 58, 147–9, 205, 210; in
    nature 21, 23, 147, 148
Melucci, A. 68
Merleau-Ponty, M. 17, 23–4, 25
metaphors 4, 192–3; of performance 3,
    78, 79, 114
Michael, M. 150
micropolitics 25–6, 28
milk, choices in consumption, for
    environmentalists 69
Miller, G. 20
modernity 170; Arendt and 210–15
Mol, A.-M. 98
Moore, N. W. 155
mountains: classification of 133–6;
    embodied performance on 138–40;
    as facts 133; navigation 136–8,
    140–2
movement: classification of 116–17,
    122–4; in mountains 138–40
Munro, Sir H. 132–3
Munro-bagging 8, 134–5
Murray, W. H. 138

Naismith, W. 136
Naismith's rule 136, 137
narratives 54, 184, 193–4, 195
nature 2, 17–18, 212; 'acting into' 213,
    214–15; as process 2, 3, 207
Nature Conservancy 155
nature conservation 154–5
nature reserves 145–6, 158–9
navigation 136–8, 139–42
New Zealand: agriculture in 171, 175;
    colonization of 163–4, 171
Nicholson, M. 155
normalization of danger 7, 80–1,
    88–9
numbers 131, 137, 142, 143

objectivity, objectification 131–2, 143,
    212, 214–15
obligation 40, 41; to hunt 53
orderings 112, 113, 114, 116
organizational behaviour, impression
    management 80, 82, 83, 84–5, 87
Otto, R. 41

Palmer, H. 18, 19, 21, 24
Patton, C. 26
Peacock, J. 58
performance 2–3; biological life as
    167–9, 205, 207–12, 215; creating
    presence 47–8; as creative 5–6, 9, 26,
    99, 165, 173, 184, 186; as embodied
    practice 23–4, 134; as event 3, 9, 12,
    35, 52, 116, 183, 186, 188, 192;
    Goffman and 78–81; knowledge
    production as 111–6, 120–2, 124–6,
    143, 153–7, 214–5; misperformances,
    failed performances 68–9, 81, 87,
    89–91; Schechner and 35, 52, 99,
    100, 127n; semantic instability 84–6;
    of place 145, 146, 157–8; and
    practice 17, 114; and ritual 34–5,
    40–41; theatrical 3, 12, 26, 34, 35, 52,
    79, 80, 166, 186, 196, 198, 206
performance artists 19–21, 79–80, 166,
    172–5, 178, 180, 196–7
performative capacity 106
performativity 2–3, 9, 11–12, 98, 112;
    and Butler 26, 167–8; Goffman and
    79–81, 89; of life 165–6, 167–9,
    212–13
persuasion 183, 184, 190, 194–6, 198
phronesis 195
place 145, 158–9; constitution of 148–9,
    150–1, 157; relationality of 153, 156,
    157–8
  memory of place 50
planning 10
PLATFORM 9–10, 184–5, 193, 194,
    197
policy making 10, 11
Poovey, M. 133
practice 2, 5, 17; embodied 17, 22–3, 24;
    place and 149; nature understood
    through 5, 18–29
presentation of self 79
process, nature as 2, 3, 207
public dialogue 183–4, 186
public participation 7, 94–7; performance
    and 98–100; in stormwater
    management 101–6

Radley, A. 24, 25
Rappaport, R. 6, 39–43

reality 11, 98, 100
Reason, D. 116
Reclaim the Streets 65
recognition 191–2
reflexivity 126, 135; collective 99
regulation 10
relational materiality 98, 105, 158
religion, ritual and 32, 34, 41, 42–3, 44
Renn, O. 97
repetition 3, 9, 17, 26, 83, 165, 166;
    landscape and life as 209–10
replication 8, 112, 114, 125, 126
resistance 17, 18, 25–6, 132, 135, 168
rhetoric 192, 195–6
Ricoeur, P. 192–3
risk 214; coping strategies 90; definition
    of situation 86, 89–90, 90–1;
    manufactured 164
risk management 82, 84, 85–6
ritual 5–6, 31–4, 47, 71, 80, 84–5;
    and biogenetic structuralism
    37–8; and ecological anthropology
    39–43; efficacy of 34–5; foxhunting
    as 52–3; safety practices as 85,
    88–9
ritual theory 34–6
ritualization 36–7, 43–4
Roberts, J. 20
Rodwell, J. S. 125
Rose, G. 1, 79, 176
Rosenhek, R. 31–2
Ryan, R. 101, 102, 105

sacrality 41
safety 7, 80, 89; performance of 81–6,
    89–90
Schafer, M. 32
Schechner, R. 35, 52, 99, 100, 127n
Schiefflen, E. 47–8
scientific knowledge 213–14
scripts 3, 6–8, 31, 68, 73, 75, 84, 86, 114,
    120, 122, 125
Scotland, hill-walking in 132, 133–43
Seed, J. 31–2
self, presentation of 79
self-identification 22
Sheets-Johnstone, M. 116, 124
shopping, and green identity 70–4
Shotter, J. 25

Simmons, P. 7, 11
Smith, P. C. 192, 195, 196
social conventions 40–1, 42
social encounter 22, 28, 79
social movements 63, 66
social norms 167–8
social practice art 183, 184–7, 189–92
social sciences 12
Solnit, R. 138
species introduction 163–4, 166, 170, 175, 178, 180
stability 207–10
stage-setting 95, 98, 100, 102–3, 104, 105, 106
Star, S. L. 113, 125
States, B. O. 186
Stewart, N. 111
stormwater management 101–6
Stott, J. G. 130
Studland, ecological survey 153–6
Suchman, L. 115, 124, 137, 140
sustainable culture 75
Swimme, B. 31
Szerszynski, B. 10, 12

Tambiah, S. 34
taskscape 150, 158, 209
taste 67
taxonomies 153–4
technological development 141–2, 210, 211–13
territoriality 176–7

theatrical performance 3, 12, 26, 34, 35, 52, 79, 80, 166, 186, 196, 198, 206
Thomas, K. 113
Thomas, W. I. 79
Thrift, N. 1, 26, 145, 149, 158
transformation 37, 131, 170, 186
translation 153–7
Trowell, J. 184
Tuan, Y.-F. 52
Tulloch, J. 26
Turner, V. 40

Urry, J. 1, 18, 25, 149
utility 205, 210–11

values, green 6–7, 22, 25
Van den Berg, J. H. 138
Verran, H. 123
Vico, G. 214
visualization 136–7

Waddington, C. H. 180
Waterton, C. 8
Watson, M. 8
Weyer, J. 213, 214
Whiteside, K. 208
Wilson, E. A. 168
work 204, 205, 206–7, 208
world, earth and 210, 211, 212
Wright, J. E. B. 138

Zonabend, F. 84, 85